P9-DNU-526

Feb. 19, 1986

Dearest Eve,

Happy Birthday Honey.

Love & Kisses,

Mom

Making Old-Fashioned Dolls

Venus A. Dodge

Making Old-Fashioned Dolls

Venus A. Dodge

With drawings by Martin Dodge

Sterling Publishing Co., Inc. New York

Photographs by Jonathon Bosley

Library of Congress Cataloging in Publication Data

Dodge, Venus
    Making old-fashioned dolls.
    Bibliography: p.
    Includes index.
    1. Dollmaking.   I. Title.
TT175.D563   1985   745.592'21   84–26788

ISBN 0-8069-5716-6
ISBN 0-8069-7974-7 (pbk)

Published in 1985 by Sterling Publishing Co., Inc.
Two Park Avenue, New York, N.Y. 10016
First published in Great Britain under the title
Making Old-Fashioned Dolls
by David & Charles (Publishers) Limited, Newton Abbot

Copyright © Venus Dodge 1985

All rights reserved.
No part of this publication may be reproduced
or transmitted in any form or by any means,
without permission.

Distributed in Canada by Oak Tree Press Ltd.
c/o Canadian Manda Group, P.O. Box 920, Station U,
Toronto, Ontario M8Z 5P9

Printed in Great Britain

CONTENTS

INTRODUCTION

In the course of my work as a dollmaker, I am often invited to address groups of people such as Craft Guilds, Women's Institutes and Dollmakers' Clubs about the history of dolls and the methods I use to make my own dolls. I enjoy this part of my job very much and learn a great deal from the people I meet. In the last few years a rapidly growing interest in craft work of all kinds and in dollmaking in particular has become very apparent. Obviously, more and more people are discovering the intense pleasure to be found in making things for themselves; the dollmaker is no longer regarded as mildly eccentric but her craft is becoming well respected, and her goods are in demand. As a result of the current trend for nostalgia, prices of antique dolls have rocketed to absurd heights and there has been a consequent interest in reproduction and old-fashioned-style dolls. Even the commercial doll manufacturers have recognised this interest and are producing vinyl dolls dressed in 'Victorian' costumes. Most of the home dollmakers I meet produce dolls in retrospective styles, as they feel that modern fashions are boring and that period costumes are far more challenging and rewarding to make. Some of the questions they ask me include how to achieve a desired authentic effect, where to buy a ringlet wig, what kind of drawers did dolls wear in 1870, and how to make leather shoes. I am also asked how best to set about selling dolls, whether porcelain doll kits are a good buy and for information on dollmaking courses. Hopefully this book will answer all of these questions, and many more.

I have chosen to cover the period 1750 to 1950 as a wide variety of dolls were made during this time in various materials including cloth, felt, wood, wax and clay. The dolls range from wealthy children's toys like the Georgian wooden doll (page 34) and the French fashion doll (page 58) to the simple rag dolls and 'penny woodens' which would have been available to all children. I have also included some dolls in sympathy with modern taste, such as the Bye-lo baby (page 117), and quaint examples like the Victorian china doll (page 59).

I repair and restore a number of antique dolls, so have had the opportunity to study them closely and see how they were made. In most cases the style and proportions of the old dolls were very different from modern ones as tastes have changed a great deal over the last two centuries. It is details such as the shape and size of the head and the proportions of the body which make a doll look authentically old fashioned; simply dressing a modern doll in old-fashioned clothes will not produce the desired effect. For example, the long torso and deep bosom on the Georgian wooden doll make the costume 'sit' perfectly, an effect which could not be achieved by putting the same clothes on a modern Sindy doll, as her modern figure would distort the shape of the costume. In the same way, the kid body of the fashion doll with its wide shoulders, small waist and large hips dictates the shape of the costume, by representing the figure which was fashionable at that time.

The costumes are still important however; the fabrics, trimmings and styles should be correct for the period, but most important is the way the garment is cut. Victorian clothes were simply not made in the same way as modern clothes, and Georgian clothes were not made like Victorian ones. I like authenticity, but I am not a slave to it. Wherever it is reasonable to do so, the patterns are cut exactly as the originals, as in the case of the Georgian doll, because I feel that many dollmakers will enjoy the challenge of recreating a completely authentic costume. However, for some of the simpler dolls, eg the rag dolls, I have simplified the patterns, without, I hope, losing the correct shape for the period. Where I have altered or simplified the patterns, you will find notes in the text, so if you prefer to make every costume in exact detail, you can still do so.

It has not been my intention to make reproduction dolls. This would be impossible with modern materials such as self-hardening clay. I have chosen each doll as being typical of her period, but have offered a variety of different types, made in a variety of materials and for a range of skills.

In my earlier book *Making Collector's Dolls* I showed the reader how to make a variety of simple dolls in cloth, felt, sculpted clay and wax. This book has been written for the dollmaker who wants to make something more ambitious, and anyone who has made dolls from my previous book should have little difficulty making most of these. The materials used are all readily available and no special equipment is needed. The patterns vary in the degree of skill required and have therefore been given a 'difficulty' rating of 1–5. I recommend that you start with one of the simpler dolls and, as your confidence grows, move up the scale. Suggestions are offered for adapting many of the dolls to make other types, and detailed notes for fabrics, trimmings and accessories are given in each chapter as well as the historical background to each doll.

In Chapter 14 you will find a range of dollmaking kits which are discussed in detail, and suggestions for adapting commercial doll parts to make original dolls. There is also a résumé of the wigs, eyes and other dollmaking materials which are currently available. Chapter 15 outlines dollmaking courses and doll fairs and offers suggestions for the dollmaker wishing to sell her own dolls. It also details the various doll publications which are available. At the back of the book you will find a comprehensive list of stockists and suppliers of dollmaking materials and accessories. I am often asked for such a list as many people are unaware of these specialist suppliers' existence, let alone the wide range of goods they stock. I have also included a full list of the books I have found helpful. Some of them, sadly, are out of print, but your local library can probably be of assistance.

Dollmaking is a highly personal craft and each dollmaker has her own tastes and talents, therefore this book does not set out to dictate, but merely to guide, and to demonstrate methods I use myself and have found successful. I hope, however, that the variety of methods described here will offer something for every dollmaker and encourage you to experiment and produce satisfying results. All patterns drawn on grids should be enlarged to 1in.

1

MAKING THE DOLLS

To make satisfyingly authentic old-fashioned dolls, it helps to know something about antique dolls. Most home dollmakers have a more than passing interest and many are very knowledgeable, so it is not my intention to write a detailed 'history of dolls' but rather to provide a little background information which relates to the dolls in this book.

Obviously dolls were in existence before 1750, though there is little information about them and few examples survive. There is at least one logical reason for starting at this date. The 'Queen Anne' doll described in Chapter 3 is the earliest type of doll of which a good number of examples have survived, and though many are in museums, they still turn up occasionally in auctions and sales. In 1982 a Georgian wooden doll in pristine condition with an extra set of clothes appeared on the television programme *The Antiques Road Show*. The gentleman who owned it had found it in the attic, and brought it, wrapped up in old newspaper, to 'see if it was worth anything' before he 'threw it away'! The team of experts were delighted to see such a superb example and the owner must have received quite a shock on being told that his old doll was worth around £8,000! Such 'finds' are rare, but they do happen. Enormous quantities of dolls were produced during and before this time (even as long ago as 1750 mass production methods were being used) particularly by the doll-making industry in Germany and the strange thing is not that such old dolls survive, but that so few have survived. It is a reflection on how little value was placed on children's toys at the time. To parents who could face with equanimity the prospect of losing several of their large brood in childhood, the doll, though expensive, would have had little sentimental value. Probably the child herself was not particularly fond of it; these dolls are hardly cuddly, and with their stylised painted faces and elaborate clothes there is little about them which would

appeal to a child. The little girl might hold the doll as she posed for a stiff formal portrait, but it is unlikely that she was permitted to 'play' with it. They were bought more as status symbols, expressions of the parents' wealth, than as toys in the true sense of the word.

Things began to change as the eighteenth century drew to a close. Inspired by books like *Emile* written by Rousseau in 1762 which advocated a less restricted lifestyle and special clothes for children, many parents began to think of their children as real people and take an interest in them. Toys began to be regarded as an essential part of childhood and by the early nineteenth century, dolls, though still made to represent ladies, were much simpler and cheaper. Most families, except the very poor, could afford the wooden Grödnerthals and the papier mâché heads on kid bodies which were made in Germany. The Grödnerthals were well-made turned wooden dolls with pegged or ball-jointed limbs and made excellent play dolls. As a child, the young Princess Victoria dressed dozens of them, and must have had fun doing so, and surely what was good enough for the heir to the throne must have been good enough for the middle classes! The dolls with papier mâché heads of the 1830s have a charm peculiarly their own. The head is modelled with the elaborate hairstyle of the period on a shoulder-plate which is glued onto a very simple stiff kid body with wooden lower arms and legs. In the nice tidy Victorian manner, the joins between wood and kid are covered with neat strips of coloured paper. Sometimes the basic doll is embellished with curls of real hair, and some examples have modelled bonnets or ribbons. These dolls usually have dark hair and blue eyes, and the varnish with which the head was finished mellows with time to a lovely soft gold. Sadly, very few are found unbroken as the papier mâché is susceptible to changes in temperature and the shoulder-plate cracks; but simple though such dolls are, and certainly designed as play dolls, they are delightful – unpretentious, well made and so typically early Victorian.

By the time Queen Victoria was on the throne, the china dolls had arrived. Most people think of these as the typical 'Victorian doll'. Attitudes were becoming increasingly prim; legs could no longer be mentioned in polite society and the china dolls with their prissy expressions and immaculate painted coiffures reflect the ultra-respectable middle-class attitudes of the time. Their pale faces and tiny hands and feet represented the mid-Victorian ideal of feminine beauty and their long full skirts emphasised the small waist, but decently covered anything that might possibly exist below. Just in case any passing male might be tempted to peep at an exposed ankle, all the dolls wore boots! The china heads and limbs on cloth bodies made satisfying but fragile play dolls and they were still being made at the end of the century, though by then they were thought very old fashioned. By this time, the pious middle classes would not permit their children to play with toys on Sundays, except in more liberated households where toys with some religious significance, such as a Noah's Ark, or certain books were acceptable. The dolls, too, were expected to provide something of educational value and many young hands were kept busy with hemming, run-and-fell seaming and feather-stitching dolls' clothes, which is why so many of the surviving china dolls are so well dressed!

While the middle-class Victorians were buying china dolls, the upper classes wanted something more luxurious, and found what they were looking for in the workshops of Montinari, Pierotti and Lucy Peck in London. These and others made fabulous wax dolls. The first proper baby dolls were made in wax, and were much admired at the Great Exhibition of 1851 though they were thought rather too life-like. The most popular wax dolls were the chubby idealised children with inset glass eyes and real hair implanted in their wax scalps. These 'little angels' were the epitome of the sentimental romantic view of children which many Victorian adults had – an easier view to hold in the days when children were cared for by nurses and governesses and merely met their parents once a day, well scrubbed and dressed in their best! The dolls were made of poured wax (liquid wax poured in layers into a mould and allowed to cool to form a thick shell-hollow inside), with heads on deep shoulder-plates and lower limbs attached to cloth bodies. Each manufacturer had his own formula for the wax – usually a blend of pure beeswax with additives for strength and colour – and many examples are recognised and attributed as much by the wax as the style of modelling. For example, the Pierottis favoured a rather alarming purplish pink colour and the Montinari dolls have modelled rolls of fat at the neck and wrists.

The methods of production used for the poured-wax dolls were time consuming and exacting and the dolls were very expensive, but waxed composition dolls were made in Germany in imitation of the fine English dolls and were a great deal cheaper. Generally the poured wax dolls have survived the ravages of time and central heating better than the wax-over compositions. The earlier type of waxed composition, known as 'slit heads' because the hair was inserted in a slit cut across the top of the head, are usually horribly crazed; the later 'pumpkin heads' with modelled hairstyles survive better. Waxed compositions which had wigs tend to have survived best of all, many of them still in good condition, testifying that wax is more durable than most people think. Presumably because they were so expensive, the poured-wax dolls were well cared for and that has contributed to their preservation. Many of them are still around, often in their original clothes, and one has to admire and marvel at the skill and patience of the girls who inserted the hairs one at a time into their little heads.

While Germany was producing simple china and composition dolls, and England elaborate wax dolls, France had been getting her act together and at the end of the 1860s launched the French fashion dolls or 'Parisiennes' on an enthusiastic world. These fabulous ladies with their trousseaux of expensive clothes were luxury dolls, and as expensive as the English wax ones. They had bisque heads on shoulder-plates, often with swivel necks, and jointed wood or kid bodies. Inspired by the elegant Empress Eugenie, the French dollmakers had been producing fashionable lady dolls for some time, but the 1870s were their golden age. Perfectly made in every detail, from their elaborately styled wigs and beautiful glass eyes to their tiny hand-made leather shoes, they offered the perfect opportunity for rich parents to demonstrate their wealth. By this time, thanks to the Industrial Revolution, many members of the middle class were also extremely well off. They liked to display their wealth with ostentatious furnishings and rich clothes and by purchasing an elaborate Parisienne for their child they were able to show the world just how much they could afford to spend on a 'toy'. However, woe-betide the little girl who actually played with her doll and messed it up! This attitude was condemned by many and not just those who could not afford such dolls. Lady Lewis, writing to her daughter in 1874, bitterly condemns the lavish French dolls and recommends that her daughter buy her grandchild a 'simple baby' and 'teach her to sew garments for it'. In spite of such comments, the French fashion doll was the doll of the 1870s among the rich and the poor had to be content with the china dolls, by now very cheap, and the even cheaper wooden Dutch dolls.

By 1880 tastes had changed again and the still lavish but relatively simpler French bébés became fashionable. Here was the idealised child of the rich middle classes with her beautiful solemn face, large glass eyes and immaculate clothes. This was a miniature version of the kind of little girl everyone admired, and modern collectors still admire them – they are the most coveted of all antique dolls. This was the first time that dolls representing children had been really popular and the bébés set the fashion for the next twenty or thirty years. Throughout the 1880s and 1890s and well into the twentieth century, little girl dolls outsold every other type. The French manufacturers concentrated on high-quality dolls with beautiful clothes. By providing the bébé with a wardrobe, one could teach the child what was suitable wear for any occasion and develop her taste. Such was the 'sales talk' of the time and it sold a lot of dolls' clothes! The shops which sold the dolls and their clothes held competitions to persuade the child or her parents to buy even more clothes in order to win the prize for the best-dressed doll.

The German manufacturers joined the bébé craze, producing dolls which were perhaps less beautiful than the French dolls but were certainly a lot cheaper, and by the end of the nineteenth century they had virtually commandeered the doll market. Despite the French firms suspending their internal rivalries and pooling their resources to compete with the Germans, the German dolls were produced in such vast quantities and at such low prices that the French simply could not compete. Nowadays, when antique dolls are comparatively rare, it is hard to believe that the bébés, both French and German, were produced in millions. The Jumeau firm claimed that in the year 1897 it made more than three million dolls and the German company of Armand Marseilles had an output much greater than this. One cannot help wondering what happened to all those dolls. Probably most of them were broken. Despite the claims that the dolls were 'unbreakable' (bébés incassables), bisque heads are very fragile, and of what use was the sturdy composition body once it had lost its head? The German dolls were so cheap that children could play with them properly rather than treat them with reverence, so casualties were inevitable. Innovations such as sleeping eyes with a counterweight and open mouths with teeth kept the Germans ahead – they were far more ready to experiment with new ideas than the French. As one manufacturer came up with an idea which proved popular, so the others would copy and by the first decade of this century there was a definite 'sameness' about the dolls. Generally they had bisque heads with sleeping glass eyes, open mouths with teeth, and mohair wigs. Their bodies were ball-jointed composition and their expressions pretty and rather vacant.

Despite the rather tiresomely reverent attitude some modern collectors have towards all old dolls, it should not be forgotten that the bisque dolls were mass produced in vast quantities in factories by grossly underpaid workers. The quality varies enormously from one manufacturer to another and within the range of dolls produced by any one firm. Some dolls are exquisite, others indifferently good and some quite awful. An odd kind of snobbery exists among some collectors whereby they regard all French dolls as superior to German and will pay twice as much for a poor-quality Jumeau than for a fine-quality Armand Marseilles. The values of old dolls are purely artificial, decided by the availability of a certain type, the current taste and an interest in keeping the market alive. As certain types of doll become very rare and therefore very expensive the fashion turns to another type and so the price of examples of that type begins to rise. Doll collecting is becoming more popular each year and so the range of 'collectable' dolls has to widen. It now includes celluloid and even 1950s dolls which a few years ago would have been regarded with contempt!

As the buying public got bored with the little girl dolls with their 'dolly' faces, the inventive Germans were ready with a new type of doll. Although they were never as well liked as the 'dolly faces', the character dolls, made to represent real children, were very popular. It was becoming fashionable to think of toys in educational terms and, thanks to Freud, parents were concerning themselves with their children's emotional development and the need for them to play with the 'right' kind of toys. Many of the character dolls were delightful and made super toys, offering the child a 'real' enough doll to identify with. Others must have been tiresome with their permanently scowling, whistling or crying expressions and probably appealed far more to adults than to children. The first realistic baby dolls were produced before the First World War but were not really popular until the 1920s following the fantastic success of the Bye-lo baby. The early character dolls had bisque heads on jointed composition bodies; later, composition was used for the heads as well and proved less fragile and cheaper to produce than bisque, though both materials were used until plastics began to take over.

Soft dolls too became popular early in the twentieth century. They developed rapidly from simple rag dolls to sophisticated toys with faces shaped by pressing in moulds, and realistically painted features. The soft dolls were popular with small children as they were cuddly, and with their parents as they were unbreakable! The English companies like Chad Valley and Deans produced ranges of charming dolls in cloth and felt. The Italian firm of Scavini produced the felt Lenci dolls, Germany the Kathë Kruse dolls and America the Kamkins Kiddies. All of these dolls were designed to represent children, and dressed in simple realistic clothes. They were not cheap, especially the Lenci and Kathë Kruse dolls, but they were popular with small children and with middle-class parents who could

afford them and felt that they were good for their offspring.

After the First World War, the centre of the dollmaking industry moved to America, though at first the dolls were largely made in Germany and distributed in America. Gradually celluloid and plastic took over from bisque and composition and by the 1950s virtually all dolls were made in some kind of plastic.

Plastic, especially vinyl, has proved to be the 'perfect material' from the doll manufacturers' point of view and the end of a search which has lasted for hundreds of years to find a material which was cheap, unbreakable and could be moulded into an infinite variety of characters. How very perverse of the buying public to be bored with plastic dolls, so that some manufacturers have begun to make porcelain dolls again, and how ironic that plastic dolls will be the antiques of the twenty-first century and probably as rare as bisque dolls are today! Incredibly, the early 1950s American 'Barbie' dolls are already highly priced and much sought after.

The modern dollmaker has one great advantage over the dollmakers of the past in that she alone is responsible for the creation of the doll and its manufacture from beginning to end. The antique dolls each passed through many hands, one person making the head, another the limbs, another painting the face and yet another setting the eyes. Each person did only their own job, over and over again and probably with very little 'job satisfaction'. In spite of this, the dolls they produced were often very beautiful, and we are fortunate that so many of them have survived for today's dollmakers to use as inspiration, to copy or to interpret in whatever way they wish.

When making copies of old dolls, the first problem which arises is the question of how authentic the copy should be. The issue is usually decided by personal taste. Many old dolls appear quite ugly to the modern eye; their faces and proportions are those which pleased the taste of their times or reflect the skill (or lack of it!) of the dollmaker. For example, home-made bodies on the china-head dolls were sometimes quite grotesque and I see no reason for taking 'authenticity' to such extremes. However, as I said in my introduction, one cannot simply put old-fashioned clothes on a modern doll and expect it to look Victorian. There is also the question of the materials used to make the dolls; self-hardening clay is very versatile and can be painted to imitate china, bisque, papier mâché and composition very effectively, but it is still self-hardening clay! Few of us have the skills or the facilities or even the inclination to make totally authentic copies of old dolls in the original materials and by the original methods, even assuming that it was possible.

This book is a reflection of my own compromise – the modelled dolls are made in Fimo and Das (see page 12), but modelled, as well as my own talents permit, to resemble the originals as closely as possible. The eyes are acrylic rather than glass because they are the right shape to suit the method (flat-backed) and glass eyes are very expensive. I prefer real hair and mohair wigs to acrylic and I copy the original colours and methods of face painting as closely as possible. I use unbleached calico for the bodies because linen is expensive, but I prefer sawdust for stuffing because it gives the doll weight and the right 'feel'. I'm all in favour of using modern equipment; the sewing machine was not in common use until the 1850s, but I see no reason to hand-sew just for the sake of it, and I wouldn't dream of turning a Georgian doll on a pole lathe when an electric lathe is so much more efficient! Each dollmaker will decide for herself which methods and materials she prefers, and how far she wishes to go towards authenticity. For the purist, the Georgian wooden doll comes closest to the 'real thing'. Despite it being turned on an electric lathe and painted with modern enamel paints, all the materials used are natural: wood for the doll, animal wool for the wig and cotton and silk for the clothes.

Modelling

There is now a variety of self-hardening or oven-fired clays available in this country. I have tried most of them, but the two I find most satisfactory are Das and Fimo. Das is a clay-like modelling material which is relatively cheap, available from most art and craft shops and stationers and is probably the best material for the beginner to use. It is moist, grey in colour (drying to almost white) and works very like ordinary clay. It will not take such sharp definition as Fimo but will sandpaper very smoothly. Das dries in the air, a process which can take up to a week, but more clay can be added at any stage if the surface is dampened to receive it. A head modelled in Das is quite strong (certainly stronger than porcelain) and provided the clay is not used too thick, the head is reasonably light. The drying time can be speeded up by leaving the modelling in a warm atmosphere, such as the airing cupboard. If cracks appear in the surface during drying, simply dampen the area and rub in a little more Das to fill the crack.

Fimo is available in a wide range of colours from some art and craft shops, and is considerably more expensive than Das. It is more like Plasticine than clay in texture and must be thoroughly kneaded before use, which is tiresome. However, it will take very finely detailed modelling and has a smoother surface finish than Das. Fimo is baked in an ordinary domestic oven at a low temperature for approximately twenty minutes to harden it, after which it is quite strong and waterproof. Of the colours available, I have used transparent, white and flesh for dollmaking. Each colour has quite different properties from the others. The transparent, which is in fact a 'marble-effect' white, is easier to knead than the white, and would make a beautiful head – unpainted – except that it seems to get extremely dirty during the modelling! The white is harder to knead, but it sandpapers well when baked (sandpaper seems to have little effect on the other colours) which does make a very smooth finish. The flesh, which would seem the obvious choice, is in fact a rather unpleasant colour and could not be used unpainted as it is too dark. All things considered, the white Fimo is the most practical choice despite the extra effort required to knead it; the advantage of a finished surface which can be sandpapered very smooth outweighs the inconvenience. The biggest argument in favour of Fimo is that it is baked hard so you do not have to wait days for the head to dry – in fact you can paint it and finish it in a day. I suggest to anyone who has not modelled in either material (and who does not already have a preferred alternative) that you try both, and see which suits you best.

I use the 'ball and bottle' method described below, but I also describe an 'all-in-one' method which some readers may prefer. You may also have – or devise – your own method. Modelling in clay is not difficult and making an acceptable doll's head is much easier than you may think. Patience, rather than skill, is required to make a well-shaped, symmetrical head with correctly positioned features. I strongly recommend using a doll, real model or pictures as a guide. Different dolls require different shaped heads and I have gone into more detail with regard to shaping etc in the later chapters. The instructions which follow are general rather than for a specific doll and should be adapted to the individual doll you have chosen to make.

The head is modelled over a removable core, so that it is hollow. A head made of solid clay – other than a very small one – would be impossibly heavy. To give access to the core, the neck is also hollow, modelled around the neck of a bottle or a cardboard tube. To attach the head to the body, the neck has a flange at the lower end, or is mounted on a shoulder-plate. Many antique dolls had a socket neck set into the shoulder-plate which allowed the head to turn, but I have not yet found a way of adapting this to self-hardening clay successfully, so all the dolls in the book are made with either flange necks or shoulder-plates (except the porcelain kits in Chapter 14). Modelled lower arms and legs have grooves scored around the upper ends so that they can be tied onto the cloth upper limbs in the traditional manner.

The core-ball may be compressed cotton or polystyrene and these are available from most art and craft shops. To make the ball a more natural shape, slices are removed from both sides and the front (Fig 1a). The size of the core-ball depends on the doll you are making (see the individual chapters). For those dolls with inset eyes I use oval, flat-backed acrylic eyes available from the specialist stockists. These eyes are now quite cheap and I recommend buying several pairs in different sizes so that you can choose whichever size best suits the individual doll. I have noted the sizes I have used in each chapter, but as individual modelling varies, you may prefer slightly larger or smaller eyes. Tools are a matter of personal choice – I find that I do most of the work with my fingers but a few simple tools like a wooden toothpick, paintbrush handle and small spatula are useful. I also find cotton buds very useful for a number of things – smoothing small areas of modelling, cleaning eyes and later during painting.

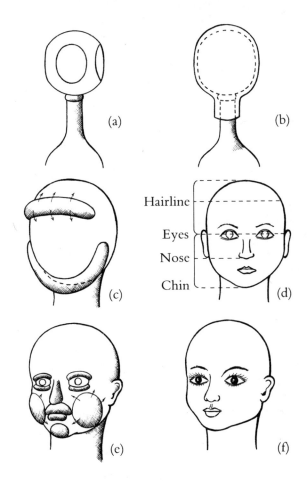

Fig 1 (a) The core-ball showing slices removed for shaping
(b) The head and neck covered with clay
(c) Rolls of clay applied to shape forehead and chin
(d) Proportions of adult head
(e) Building up the features
(f) The finished head

Ball and bottle method
Choose a bottle with a long slim neck without prominent ridges, such as a wine or fruit squash bottle. If you are using Das, grease the neck of the bottle liberally with Vaseline; for Fimo, cover it with aluminium cooking foil, so that the modelling can be removed easily. Place the pared core-ball on the neck of the bottle and cover the ball and neck with rolled-out clay, approximately ¼in thick (Fig 1b). Add 'sausages' of clay to the head to build up the forehead and the chin (Fig 1c). Smooth the added clay well into the head and check that the head is completely symmetrical, looking at it from both sides, above and below. Make sure that the basic shape of the head is correct before building up the features (Fig 1d shows the proportions for an adult

head). The eyes are about halfway down the head, the nose halfway between the eyes and chin and the mouth halfway between the nose and chin. The most common mistake made by the beginner is to place the eyes too high, so check these proportions carefully and mark them on the head. Apply a wedge of clay for the nose and push in the eyes. (For dolls with painted eyes, make a smooth shallow area which will provide a flat surface for painting, or if you prefer, mark the outline of the eye with a small pointed tool.) Push the acrylic eyes well into the clay, checking that they are straight, level and evenly spaced. Apply flattened balls of clay for the cheeks and smooth into the face, add a small flattened ball for the chin, a curved wedge for the upper lip and a straight wedge for the lower lip (Fig 1e). Check again that the head is completely symmetrical and properly proportioned before refining the modelling. Look at the head from above – are the nose and chin central and the cheeks both the same size and shape? Does the forehead recede? Look at the head from below – is the jawline symmetrical? Check the back of the head – is it a good shape? Check the profiles, are they attractive? Does the forehead or chin recede?

Once the basic shape is satisfactory, refine the modelling. Shape the nose, and push out the sides of the nostrils. Shape the lips into smooth curves. Check that the eyelids curve smoothly around the eyes and do not show too much white on them. Add small ovals of clay to either side of the head (Fig 1d) and shape the ears (pierce the earlobes for earrings if required). If the head is to have a flange neck, add a roll of clay to the lower end of the neck and ensure that it is well joined to the main body of the clay (Fig 2a). If the head is to have a shoulder-plate, cut a clean edge around the lower end of the neck (Fig 2b). Check the modelling very carefully from all angles. It can be helpful to hold a mirror to the head, and look at it in reverse. This often shows up mistakes which you would other-wise miss. When you are satisfied with the modelling, smooth it as thoroughly as pos-sible. In Fimo, the smoothing must be done lightly with your fingers and slightly dam-pened cotton buds. With Das, smooth with wet fingers and a paintbrush and water. The smoother the head at this stage, the less the work that will be required later. Do not for-get the back of the head; if it is to be covered

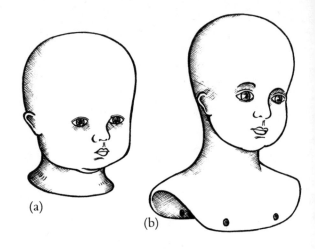

Fig 2 (a) Head with flange neck
(b) Head with shoulder-plate

by a wig it is not so important, but a baby with painted hair must have a good smooth head. Leave a Das head on the bottle in a warm place to begin drying out. Remove a Fimo head carefully, and put it in a baking tin lined with wadding (resting on the back of the head) and bake at a low temperature for approximately twenty minutes.

To make a shoulder-plate, cut a rectangle of rolled-out clay (approximately ¼in thick) and round off the corners. Cut out a circular hole from the centre to fit the lower end of the neck (Fig 3a). Mould the piece over the doll's shoulders (Fig 3b) or a cardboard tube or bottle to shape it and leave it to dry or bake. (If you intend to sew the shoulder-plate to the body rather than glue it, pierce sewing holes back and front.) If working in Fimo, join the neck into the shoulder-plate with a roll of clay well smoothed out on the outside and inside of the piece and bake again to harden the join. (Fimo can be re-baked several times – it seems to get harder and stronger each time.) Allow Das pieces to dry out for a day or two so that they can be handled easily, then remove the head from the bottle and join the neck into the shoulder-plate with a clay roll. Dampen the end of the neck and the centre of the shoulder-plate thoroughly so that the clay will stick properly and smooth out the clay roll on the outside and inside of the piece, then leave the head to dry thoroughly (Fig 3c).

All-in-one method
First make a modelling block (Fig 4). The block is made of round section wood, with

14

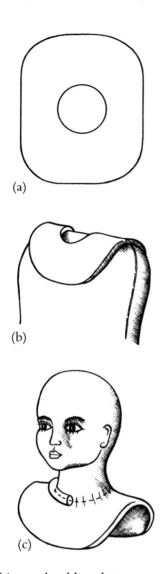

(a)

(b)

(c)

Fig 3 Making a shoulder-plate

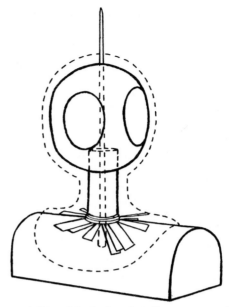

Fig 4 Modelling block for the all-in-one method

the lower edge planed flat. A hole is drilled into the top of the wood at the centre to take a meat skewer. For the neck, roll a tube of cardboard and cut the lower edge to splay out over the wooden block. Push the upper end of the neck tube into a hole bored in the core-ball (with a potato peeler) and push a meat skewer through the core-ball and neck and into the wooden block to hold everything steady. Cover the entire thing – core-ball, cardboard tube and wooden block – with aluminium foil or cling film pressed tightly in place so that the modelling can be removed easily. Model the head, neck and shoulder-plate (or flange neck) as previously described. Leave Das on the block to dry, remove Fimo carefully and bake. When you pull out the meat skewer (which should be done immediately with Fimo before it is baked, and

after one day's drying out with Das) fill the hole in the top of the head (that is, if the doll is a baby with painted hair, for example, and does not have a wig).

I have given only brief modelling instructions and not gone into great detail because I have found after a couple of years of teaching people to make dolls in self-hardening clay that everyone has his or her own method. There are, of course, rules about proportions which should be followed, but each doll-maker develops her own methods for shaping a nose, a mouth or an eyelid and it can be counter-productive to try and follow someone else's methods. Therefore, follow my instructions if you wish, or experiment alone if you prefer. Modelling heads is enormous fun, very satisfying and not difficult.

If your first effort is not all you would wish, keep at it. It's not always the 'real' faces which make the most attractive dolls; very few children actually look like French bébés. The more heads you make, the more competent you will become. When I began, I was happy to settle for something which looked vaguely human but one learns something from every head one makes and every mistake. You will need patience, but given that and an 'observing' eye I believe anyone can model dolls' heads. The beginner should concentrate on getting the proportions right, making the head symmetrical and getting a smooth finish. Keep the modelling simple to

15

begin with and put in more detail as your confidence grows. If the head is nicely shaped and symmetrical, beautiful faces can then be painted on without the need for very detailed modelling. The character doll in Chapter 10 has a very simply modelled face: just cheeks, a chin and nose, and the rest of the detail is painted. As you become more skilful you can copy the shapes and proportions which give the old-fashioned dolls their own characters, ie the heavy faces of the bébés or the aloof expression of the fashion doll. You will learn to observe the difference in proportions between the heads of babies, children and adults. For example, a baby's features occupy only a small part of the head, the eyes are set further apart, the nose is small and fleshy with virtually no bridge and the head is beautifully rounded. If you want to make old-fashioned dolls, look at as many pictures and study as many old dolls as you can. They are different from modern dolls and it is only by studying and comparing them that you will see how different.

Modelled lower limbs can be made for any doll with a modelled head, either just hands as for the Bye-lo baby (page 117), or lower arms and legs as for the Edwardian child (page 110) and the small bébé (page 96). Make the limbs in the same clay you have used for the head. Be careful when modelling limbs that you do not make them too long, so that the finished arm or leg cannot bend at the natural place for the elbow or knee. Arms should be modelled to just below the elbow, and legs to just below the knee, so that when they are tied on the 'bend' is in the cloth upper limb, just above the top edge of the modelled lower limb. As a guide, the elbow is roughly level with the waist and the hands with the crotch; the knee should be slightly lower than half-way down the leg.

The arms and legs are made of solid (not hollow) rolls of clay. To model the arms, roll a 'sausage' of clay of the appropriate thickness, long enough to make the arm and hand in one piece (Fig 5). Pinch and roll the clay to narrow the wrist and flatten the hand into a spoon shape. With a small sharp knife, cut out a wedge between the thumb and fingers and separate the fingers. Roll the thumb and fingers gently to shape, cutting off clay from the ends until they are the right length. For small hands, press the fingers gently together so that they are not separate otherwise they

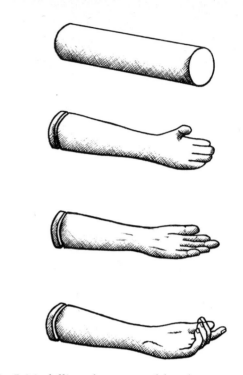

Fig 5 Modelling the arm and hand

would be too fragile. Larger hands may have the fingers separated. The thumb should be long enough to reach to the first joint of the index finger. (Study your own hands to get a better idea.) Add a little clay to the inside of the hand to make a cushion around the thumb, hollow the palm of the hand and push the thumb gently in towards the palm. Curl the fingers slightly into a natural position. Score grooves around the arms, about ¼in from the ends for tying on. Smooth the arms thoroughly and leave to dry or bake.

To model the legs, roll a 'sausage' of clay of the appropriate thickness, long enough to model the leg and foot in one piece (Fig 6). Pinch and roll the clay to narrow the ankle and bend the foot forward, flattening the sole. Round off the toes and heels, pinch to shape

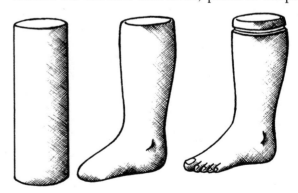

Fig 6 Modelling the leg and foot

the insteps and separate the toes with a small sharp knife. Check that the feet are the same shape and size by putting them together sole to sole. Score grooves around the legs, about ¼in from the ends for tying on. Smooth the legs thoroughly and leave to dry or bake.

When the head and limbs are thoroughly dry, remove the core-ball from the head. Compressed cotton balls can be picked out with your fingers, and will pull out quite easily. Polystyrene must be broken up inside the head using a small screwdriver or something similar and will come out in small pieces. Take care not to damage the head or shoulder-plate as you work. A pair of long tweezers might be useful for pulling out the bits which are hard to reach. If the inside of a Das head is still slightly damp when the core-ball is removed, leave it to dry thoroughly before sanding and painting.

Das parts should be sanded with a fine-grade abrasive paper, taking care not to scratch the eyes. If you wish, the eyes may be covered with small pieces of tape to protect them while you sand. Lumps and bumps may be pared away with a craft knife with a sharp new blade, which may also be used carefully to refine the modelling. Sand the pieces very thoroughly – the smoother they are at this stage the better the finish will be when the doll is painted. White Fimo can also be sanded with fine-grade abrasive paper, but other colours are better smoothed with 000 grade wire wool. Work carefully around the fingers so that you do not snap them off and smooth a clean rounded edge on the flange neck or shoulder-plate. Check that the holes for pierced ears and sewn-on shoulder-plates are clean. When the pieces are sanded as smoothly as possible, you are ready to start painting.

Painting

You can use virtually any type of paint – poster colour, acrylic or bisque paint – for these dolls, but the type I use myself and recommend is Humbrol enamel. Small tins are available from art and craft shops and Woolworths, and you will need the flesh shade and white, both matt. For 'bisque' dolls, mix the flesh with at least as much white, remembering that the colour dries one shade lighter.

When you paint an old-fashioned doll, you are painting it to imitate the material from which the original doll was made. For example, the china doll in Chapter 5 is painted with matt white paint to represent white porcelain and given several coats of high-gloss varnish over the painted hair and features to represent the china glaze. Bisque dolls were made of porcelain which was given a wash of flesh-coloured paint and fired to fuse the matt colour into the porcelain. Bisque varies in colour from one doll to another, but generally the best-quality bisque is a fine pale flesh shade. Composition, which was made from a variety of ingredients including sawdust, plaster, glue and flour, was usually painted a slightly darker matt flesh shade than bisque.

Use fine-quality artist's paintbrushes which will not shed hairs – a ½in wide brush for the flesh painting, and very fine brushes for the details. Cotton buds are useful for cleaning up mistakes. I suggest covering inset acrylic eyes with small pieces of surgical tape (available from chemists) carefully cut to shape to protect them during painting. The modelled parts will require three coats of paint for a really smooth finish to imitate bisque and each coat should be allowed to dry thoroughly before the next is applied. On Das parts, the first coat of paint will raise a suede-like grain in the clay. Leave the paint to dry, then rub the parts with a rough cotton cloth such as a teatowel to smooth them before the second coat is applied. When the paint is thoroughly dry, peel the tape away from the eyes and, if necessary, clean them with a wooden toothpick.

I recommend acrylic paints for the features, because being water-based, mistakes can be easily wiped off. Use very fine brushes, and follow the directions given for the individual dolls. You might prefer to use a drawing pen (eg a Rotring) for the eyelashes, as they need to be fine straight lines and can be tricky to paint, however fine the brush. Fingernails and toenails may also be defined with an outline of pink. I have found that it is best to water down the paint so that the colour is less dense, as this is the way the original dolls were painted. For dolls with painted eyes, mark the eye lightly on the face in pencil (mistakes can be removed with a pencil rubber) then paint the whole area white. When this is dry paint the iris in a watery colour, shading the colour from darker at the top to lighter at the bottom to give the effect of the eye being shaded by an eyelid. Paint in the pupil and, if you wish, add a touch of white to each eye for a high-light. Outline the eye and add lashes as appropriate. Paint the eyebrows to suit the doll, for example the bébés have heavy brows in two tones of brown painted with feathery brush strokes. For bisque dolls, mix flesh, red and a little brown to make a soft warm rusty-red colour for the mouth – bright pink colours do not suit old-fashioned dolls. I find that powder blusher rubbed in with the fingers colours the cheeks more naturally than paint – choose a soft rusty pink shade which matches the lips. If, during the course of painting, the inset acrylic eyes have become dull (through being paint-smeared and cleaned), paint over them with a thick coat of gloss varnish (Das varnish is ideal) to make them bright again.

Wax-dipping

Several of the dolls in the book may be adapted to make wax dolls using the dipped-wax method. Make the head and limbs as described in Das or Fimo (see pages 12–17) and paint them flesh colour. Make a support for the head by gluing a piece of foam tightly around a length of dowelling or the handle of a wooden spoon (Fig 7). Tie on the modelled lower limbs to the cloth upper limbs, so that you have something to hold while dipping the limb.

When working with wax, the following safety precautions should be observed.

1 Never work when small children and pets are around.
2 Always use a double boiler or a pyrex jug or basin in a saucepan of hot water. Do not heat the wax directly.
3 Heat the wax slowly – do not be tempted to turn the heat up to speed things along.
4 Never leave melting wax unattended.
5 Do not let the temperature of the wax exceed 260°F (126°C).
6 If the wax should catch fire, douse the fire with baking soda, not water.
7 Turn off the heat before dipping.

Provided that these precautions are observed, there is no danger in using wax for doll-making.

I suggest a mixture of beeswax and candlewax for dipping old-fashioned dolls as the blend produces a good colour and consistency. You will need a vessel which is large enough to dip the head – and which, when filled, is no more than two-thirds full to allow

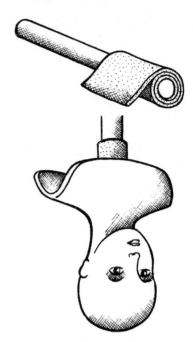

Fig 7 Support for wax-dipped head

for displacement. The quantity of wax will thus depend on the size of the vessel. As a guide, 1lb of wax will melt to about ¾pt. Melt the wax slowly, and when it is completely dissolved, turn off the heat. Check that the head is securely wedged onto the support, then, holding the handle firmly and, with the face uppermost, lower the head into the wax for a few seconds and lift it out again in one slow controlled movement. As the face is uppermost, any blobs or drips should run to the back of the head, and at this temperature the wax will begin to harden immediately. (If you wish to practise this procedure before dipping the head, spear a ball of waste clay or an apple or something similar on a knitting needle and dip this so that you can see how the wax will behave.) Dolls may be dipped once, twice or three times, depending on how thick you wish the coating to be, but definition in the modelling will be lost under a thick coat and a build-up of wax will occur in areas of undercutting such as the nostrils and lips. When the dipping is satisfactory remove the support, then pare away any lumps and bumps with a sharp craft knife and smooth with a little turpentine and a piece of nylon stocking. Scrape off any wax which has seeped under the shoulder-plate with the craft knife, and carefully cut away the wax from over the eyes. Use a wooden toothpick to remove small pieces, then clean the eyes with a little turpentine on a cotton bud. Dip the lower limbs by holding the upper limbs and pare and smooth any blobs as for the head.

Paint the features with oil paints and very fine brushes. Mixing a little turpentine into the paint will speed up the drying process, but it will still take up to a week. Colour the cheeks by rubbing a little colour in with the finger rather than painting it on.

Consider wax-dipping any modelled head which has not turned out as well as you would like. The soft pearly coating will greatly improve an ugly doll and will completely conceal a rough finish. If you make a complete mess of the dipping, don't panic! Re-heat the wax slowly and allow it to get quite hot (but not exceeding 260°F [126°C]). You can smell when it gets hot! Lower the head back into the hot wax and the coating will melt away. Remove the head and wipe it clean with a soft cotton cloth, then allow the wax and the head to cool again before re-dipping. (See *Making Collector's Dolls* for more information on using wax for doll-making.)

Bodies

The dolls with modelled heads and limbs have stuffed cloth bodies. Linen is the ideal fabric for old-fashioned dolls' bodies, but it is very expensive. Any strongly woven cotton fabric can be used, and calico, bleached or unbleached, is a good choice. Some antique dolls had bodies made of cotton-print fabrics, but plain white, cream or beige is more in sympathy with modern taste. Despite the fact that all sewing was done by hand until the 1850s, I prefer to machine-sew the seams on bodies both for speed and strength, and I double-stitch all the seams because they are exposed to some strain during stuffing. Some of the dolls in the book have simple bag-shaped bodies (the type used on the early homemade dolls), while others have shaped bodies with darts and a gusset in the lower back which forms a seat. Elbow, knee and hip joints are made by stabstitching through the body. The lower limbs are tied on with strong button thread into grooves scored around the ends before the doll is stuffed (Fig 8). Always check that you have tied the right and left arms and legs to the correct sides of the body – it is easy to attach them the wrong way round and very annoying if discovered after the doll is stuffed.

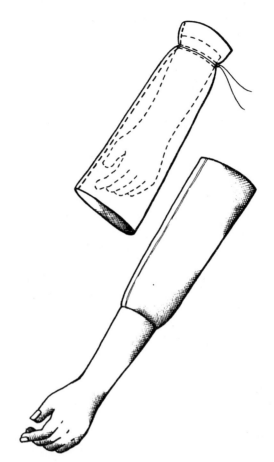

Fig 8 Tying on modelled lower limb to cloth upper limb

Heads with flange necks are also tied on using a strong tape run through the casing at the top of the body. Two people are needed to tie on a flange neck efficiently – one to hold the head, the other to pull up and tie the tape as tightly as possible. A flange neck will allow the head to turn, but should be tied in very tightly so that it is secure. Shoulder-plates may be glued onto the body with UHU or a similar glue or sewn on through holes bored in the lower edges of the shoulder-plate during modelling. I recommend narrow tape rather than button thread for sewing on the shoulder head as it makes a stronger tie with less strain on the holes. The tape, threaded through a darning needle, is passed through the body and one end is pulled through the hole in the shoulder-plate. Knot the tape ends securely and trim (Fig 9). This method is particularly useful for the doll kits in Chapter 14, most of which have shoulder-plates.

If you wish to make the doll poseable, the limbs may be wired. Plastic-covered garden wire serves the purpose very well. I suggest

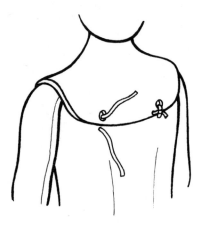

Fig 9 Tying on a shoulder-plate head

drilling a hole down into the centre of the modelled lower limb and gluing one end of the wire into it. When the upper limb is stuffed, care should be taken to ensure that the wire is in the centre of the stuffing and the top end should be bent over to form a loop so that the wire cannot pierce the cloth (Fig 10). I have used this method on several of the dolls in the book, including the fashion doll in Chapter 8. She has a kid body, and you will find notes on making leather bodies in that chapter. Dolls with cloth limbs, such as the felt children (Chapter 13) may also be wired; in this case, both ends should be looped to prevent them piercing the cloth and the wire should be carefully positioned in the centre of the stuffing. A wired limb can be bent to hold a pose, and makes an attractive alternative to arms which simply hang by the doll's sides.

An extraordinary variety of stuffing has been used in antique dolls including seaweed, hemp, bran and cow's hair as well as the more usual sawdust, kapok or powdered cork, but, of these, sawdust is probably the only practical proposition for today's dollmaker. The sawdust should be clean, absolutely dry and sifted to remove impurities. I suggest using a length of dowelling to tamp it down as anything with a point, such as a knitting needle, is likely to punch through the cloth. Stuffing with sawdust needs patience as it must be packed in very firmly for the best results and this takes time. I find a small funnel useful for getting the sawdust into the limbs but put it in by hand in larger areas of the body. Use a little at a time and tamp it down as hard as possible before adding more. The stuffing should be so firm that the doll's body virtually feels as though it is made of wood.

As an alternative to sawdust, many modern dollmakers prefer soft stuffings, and you can if you wish use a soft stuffing for all of the dolls in the book. I strongly advise that you use only a good-quality acrylic or polyester and particularly recommend the CLS quality polyfibre filling supplied by Ridings Craft (see Stockists) which I use myself. Cheap stuffing is false economy – the doll soon becomes limp and droopy! The beginner often has a tendency to understuff; the more firmly the stuffing is packed in, the better the finished doll will look. Remember that a doll's body can swallow an amazing amount of stuffing and limbs and bodies should be plump and well rounded, especially for felt dolls, so don't skimp!

Wigs
With the exception of the china doll in Chapter 5 who has painted hair, all the dolls in the book have wigs. I have used traditional materials for all of them except the felt children who have wigs made from fur fabric. The rag dolls have mohair wool hair, the character doll and Little Women have mohair wigs, and the fashion doll and the bébés have real hair wigs. Many of the specialist suppliers sell wigs in acrylic, mohair and real hair in a variety of shades, styles and sizes, but you may prefer to make your own. For old-fashioned dolls, the material should be suitable to the type of doll. Rag dolls in the past have had wigs made of tow, hemp, linen or silk yarn and human hair, but wool is probably the most common. Use a pure wool rather than a nylon or acrylic yarn in a natural

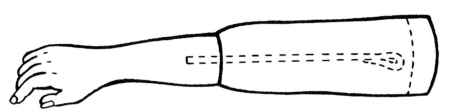

Fig 10 Wiring a limb to bend

hair colour. I particularly recommend mohair wool because the fluffy strands cling together on the doll's head and do not separate to reveal bald patches. Mohair is available from several stockists by the yard (the quality and colour range sold by Hello Dolly [see Stockists] is particularly good) and makes beautiful old-fashioned wigs. Real hair can be bought as wefting (see Stockists), as hair switches, or cut from life-size wigs. As it is one of the oldest materials used for wigs it is suitable for most dolls. For special effects (for example the hair used on the Georgian wooden doll) you can use animal wool which handles very like mohair and is useful for old lady dolls, pedlar dolls etc as well as for 'powdered' hair. Embroidery silk can be used with excellent results, particularly on small dolls, and would make a good alternative to the mohair wigs on the Little Women.

To make a style with a simple parting, measure over the doll's head from the forehead to the centre back of the head and cut a piece of ½in wide cotton tape to this length in a colour which matches the hair. Cut sufficient hair to cover the tape evenly but not too thickly and machine-stitch the parting through the hair and the tape. For a soft doll, stitch the hair to the head through the parting, and for a modelled head, glue the tape to the head. Brush the hair evenly down around the head, then lift one section at a time and coat the head lightly with glue. Smooth the hair down and leave it until the glue is dry. This style may be created with yarn, mohair or real hair and is suitable for Victorian children and lady dolls. If the hair is cut sufficiently long, it may be plaited, curled or twisted into ringlets for a more elaborate style. A fringe strip could be applied across the forehead before the main hair is added, and a small plaited bun might be attached to the back of the head. I have used this method in wool for the child rag doll in Chapter 4 (using wool with the ends twisted into ringlets), and for Beth (using mohair) and Amy (also in mohair with the ends plaited) in Little Women in Chapter 7.

To make a cap-shaped wig which may be sewn onto a cloth doll's head or glued to a modelled head, the toe of a nylon stocking makes a good base. Stretch the toe cap over a polystyrene ball the same size as the doll's head and pin it in place. To make this type of wig you will need strips of hair. These might be machine-stitched lengths of mohair or wool (with or without a narrow tape binding according to preference) or strips cut from a life-sized wig. Working in a spiral from the lower edge up to the crown, oversew the hair strips to the nylon base (Fig 11). When you reach the crown, make a small hole through the base and pull a top-knot of hair through the hole, stitching it securely to the inside. This type of wig may be styled in a variety of ways depending on the length of the hair and the type of doll, but it looks most attractive in long curly styles.

If you have an old wig of the appropriate colour, the method described above makes an excellent alternative to a bought doll's wig, or more simply, you might prefer to cut the crown section from the wig and trim this to fit the doll. Long real hair switches which were fashionable a few years ago can be bought very cheaply from jumble sales and other such sources and make excellent dolls' wigs. I recommend washing the hair switch with shampoo, applying a hair conditioner and then brushing it out flat on a towel. When the hair is almost dry, place it on the doll's head and mould the damp flat base to a dome shape to conform with the doll's head. Keep smoothing and pressing the base to the head until it is dry, then glue it in place and style the hair. This method is very good for smaller, modelled heads, and as the switch is made of real hair you can use any of the methods you would use to style your own hair such as heated rollers, setting lotion or pin curls. I have used commercial dolls' wigs in mohair and real hair for the dolls in the book to show the range available. Full details of wigs and other dollmaking materials and accessories currently available will be found in Chapter 14.

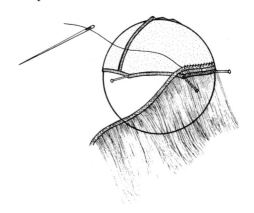

Fig 11 Making a cap wig

2
MAKING THE CLOTHES

The original clothes of antique dolls are of interest not only to the dollmaker and collector but also to the costume historian as they are in many cases the only surviving examples of the type of clothes which were actually worn at the time. Very few examples of full-size costumes dating from before the latter part of the nineteenth century have survived in their original condition, and items of underwear and costume accessories are equally rare. For this reason, the dressed doll is a valuable aid to the student of fashion, showing, in three dimensions, the styles and fabrics used, the cut of the garments and the underwear worn beneath them in a way no painting or fashion periodical can.

Dolls' clothes fall into three main categories – homemade, professionally made and commercially made, and the dollmaker should choose not only the correct style of clothes for the period, but also the type of clothes appropriate to the particular old-fashioned doll she is making. It is almost impossible to recreate antique dolls' clothes totally authentically, even if one uses old materials and copies old patterns, because each generation is so strongly influenced by the tastes of its own time, and has its own feelings about what looks 'right'. This particular problem is not confined to the twentieth century – many Victorian dollmakers chose to costume their dolls in retrospective styles and their versions of seventeenth- and eighteenth-century fashions have an unmistakably Victorian air about them. However, given some research and an eye for detail, the modern dollmaker can produce very attractive clothes for dolls which, though made in modern materials and using modern methods, are quite satisfyingly authentic enough to please most of us and perfectly appropriate for the old-fashioned dolls in this book.

To be successful, the costume must be of the appropriate period, it should be suitable for the 'age' of the doll, and it should be suited to the type of doll. The choice of fabrics, trimmings and fastenings is also important and the underwear beneath the clothes and the accessories should also be appropriate. The fashions in dolls' clothes broadly follow the fashions of real people, which in most cases were not the high fashions of the period. Only the rich wore the very latest styles; most people and dolls wore simplified versions of the current styles or slightly older fashions. A mistake often made among amateur dollmakers is to overdress an old-fashioned doll in very elaborate clothes, fussily trimmed, and often in quite inappropriate materials. With the exception of luxury dolls (eg the poured waxes, the French fashion dolls and the bébés), most nineteenth-century dolls wore relatively simple clothes.

The exceptions to this rule were the commercially dressed dolls which usually had superficially elaborate costumes, generally made from cheap fabrics and trimmings, and very often extremely crudely sewn or glued together. These rather tawdry clothes would not have survived long, so the doll was often re-dressed. Not all commercially made dolls' clothes were poor, especially by the twentieth century when the majority of dolls were sold dressed and the standard of workmanship of the factory-made clothes was often good, but commercial clothes were deliberately designed to be eye-catching, and mass-production methods dictate an economy of fabric and trimmings which does not apply to homemade or professionally made clothes. The Chad Valley Bambina in Chapter 12 is an example of the sort of commercially dressed doll produced in the 1920s–1940s. Her clothes are simple designs, machine-made in brightly coloured felt, simply trimmed with bands of a contrasting colour and felt roses. Her underwear is minimal – just a pair of knickers. By contrast, the sort of dolls which would be sold undressed, like the character child in Chapter 10 and the china doll in Chapter 5, were dressed in homemade clothes. The styles are simplified versions of the current fashions, simply trimmed and with a complete set of underwear.

The Georgian wooden doll, the fashion doll and the French bébés are dressed in 'professionally made' clothes. In the case of the Georgian wooden, the clothes would probably have been made by the family dress-maker in the very latest fashion. The fabrics and trimmings would be of fine quality, the detail accurate and the costume complete with underwear and accessories. The French fashion dolls and bébés were dressed by pro-fessionals who made nothing but dolls' clothes. An entire industry in Paris in the 1860s–1890s was devoted to dressing and equipping these luxury dolls. The standards of workmanship were very fine, the fabrics and trimmings were of the best quality and the doll had every conceivable accessory from hats and parasols to gloves, boots and fans, though oddly, her underwear was often less perfect than her costume!

Notes on the type of costumes appropriate for each period follow, but the serious doll-maker will also find costume reference books useful. Paintings, fashion journals and plates tend to show high-fashion garments rather than the type of clothes worn by most people, but old photographs are an invaluable source of reference for everyday clothes and give a far more accurate picture of what was actually worn. Pictures of old dolls in original clothes and the dolls themselves are the best reference of all, and fortunately there are enough of them in museums and private collections for the modern dollmaker to study in detail. It might come as a revelation to find that not all old dolls wore the sort of exquisitely made lavish clothes in beautiful fabrics that we would imagine them to have worn; in fact many of them, especially cheaper dolls like the peg woodens and those dressed by children, wore very plain, poorly made clothes.

During the eighteenth century, the type of turned wooden doll shown in Chapter 3 was expensive, and was costumed to represent an upper-class lady. Silk was the most popular fabric, either in a plain colour or brocaded with a flower-spray pattern or stripes. Popular trimmings included lace, galloon (a metallic-thread braid), metal sequins and em-broidery. The fashion of the period was the saque-back open robe worn over a matching petticoat, but for informal occasions the 'round gown', which consisted of a stiffened bodice and skirt, was popular. A shift and several petticoats would be worn under the gown, though drawers had not yet come into fashion. Fine linen or cotton was used for underwear. Muslin caps trimmed with lace and ribbons were worn on the towering coiffure, and costume accessories such as fans and long walking sticks were the mode.

By the end of the eighteenth century fashions had become a great deal simpler and many of the wooden Grödnerthal dolls are found dressed in clothes of the Regency period. Lightweight silks and cottons were most popular for these simple high-waisted dresses with puffed sleeves in plain pastel colours and white. Flower-sprig and striped patterns were popular for day wear and poke bonnets, small capes and short jackets were worn outdoors. Drawers made their first appearance in the form of 'leglets' which were cotton tubes tied above the knee. The fine fabrics and lack of concealing petticoats made some form of leg covering essential for modesty and the leglets developed into pantaloons which consisted of two quite separate ankle-length legs, joined at the waist by a casing or waistband. Because they resembled men's trousers, pantaloons were considered very 'fast' at first, and were thoroughly disapproved of by the older generation, but by the 1820s they were generally worn. Cotton and linen were still used for underwear and the early pantaloons were untrimmed, though by 1820, broderie anglaise, tucks and lace edgings were popular. Leglets continued to be worn by those who could not afford pantaloons, and were popular for small girls. Most dolls' clothes at this time were homemade, though some commercially dressed dolls were available.

By 1830, clothes were becoming more elaborate. It was fashionable to have a small waist again and the large gigot sleeves and full skirts emphasised it. Most of the dolls with moulded papier mâché heads, simple kid bodies and wooden lower limbs were dressed in the style of this period. Silk and cotton were still the most popular fabrics, and ribbons, embroidery and fringes were used for trimmings. The first machine-made cottons became available and were relatively cheap as a result of which the upper classes and richer middle classes wore silk! The Grödnerthal dolls had become simpler but were still popular and, like the papier mâchés, were dressed in ladies' fashions, although occasional examples are found dressed in girls' styles. Girls continued to wear pantalettes (as they were now called) but their mamas wore drawers – basically the same garment but now just below knee length. The drawers were still made as two separate legs, joined only at the waist.

Corsets were rarely worn during the Regency period but became popular again when waists came back into fashion. They were rigid and unyielding, and were worn very tightly laced by young girls as well as women, though few dolls wore them. A stuffed bustle pad was often worn to push out the skirts, and similar pads were worn on the shoulders to support the sleeves. The majority of homemade dolls' clothes are simplified versions of the fashion; the waists are small, the sleeves and skirts wide, but there is little sign of the absurdity of the extreme fashion shown in fashion plates of the period. Girls' clothes were basically the same as women's, but the skirts were shorter, showing pantalettes to the ankles.

The 1840s brought wax-over-composition dolls with cloth bodies and dolls with china heads. Small waists and full skirts were still fashionable, but sleeves were smaller and the armhole had dropped well below shoulder level. Some of the more expensive waxed dolls were commercially dressed in silks and laces, but the majority of the china dolls were dressed at home in printed cottons. Underwear was still white and on most dolls consisted of a chemise, open drawers and several petticoats fastened by drawstrings. Few home-dressed dolls wore corsets, and underwear was usually plain and untrimmed. During the 1850s and 1860s, skirts became fuller and fuller and the cage crinoline was introduced, though very few doll-size versions have been found. Underwear remained basically the same though by now it was trimmed with frills, broderie anglaise and lace, and decorated with a little coloured ribbon insertion.

The first commercial patterns for dolls' clothes were published in the 1860s, the domestic sewing machine came into common use and a wide variety of fabrics and trimmings were now available. Lady dolls were still the most popular, some commercially dressed in fashionable clothes, others more simply dressed at home. Many dolls were dressed to represent girls, with very full calf-length skirts showing pantalettes, a little longer than the skirts. The expensive French dolls were dressed in very elaborate professionally made clothes, either as ladies or girls, in silks trimmed with ruching, rosettes and silk braid. They wore hats trimmed with feathers and flowers and the fashionable elastic-sided boots. The baby dolls of the period, usually made of poured wax or wax-over composition, were dressed in the very long baby clothes worn by real infants at that time. Baby clothes were always white, usually cotton lawn trimmed with rows of pintucks and broderie anglaise. All dolls wore layers of clothes – chemise, drawers, several petticoats, dresses and often cloaks and hats as well. The china heads and the wooden Dutch dolls, which were the everyday dolls of the period, were almost invariably home-dressed in simple styles in printed cottons. The composition and wax-over-composition dolls were often commercially dressed in taffeta and silk with net and ribbon trimmings.

During the 1870s, the fashionable and expensive French dolls were popular with the richer upper classes who could afford them and their lavish wardrobes. Fine fabrics and expensive trimmings were used by the professional dolls' dressmakers and milliners to produce the latest styles in miniature. The dolls' clothes were accurate copies of the fashions worn by ladies of the time, made in exactly the same way as the full-size versions and largely hand-sewn. Underwear was usually made of white cotton, the drawers were now usually closed at the back, front or all the way round, and combinations had come into fashion. The chemise and several petticoats were still worn, though by now pretty underwear was popular and no longer thought of as improper. The 'Parisiennes' wore clothes of silk, satin, velvet and fine wool. Pleats, flounces, velvet bands and silk fringes were popular trimmings and it was fashionable to use two different fabrics for the outfits. The styles were elaborate and often very fussy – the basque jacket worn over a bustle skirt was very fashionable; the princess dress and long tunic worn over a trained skirt were also popular. Every item used by the fashionable lady of the time could be bought in doll's size, even horsehair and wire bustles, spectacles and manicure sets!

The bébés of the 1880s and 1890s were also lavishly dressed and equipped. During the 1880s they wore the fashionable low-waisted dresses with short pleated or gathered skirts and fullness at the back of the skirt to represent a small bustle. The bébés also wore chemises and closed drawers or combinations in white cotton trimmed with lace, and strapped leather shoes. During the 1890s, girl dolls often wore long dresses influenced by the Kate Greenaway styles though shorter skirts were also popular. The bébés often wore large brimmed bonnets trimmed with ribbons, flowers and feathers.

The standards of the professional dolls' dressmakers had dropped somewhat since the 1870s, and most of the clothes were now machine-sewn, but they were still very attractive and generally well made. Among the cheaper dolls at this time, the china heads and the wooden Dutch dolls were still dressed at home in simple clothes and the German bisque dolls were becoming enormously popular. The German bisques were usually sold wearing only a cotton chemise, socks, shoes and hair ribbon and were mostly home-dressed, though some manufacturers also produced a range of dolls' clothes. The German 'dolly-faced' bisque dolls were dressed in a wide variety of styles. The commercially dressed dolls often wore frilly, lace-trimmed dresses with ruffles and rosettes and large frilled hats. The cheaper versions wore sprigged cottons, the more expensive ones silk or imitation silk. Their underwear was usually rather poor, made from starched cotton with a little lace trimming. Home-dressed dolls might wear imitations of the commercial clothes, but were usually more simply dressed in the styles worn by children of the period, often made from the commercial dolls' clothes patterns.

The German character dolls usually wore simple, commercially made clothes designed to represent real children's clothes, though alternative outfits were often made for them at home. Knitting had become extremely popular during the First World War and post-war dolls often have knitted clothes, particularly boy dolls. The yoked dresses and white pinafores of the Edwardian period are often found on girl dolls, worn with black stockings and navy blue or white knickers. Liberty bodices became popular for girls and are often found on dolls, though more old-fashioned dolls continued to wear chemises and drawers in white cotton. White lawn trimmed with pintucks and lace or broderie anglaise was very popular at this time, and home-dressed dolls often have entire outfits made in white cotton. Dolls wore buttoned boots or strapped shoes in leather. Child dolls were the most popular type but a few fashionably dressed ladies and babies were produced. Baby dolls were still dressed all in white, but their clothes were shorter than those of Victorian babies.

The fancy-dress styles of children's clothes such as the 'highland' outfit, sailor suit, 'Little Lord Fauntleroy' costume for boys and the 'Kate Greenaway' styles for girls were also adapted for dolls' clothes and many dolls in various materials are found dressed in these costumes from the 1850s until the Edwardian period. Retrospective costumes were also popular and dolls dressed in bridal clothes were made during most periods, being particularly popular during the latter part of the nineteenth century.

As the twentieth century advanced and children's clothes became simpler, so did dolls' clothes. By now most dolls were commercially dressed by the doll manufacturers. Styles and materials varied from one type of doll to another but were usually simple. Boy dolls wore shorts and shirts, and perhaps a knitted sweater and cap. Girl dolls had short frocks with short sleeves, full skirts and often matching knickers. Babies might wear long or short baby gowns or rompers. Plastic shoes began to replace leather and trimmings on clothes and underwear were minimal. Elaborately dressed luxury dolls were still produced, though they usually wore artificial rather than real silk, and hand-made clothes were now a thing of the past.

The beginner should not be daunted by the prospect of making period clothes for dolls – in many cases they are very simple. It is the 'shape' of the garment which is important, and the correct choice of fabric and trimmings. Most of the costumes in the book are quite straightforward, some a little more difficult, and a few are recommended for experienced dollmakers. You will find that the difficulty of the costume is related to the difficulty of the doll, so I would recommend that a beginner starts with something like the

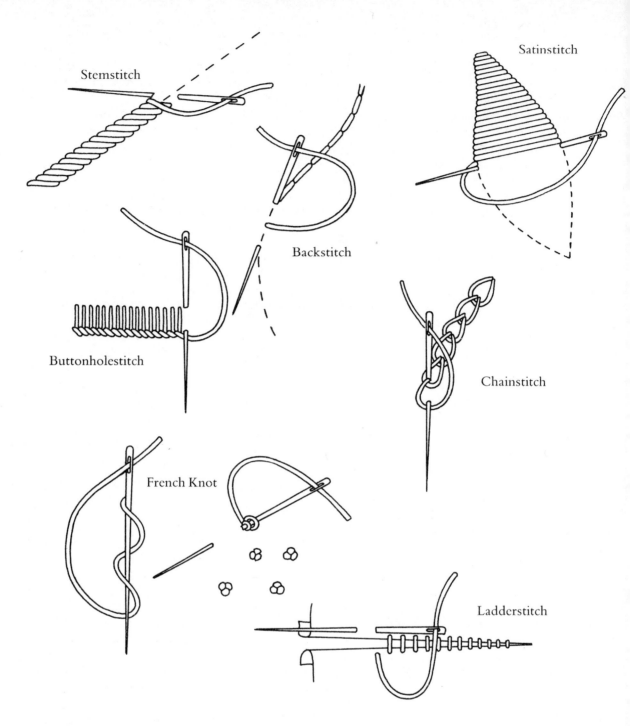

Stemstitch

Satinstitch

Backstitch

Buttonholestitch

Chainstitch

French Knot

Ladderstitch

rag dolls or the china doll and as confidence grows, she can then move up the scale. I hope the experienced dollmaker will enjoy the challenge of the Georgian wooden doll and the French fashion doll.

Materials
Obviously, none of the dolls in the book should be dressed in man-made fabrics, and trimmings should also be made of natural materials wherever possible. Most of us do

Fig 12 Basic stitches used throughout the book

not have access to unlimited quantities of old fabrics, though the occasional lucky find in a jumble sale or antiques market will often provide good dressmaking materials, trimmings or buttons. I'm not in favour of using old material just for the sake of it. It is certainly a good thing when one is re-dressing an antique doll to use a suitable fabric of the same age as the doll and to trim it with old lace, but when one is making original dolls, there is no reason to feel that the new doll must be dressed in old fabric. However, the fabric should be chosen to suit the type of doll – each chapter gives details of the fabrics most suitable for the individual dolls, but your own taste will be the deciding factor.

Most of the dolls' costumes in this book have been made in cotton. Because cotton was widely available from the early part of the nineteenth century, dolls' clothes made in this fabric never look out of place. It also demonstrates that the clothes do not have to be made in expensive fabrics to achieve a lavish effect (see the bébés, and the Bru kit in Chapter 14). I live in the country and find the range of cottons in my local town very limited, so I am delighted to recommend a firm called Village Fabrics (see Stockists) which stocks an enormous range of pure cotton fabrics of very fine quality at extremely reasonable prices. The choice of plain colours and tiny prints is so wide that the 'perfect' fabric for any doll, period or modern, can be found here. Most of the print fabrics used on the dolls in the book have come from Village Fabrics, and, as a minimum order of half a metre is accepted, there is no waste. For a nominal charge, a sample pack containing swatches of every fabric in stock will be sent so there is no guesswork involved. A range like this also means that the dollmaker can pick exactly the right type of print in the right colour for each period rather than having to compromise with what is available in the shops. The greatest advantage is that these fabrics are pure cotton rather than polyester cotton which most shops sell. Pure cotton is not only more authentic for old-fashioned dolls, it also gathers and hangs far better than man-made fibres, and will take very fine pin-tucks, tiny hems and crisp pleats.

For very elaborate clothes, silks and satins are lovely. The modern polyester-based fabrics are very different from the old ones; they are generally much lighter and do not gather and hang as well, so if you can find – and afford – pure silk it is best to use it. Often an old evening dress found in a jumble sale will provide the perfect material for a fashion doll or bébé. The fabric is generally good because such a garment is rarely worn and the silky brocades fashionable in the 1950s and early 1960s are often very similar to the patterns of a hundred years ago. Make sure that any design on the fabric is not overlarge for the doll. Old wedding dresses too can often be used for bride dolls and I have twice been commissioned to dress dolls for middle-aged ladies in the fabric from their own wedding dresses, one a soft pure silk which had mellowed to ivory, the other a stiff white brocaded satin – both delightful fabrics to work with.

Velvet will also suit many old-fashioned dolls, although old velvet is often too badly marked to be of any use and new velvet is all too often made of nylon and too thick. Cotton velveteen, although becoming hard to find, is excellent and the rich colours are those which were so fashionable at the end of the nineteenth century. Look out for old baby gowns – torn or soiled ones are sold cheaply in junk shops and antique fairs and they make lovely Victorian baby dolls' clothes and Edwardian pinafores. Do not be afraid to ask friends and relatives for material. Most people hoard things and will probably be only too willing to get rid of unwanted garments. Doll fairs can also be a marvellous source (see Chapter 15) as many stalls specialise in old fabrics and trimmings for dolls' clothes.

Underwear

White cotton lawn is probably the best choice for the underwear for all of the dolls. Many of the originals would have worn fine linen, but this is now prohibitively expensive though you might consider using linen handkerchiefs to provide underwear for small dolls, ie the Georgian wooden. The trimmings on underwear should be white cotton lace or broderie anglaise. If you have difficulty finding narrow cotton lace, I recommend those supplied by Sunday Dolls (see Stockists) which specialises in fine laces, silk ribbons and other trimmings perfectly scaled for dolls' clothes. Pintucks were a popular trimming on Victorian underwear and several rows of pintucks and a lace edging on petticoats and drawers look very pretty and very old fashioned.

Fastenings on underwear might be buttons and buttonholes, in which case try to find tiny mother-of-pearl or old linen buttons rather than plastic ones (Hello Dolly supplies pearl buttons [see Stockists]). These can also be cut from old garments found in jumble sales, or Edwardian evening gloves. I also suggest asking elderly neighbours and friends who often have button boxes – I have acquired lots of tiny old buttons this way. If you must use plastic, choose the smallest size you can find, usually sold for baby clothes. The majority of antique dolls' underclothes fasten with strings, usually made of narrow white cotton tape which is virtually the same as that found in haberdashery departments. The strings are stitched to either side and then tied, as on the back of a petticoat bodice, or threaded through a casing and pulled up, as on drawers or waist petticoats. For strings for small dolls, I recommend cotton candlewick which is available in several thicknesses from art and craft shops or candlemaking suppliers. (Candlewick is also useful for tying in flange necks and sewing on small shoulder-plates.)

Feather-stitching was a particularly popular trimming on Victorian underwear. This was usually worked in white, or occasionally a pastel colour, and on the better-made underclothes the seams were usually felled (sewn down flat on the inside with hemming), though this is a refinement the modern dollmaker might be happy to dispense with!

Petticoats varied in style and quantity according to the garments worn over them. The Georgian lady usually wore two, one narrow and fairly short, one full and longer under the dress petticoat. By the 1840s, the enormous skirts needed up to six petticoats to hold them out before the cage crinoline was introduced. Flannel was popular for at least one of the Victorian petticoats which was usually white, with the hem often scalloped and embroidered in white. Quilted eiderdown petticoats were fashionable among the rich as they were light and very full. Red flannel petticoats were also the vogue as it was believed that red flannel had healthful properties. The type of flannel used for these petticoats seems to have disappeared, but I have found that flannelette and winceyette make good dolls' petticoats as they are not too bulky. Obviously it is not practical to put six petticoats on most dolls, but Victorian dolls should have at least two. As the object of the exercise was to make the skirts stand out as much as possible, the cotton petticoats would be stiffly starched and various devices such as deep tucks, deep double-thickness hems and rows of piping were all used. The weight of all this must have been considerable – no wonder Victorian ladies drooped!

The cage crinoline dispensed with most of the petticoats, but brought its own problems. It took up an enormous amount of room and ladies were advised not to venture out in a high wind or to attempt climbing stiles in one! Although most women wore one, very few are found on dolls. Some of the fashionable French dolls had them, but the simpler home-dressed dolls made do with petticoats. I have made both a crinoline and the hooped 'panniers' of the eighteenth century for dolls and, though fun to make, they do not look attractive. The crinoline needs the movement of a live woman inside it to bob and sway – on a doll it just looks odd. However, if you want to try it, I recommend millinery wire (available from haberdashery departments) and cotton tape. Make eight or ten hoops of wire, graduated from waist to hem in a smooth bell shape and stitch them to six lengths of tape, evenly spaced around the bell. Make a wide tape casing at the waist edge and thread a drawstring through. The structure rather resembles an uncovered lampshade and wearing it the doll is forced to stand, as sitting her skirts fly over her head in a most unladylike fashion!

I have not used corsets on any of the dolls in the book, though the Georgian wooden has stays and the Edwardian child a liberty bodice. If you want to make corsets, consult *The History of Underclothes* or similar (*see* Bibliography) and choose those appropriate to the period. Although whalebone no longer exists, dolls' corsets can be stiffened by using boning salvaged from old clothes, or modern nylon boning. Collar stiffeners are useful for smaller corsets and petticoat strap clips (available from haberdashery departments) make excellent suspenders.

'Bust improvers' (false bosoms) and hip pads have been used throughout history at various periods when fashion decreed that art should improve on nature. Similar devices are also found on dolls and can be useful to the modern dollmaker in achieving the correct 'shape' for the period. A bust improver (Fig 13a) can be used to round out the bosom on the fashion doll or any other lady doll who needs a little help in this direction. Make little round bags of fine lawn or silk and stuff with a soft stuffing. The original devices were usually pinned to the chemise or tucked into pockets in the dress lining – both methods which can easily be copied. The bustle pad (Fig 13b) is made in the same way and tied

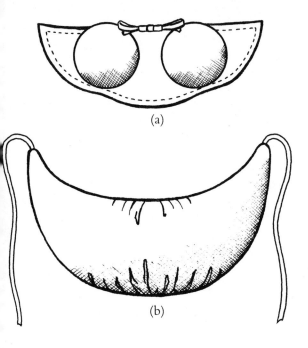

Fig 13 'Bust improver' and hip pad

around the waist with tapes. Such pads, worn on each hip, were also used to support the Georgian skirts, and one at the back was worn in the 1830s and again in the 1870s to 1890s.

The most popular colour for dolls' stockings has been white, though in the 1850s and 1860s horizontal stripes in red and white or blue and white were fashionable. From the 1880s, darker colours, usually black or brown, were worn for everyday, with white for evening or 'best'. Most people wore cotton or wool stockings; the rich, silk. Tubular gauze bandage (available from chemists) makes excellent stockings – the finger size for small dolls, the wrist size for larger ones. You might like to embroider simple flower shapes (clocks) on the outside of Georgian stockings, which were tied above the knee with ribbons, garters being the method most commonly used until suspenders were invented in the 1870s (children continued to use elastic garters). If you prefer to buy stockings, Hello Dolly (see Stockists) has a good range in cotton and nylon in black and white. The bébés usually wore socks in pastel colours in filet crochet worked in silky yarn. Some lacy babies' bootee patterns will adapt to look very like these socks, otherwise plain socks can be trimmed with coloured lace to achieve a similar effect. Edwardian children wore black cotton or

wool stockings and by the 1920s most children wore ankle socks, cotton at first, later nylon.

Trimmings

Choose trimmings as carefully as fabrics, as the wrong trimming can spoil a good costume. Few modern laces, braids and ribbons resemble the old ones so at best we have to compromise. Never use nylon lace on an old-fashioned doll as it looks hopelessly wrong – modern cotton lace may not be perfect but it looks much better than nylon. If you can find old lace so much the better, but only use it if the pattern is delicate enough for the doll – better to use a modern lace with a small enough pattern than an old one which is too large. Examine the trimmings in the local shops with an open mind as they can be surprisingly good; for example, the pleated cotton lace over satin ribbon which is used on the fashion doll was a little expensive, but so perfectly '1870s' that I designed the costume to use it. Ivory-coloured lace usually looks more old-fashioned than white, but you can soften the colour of white lace by dipping it in very weak tea. To age new cotton fabrics and laces, boil them before use.

Modern satin ribbons are often nylon or polyester but you may find that some – often the cheaper ribbons – look less like nylon than others. Very old-fashioned silk ribbons in a wide range of colours and very narrow velvet ribbon can be bought from Sunday Dolls (see Stockists). The nylon velvet ribbon sold in the shops can be very useful as it does not look too modern. Look also at the silky braids and fringes which are sold for trimming lampshades as these are particularly good for Victorian ladies' clothes. Ricrac braid was often used to trim clothes (though the modern type is not the same), particularly in the 1830s. Bands of coloured cotton tape also look very good on simple cotton dresses.

Remember also the self-fabric trimmings like ruffles, frills, pleats and pintucks which were used extensively throughout the nineteenth century. Tucks not only stiffened the skirt, but were also a practical way of allowing for growth on children's clothes, and many Victorian childrens' garments had two or three deep tucks above the hem. Piping was also a popular trimming, around armholes and waistlines in the 1850s and around flounces in the 1870s.

Footwear

Fig 14 gives patterns for a simple shoe in four sizes, which is suitable (though not totally authentic) for most dolls. The shoes should be made in leather which may be cut from old handbags, gloves or leather clothes. Pittards (*see* Stockists), which makes leather goods, will supply a bag of leather pieces in a wide assortment of colours for a very modest charge, enough to provide dozens of pairs of shoes. The shoe is made on the foot so, for modelled dolls, it is easier to make the shoes before the doll is assembled. For soft dolls, I recommend using a plastic or porcelain doll with the same size feet as a 'last' (it is very difficult to make these shoes on soft feet). Cut one upper for each shoe. Cut one sole for each shoe – with the suede outside, or in brown leather so that the shoe looks 'real'. Cut one sole for each shoe in stiff cardboard. With right sides together, stitch the centre-back seams in the uppers (Fig 15a). Working with the sole of the foot uppermost, place the cardboard sole on the foot. I suggest sticking the card sole to the foot with a tiny dab of glue to hold it steady while you work. Slip the upper down the doll's leg and pull the lower edges over the card sole (Fig 15b). Smear glue around the edge of the sole (UHU is excellent) and press the edge of the upper onto the glued area as smoothly as possible. Glue the inside of the leather sole and put it onto the shoe (Fig 15c). Leave the glue to dry, then remove the shoe from the foot. Punch holes on either side to thread the shoe ribbon ties (Fig 15d). For a really professional finish, tiny metal eyelets (available from Sunday Dolls) may be punched into the holes. The shoes may also be trimmed with ribbon bows and buckles.

Accessories

Tiny flowers, feathers, beads and buckles can all be bought from specialist shops, and sometimes in the hat department of your local store. Broken life-size jewellery makes good doll-size earrings, necklaces and brooches for many dolls. Watchstraps will make good belts for small dolls and also provide belt buckles for larger ones. Life-size earrings make doll-size brooches and tiny pearl beads make good necklaces or buttons. Simple straw hats (available from specialist stockists) can also be steamed to shape into bonnets and trimmed with feathers, flowers, ribbons and

veiling to suit a variety of periods. A feather boa of marabou or lambswool trimming would suit a lady doll of the 1890s, or a fur muff with matching cap a Victorian child. Many dolls could wear shawls, simply knitted or crocheted, or made in silky fabric trimmed with lampshade fringe. Paisley shawls which were very fashionable in the 1850s and 1860s can be simply made from a suitably patterned headscarf. Reticules (handbags) came into fashion with the slim Regency styles when pockets were no longer practical and any lady doll from this period onwards might have a drawstring bag containing a tiny handkerchief, purse and perfume bottle.

To make a simple parasol suitable for a fashion doll or Edwardian lady, cut a length of dowelling and whittle a handle at one end (or, more simply, spear on a bead) and a point at the other. Measure the length of the parasol from below the handle to the point and cut a circle of fabric or lace with that radius. Fold the cover in half and seam around the outside edge, leaving a small gap to turn through. Turn through, slipstitch closed and press. Fold the piece in half, seam the straight edges together and turn through. Trim the top edge with gathered lace. Push the point of the handle through the bottom of the cover and secure with a little glue. Furl the cover around the handle and tie with a small piece of ribbon. (This method has been used for the parasols for the dolls on page 120.)

Fans were popular accessories from the seventeenth century onwards and are particularly suitable for stylishly dressed lady dolls. To make a simple fan, cut a semi-circle of lace and bond it to iron-on Vilene. Trim the curved edge with lace and fold the piece as shown in Fig 16. Secure the folds by sewing through at the base.

To make a 'proper' fan with sticks, use fine wood strip (sold in art and craft shops) or fine strips of stiff cardboard. Pierce a hole through one end of each stick (in wood this must be done with a tiny drill bit to avoid splitting the wood). Thread fuse-wire through the holes and twist the ends together to form a loop (Fig 17a). Spread out the sticks and cut a cover (leaf) for the fan in light fabric, lace or paper. Glue carefully along each stick and place the cover in position (Fig 17b). If you

Fig 14 Simple shoe patterns

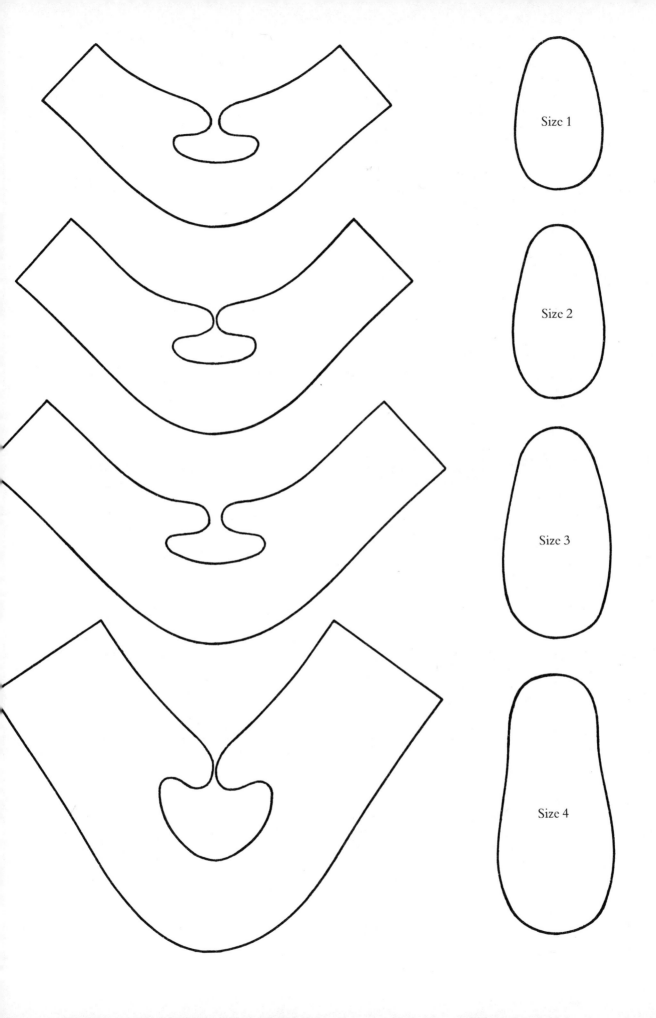

Size 1

Size 2

Size 3

Size 4

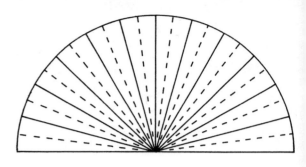

Fig 16 Simple folded fan

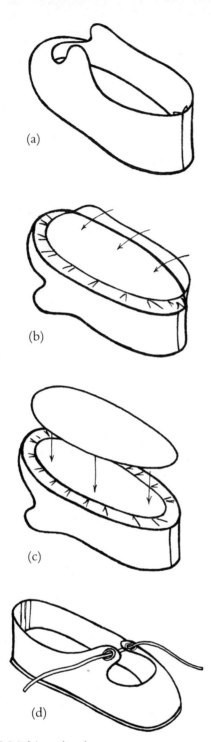

(a)

(b)

(c)

(d)

Fig 15 Making the shoes

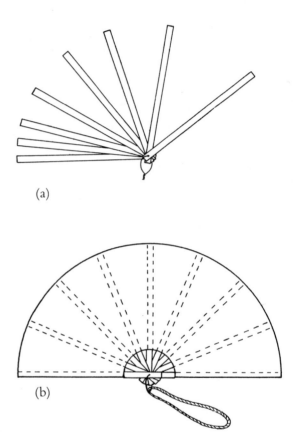

(a)

(b)

Fig 17 Fan with sticks

wish, glue a fine lace edging around the cover. This method has been used for the Georgian lady's fan (page 40), using a landscape picture cut from wrapping paper for the cover and wood strip for the sticks. If the fan is well made it will fold and open properly, but it is of course fragile. Thread a ribbon through the wire to tie around the doll's wrist.

To make the sort of earrings which the French fashion dolls and bébés wore in their pierced ears, choose glass or pearl beads (not wood or plastic) in a colour to match the costume. The earrings were usually made from one larger round or pear-shaped bead with one or two tiny beads on either side. Cut two 3in lengths of fine fuse-wire and bend one end of each piece into a tiny loop to prevent the beads slipping off (Fig 18a). Thread the first bead and bend the wire loop up over it, then thread the other beads. Push the end of the wire through the doll's ears

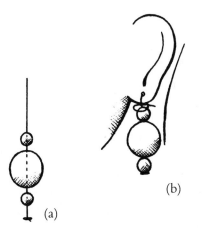

Fig 18 Bead and fuse-wire earrings

from front to back, twist the end around the earring to secure, and trim the wire (Fig 18b).

Finally a few notes for the dollmaker who wishes to make her dolls' clothes as authentically as possible. Firstly, the question of hand versus machine sewing. The domestic sewing machine was in common use by the 1860s, so homemade and commercially made dolls' clothes from this date onwards might well be machine-sewn. The fine-quality professionally made clothes were still made largely by hand until the 1890s and anything made before 1850 would be hand-sewn.

Gathers on Victorian clothes were usually sewn through a double thickness of fabric. The edge to be gathered was folded to the inside and pressed. One gathering thread was worked close to the folded edge and a second about half an inch below. The gathers were pulled up and stroked with a pin or needle to lie absolutely evenly. The bodice or band which was to be joined to the gathered part was sewn on from the outside. The edge of the flat part was also turned under and pressed, then the flat part of the work was laid over the gathers and hemmed in place, each stitch picking up one gather. As you can imagine, this method takes far more time and effort than the modern method. Tucks were made by measuring precisely and drawing threads out of the cloth to mark the line of each tuck. They were sewn along the drawn thread with tiny hemming or running stitches.

Hems on early dolls' clothes are usually very small because fabrics were expensive and could not be wasted on parts which did not show. However, after about 1835, deep hems were commonly used to help the skirt stand out. At the same time, deep tucks and corded hems were used on underwear to serve the same purpose.

Piped armholes and waist seams are found on many dolls' clothes of the 1840s–1860s. Fine piping cord was used inside a bias-cut strip of dress fabric and the piping was stitched in at the same time as the seam, sandwiched between the two pieces.

Strings were used to fasten most early dolls' clothes and continued to be used well into the twentieth century. Edges were pinned with hand-made two-part pins but by the 1830s, one-part pins, copper and brass hooks and eyes and rubber elastic were in existence, and cloth buttons with shanks were used particularly on underwear. Metal eyelets were used on corsets at this time. Safety pins and suspenders were invented in the 1870s, and zips in the 1920s.

I strongly recommend that for more complex patterns – eg the Georgian wooden and the fashion lady doll – you should cut toiles (patterns) from kitchen paper and fit them to the doll. Any adjustments can then be made to the pattern before cutting the fabric.

I suggest you use millinery wire or fine cane for wiring shirred bonnets and hats. I would also recommend lining clothes, cutting the linings from the same pattern. Most old dolls' clothes were lined in fine cotton or silk, and it does give the costume 'body'. Always pin up the hem of a dress on the doll to judge the most attractive length and always fit the clothes several times as you are making them; individual dolls will vary in size and shape according to individual modelling, sewing and stuffing. It is usually sensible to dress a doll from the 'skin' outwards, especially if it is to have several layers of clothes.

Always remember that in spite of everything the doll you are making is *your* doll. Don't be influenced by anyone else's tastes – follow your own. If the doll pleases you, then it is 'right'.

3
THE GEORGIAN WOODEN DOLL
(c1750)

Dolls of the late seventeenth and eighteenth centuries are rare and most of them are in museum collections, but it is perhaps remarkable that they have survived at all. These have probably only survived because they were, in their time, comparatively expensive toys. Wooden dolls were made both in Germany and England throughout this period, sold both dressed and undressed, but it was only the richer middle- and upper-class parents who would buy these 'babies' for their children. At the beginning of the eighteenth century, many dolls served a dual purpose. Before the advent of fashion journals they were dressed and sent out to dressmakers and milliners in country areas to show the latest fashions from Paris and London, and no doubt when they became too shabby for their original purpose were passed on and re-dressed as a child's toy. Simpler dolls were also made specifically as toys and were often sold at fairs, like St Bartholomew's Fair in London which sold the Bartholomew Babies. The simple carved wooden dolls were very much a 'cottage industry' both in England and Germany. One person or family would carve the dolls and another paint them. In the earlier part of the century most dolls sold as toys were dressed at home but by the end of the period, many were commercially dressed.

The earlier dolls, of which Lord and Lady Clapham in the Victoria and Albert Museum are a superb example, have wooden heads and bodies turned on a lathe. The legs and arms might be made of wood, peg-jointed to the body, or of cloth or leather nailed on. The heads are usually large with the features painted over a layer of gesso (liquid plaster) used to smooth the surface. Usually only the head and shoulders are painted and varnished. As the century progressed, the heads became smaller and inset glass eyes, usually dark brown or black, replaced painted ones. By the end of the century blue glass eyes were popular. The name generally given to this type of doll by collectors is 'Queen Anne', but this is confusing as Queen Anne reigned for only twelve years and the early examples of this type date from the reign of William and Mary and the latest to George IV. The American name 'Mary-Anne-Georgians' is somewhat cumbersome but more accurate.

Many of the surviving dolls have wigs of human hair, some of tow or wool. As powdered hair was the fashion, it is reasonable to assume that some of these wigs were originally powdered – indeed occasionally a doll retains the silk 'cushion' on top of the head over which the hair was drawn up to make the towering coiffure of the period, but the powder has long since disappeared.

From the examples which retain their original clothing, such as Lord and Lady Clapham and the Old Pretender doll in the Bethnal Green Museum, we see that the dolls were dressed in miniature versions of real clothes of the time, complete to the smallest details. The dolls mentioned are exceptional in that their clothing is made from the finest fabrics available, used new. Most dolls of the period are dressed in clothes made from many small pieces of fabric stitched together, probably the smallest scraps left over from ordinary dressmaking, as fabrics at this time were very costly.

The typical Georgian doll wears a knee-length shift, usually cotton and perhaps trimmed with lace; stays with shoulder straps and a stiffened front panel (stomacher); and several cotton petticoats (called undercoats at this time). Drawers were not worn during this period (except by Italian ladies). The stockings were knitted in silk or cotton, often decorated with clocks (embroidered motifs) and tied above the knee with ribbon garters. The doll's gown might be a round gown or an open robe with petticoat. The saque-back robe became very popular by the middle of the century and it is a style often found on

Fig 19 Georgian doll

Georgian dolls. One or two pockets were usually tied around the doll's waist under the petticoat. These were both fashionable and practical but were replaced by reticules when the slim dresses of the Regency period were introduced. Access to the pockets was through slits in the petticoat. Very often the pocket will contain a tiny handkerchief and pin cushion. Pins were a vital and expensive part of Georgian costume. They were made in two parts (hand-made of course) and used to pin various parts of the clothing (even babies' clothes) in place.

The quality of the dolls' clothes will vary according to where they were made. The home-dressed doll, with clothes made by the family's dressmaker or a skilled mother or aunt, will usually have beautifully sewn and finished garments with fine detail, but the commercially dressed version is more likely to be much simpler, the clothes often lined with paper and trimmed with rather tawdry

braids. The stitching and all the trimmings were done by hand. The most popular fabrics for dolls' clothes were cotton for the underwear, and silks, brocades, satin or chintz for the gowns and petticoats. Wool was considered very 'lower class' and rarely used. Colours were generally soft and patterns delicate. Green, blue, yellow and lavender were popular and stripes and floral sprays were fashionable. Cosmetics were used liberally throughout the period and this is reflected in the face painting of the wooden dolls with their rouged cheeks and black face patches.

Our doll is of the earlier type; she has a large head and torso turned in one piece. The unjointed arms are nailed to the shoulders with leather strips and the legs are peg-jointed at the hips. The features are painted onto the face over a layer of gesso and varnished, and white animal wool represents powdered hair.

To make the doll, you can use either new wood from a timber merchant or DIY shop, or old wood, perhaps the leg from a piece of furniture. It should have a straight grain and be free of knots. I would recommend pine for its availability, ease of working and light weight. The head and body are turned on a lathe, then refined to shape with a chisel. The legs and arms are turned, then shaped with a chisel and craft knife. A lathe and the right tools are essential to make this doll, though no great degree of skill in woodwork is necessary. If it all sounds a little daunting to someone who has never worked with these tools, I suggest that you try an evening class in woodwork, or more simply, coax a husband, friend or neighbour to make the doll for you! When carving the hands, remember that most of the original dolls had very crude hands, rather like wooden forks. If you prefer, you could substitute stuffed leather or cloth arms, nailed to the shoulders, but ensure that they are the same length as the pattern and not too plump.

The doll wears a lawn shift, trimmed at the neckline with lace which can be seen above the bodice of the robe, calico stays with ribbon shoulder straps and a stiff brocade stomacher-panel which laces down the back. The stockings are made from tubular gauze finger bandage (which looks very convincingly like knitted cotton) and the shoes from fine dark-red kid trimmed with tiny buckles. She wears two undercoats, both with drawstrings at the waist. One is of white calico with a deep hem to help the skirts stand out, and the other of white lawn. She also has a pair of pockets. The saque-back robe à la Française and its matching petticoat (c1750) are both made of sea-green silk taffeta trimmed with self-fabric ruching and dark pink silk-ribbon bows. The open front of the robe is pinned to the stomacher at each side. The doll wears a mob cap of white organdie with double lace frills and she carries a fan. All the clothes are removable as were the better originals and the patterns are authentic, copied from clothes of the period.

Choose the fabrics for this doll carefully. Consider only natural fabrics such as silk, silk taffeta, satin, silk brocade or chintz for the gown. Unless you can find a pattern which is *very* Georgian and perfectly in scale it is better to use a plain colour. The fabric should have some body, being fairly stiff but not thick. The lace should be a fine cotton or silk lace in white or ivory and the ribbon for trimming should be very narrow and silk – not

nylon-satin baby ribbon (*see* Stockists). The underwear and pockets should be white; lawn, calico or fine linen are all suitable and I recommend cotton candlewick for the strings. The stays may be made in cotton, calico or a brocade or silk, with or without the stomacher panel (I have used embroidered ribbon). If you choose to make a plain front to the stays you may like to lace the fronts of the robe with narrow silk ribbons (Fig 28). This looks very pretty, but it conceals the stomacher. If you wish to make the dolls' clothes as authentic as possible, they should be hand-sewn. My own instinct is to compromise – sew by machine and hem and finish by hand! It is for you to decide.

Georgian Wooden Doll (c1750)
(15in tall)
Difficulty 5/Colour picture page 49
Body: Figs 20, 21 and 22
Clothes patterns: Figs 25, 26, 27 and 28

TOOLS
lathe
woodworking chisel
woodturning chisels
fretsaw
small file
drill with 1/8in bit
vice
calipers
craft knife

MATERIALS
1 piece of wood 8×2½×2½in for head and body
2ft length of ¾in square wood for legs and arms
scrap of leather for hinges
2in piece of 1/8in dowelling for pegs
small brass pins
white woodwork glue
sandpaper
white animal wool for wig
gesso
paints
brushes
varnish
narrow white tape
thread

Working with the drawings of the doll's body (Figs 20 and 21) in front of you, centre the 8in block of wood on the lathe and turn it until it becomes cylindrical and 2½in in diameter. Mark in pencil the positions of the neck,

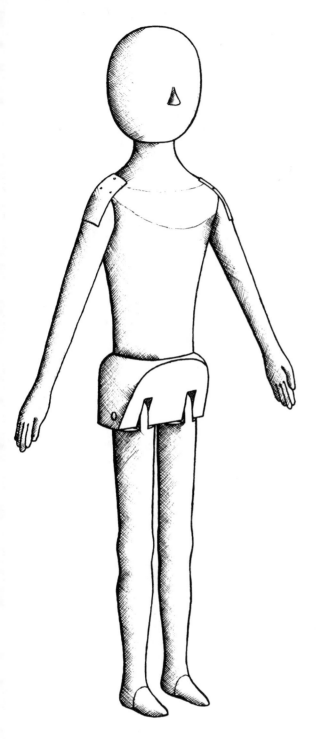

Fig 20 The assembled wooden body of Georgian doll

gouge reduce the head and hips to the required diameters. Continue with the gouge to shape the head, neck and torso. You will now have a round 'skittle-shaped' piece which resembles Fig 21a. Check that the dimensions are correct, and smooth with medium-grade sandpaper.

Clamp the hips of the piece horizontally into the vice. With a 1in woodworking chisel pare a flat plane on the back of the torso as shown in Fig 21b and smooth away the sharp edges at either side of this plane into the body. Turn the piece over in the vice and chisel away the slightly concave pelvis and the ridge above the chest. This ridge is smoothed away at back and front, the original shape remaining only at either side to form the doll's shoulders (Fig 21b).

Mark in pencil and cut the slots for the legs in the lower torso with a fretsaw (Fig 21a). Clean these slots with a small file and check that they are parallel and uniform. Using a drill with ⅛in bit drill through the hips from both sides. Do not drill right through the torso as the legs are pegged independently to ensure that they both move freely. You will note in Fig 21b that these holes are drilled to the front of the torso, not through the centre.

To make the doll's nose, glue a small wedge-shaped piece of wood to the face with white woodwork glue. When this is thoroughly dry, refine the nose shaping with a craft knife.

Cut two 5½in lengths of ¾in square wood for the legs. Turn these two pieces to represent simple legs as shown in Fig 22 (the feet are not included in the turning). To shape the feet, cut a flat plane, ⅜in high, at the lower front of each leg and glue a small piece of wood to this plane. Shape the wood pieces into feet with a craft knife. (The finished foot should be slightly less than 1in long to fit the shoe pattern.)

At the top of each leg cut away the wood at either side to leave a tenon (parallel with the foot) which will fit into the socket in the body (Fig 22a). Work gradually, paring the tenon until a snug fit in the socket is achieved. Round off the front edge of the tenon as shown in Fig 22b. To ensure free movement of the legs the tenon is not pushed right into the socket, but a small gap is left between the top of the tenon and the socket and the top edge of the leg and the hip (Fig 23a). Having adjusted the leg so that it moves freely,

shoulders and hips. With the wood turning on the lathe, use a parting tool (this is a chisel with a wedge-shaped blade) or a small gouge to reduce the wood at the neck and the waist until the required dimensions are reached. (Use the calipers to measure these dimensions at frequent intervals as you work.) With a

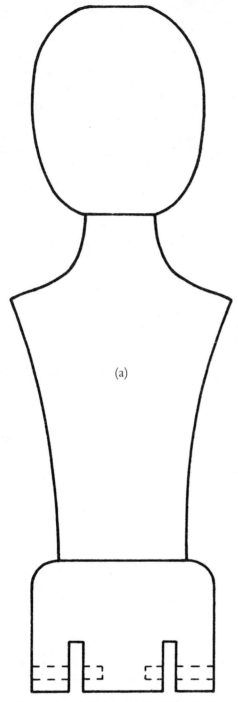

(a)

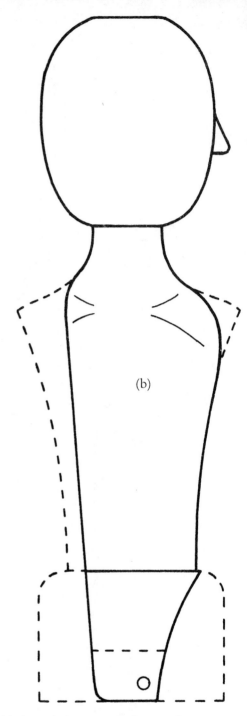

(b)

Fig 21 (a) Actual size pattern for turning head and torso of Georgian doll
(b) Side view showing areas to be pared from torso

replace the drill in the hole drilled in the hip and drill through the tenon (Fig 23b). Insert ⅛in dowelling through this hole to peg the leg. Repeat for the other leg. (If the pegs do not fit tightly, glue them in place, but ensure that the glue does not touch the tenon.)

Cut two 5in lengths of ¾in square wood for the arms. (Do not use a thinner wood, because though the arms are turned much thinner than ¾in the extra width is required for the hands.) Turn the pieces on the lathe to shape simple arms as shown in Fig 22c.

Remove from the lathe and round the top of the arm to a dome shape with a craft knife and sandpaper. Slice away the underside of the top of the arm at an oblique angle as shown in Fig 22d. Carve the hands with a small chisel and craft knife, forming a simple fork-shaped hand with separate thumb. Attach the arms to

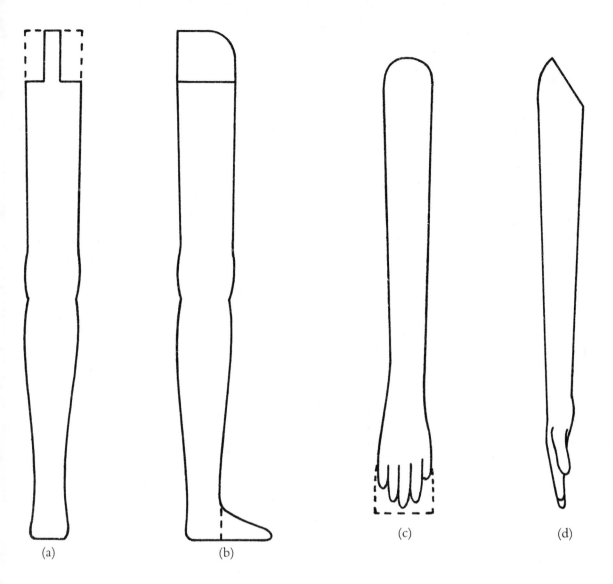

(a)   (b)   (c)   (d)

Fig 22 Actual size patterns for legs and
arms of Georgian doll

the shoulders with small strips of leather. The
leather is glued to the top of the arm and the
shoulder and tacked to the shoulder with
small brass pins. (Do not attempt to tack pins
into the arms as this would split the wood.)
Sandpaper the doll carefully with fine-grade
paper and wipe clean.

Paint a coat of gesso (liquid plaster available
from art shops) over the head and shoulder
area and the arms up to the elbow (you can
paint straight onto the wood if you prefer). If
you wish, gesso can be used to build up the
features on the face to give more shaping.
This was a technique often used on the early
dolls which produced a virtual 'mask' of
plaster with the nose, mouth and chin quite
strongly shaped. It is done by painting on a

little gesso at a time and allowing it to dry
before applying more, thus gradually building up the required shape.

When the gesso is thoroughly dry, sand it
with fine-grade paper. Paint the head and
shoulders and lower arms in a pale flesh
colour. I recommend Humbrol matt enamel
paints, mixing white and flesh colours to the
required shade. You will require two, possibly three, coats and the paint should be
allowed to dry thoroughly between each coat.
Use a very fine, good-quality brush to paint
the features. As it will be sealed with varnish,
any type of paint including poster and acrylic
is suitable. Use Fig 24 and the colour picture
on page 49 as a guide. Mark the features
lightly in pencil – mistakes can then be wiped
off with a damp cloth.

The eyes are painted in black with fine
dotted lines above and below them. The

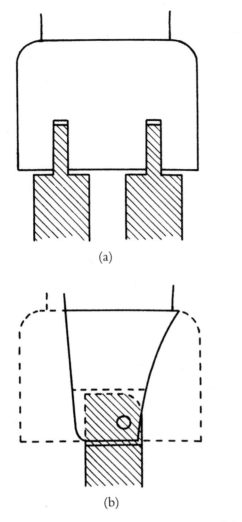

(a)

(b)

Fig 23 Showing how leg tenons are pegged into hip sockets

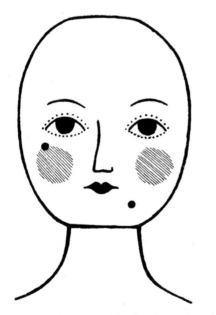

Fig 24 Face-painting guide for Georgian doll

arched eyebrows are black or dark brown. The mouth is a rather bright red and the cheeks a lighter red. Add the black patches beside the eye and mouth. When the paint is dry, varnish the head, shoulders and lower arms. I recommend Humbrol satin finish spray varnish as it is easy to use and not too shiny. Leave the doll aside until the varnish is thoroughly dry, preferably overnight.

To make the wig, measure around the doll's head at the hairline and cut a piece of narrow white tape to this length. Stitch animal wool to the length of tape. Apply glue to the hairline and stick the hair in place with the tape uppermost. Draw all the hair up to the back of the head and tie in a bunch with thread. Coil the ends into a small bun and secure. Make a ringlet and glue to the hairline so that the ringlet hangs over one shoulder (*see* Wigs, Chapter 1).

GEORGIAN DOLL'S CLOTHES
½yd cotton (36in wide) for underwear
1yd fine cotton candlewick for strings
8in tubular gauze finger bandage for stockings
scrap of thin leather for shoes
2 tiny buckles for shoes
1yd fabric (36in wide) for robe and petticoat
2yd narrow cotton lace for trimming
1yd narrow silk ribbon for trimming
scraps of organdie and lace for mob cap and fan
white button thread
thin candlewick thread
small hook and bar fastenings

To make the shift, cut the pattern in fine cotton (Fig 26). Stitch the side seams from the sleeve ends to the lower edge. Roll a narrow hem around the neck and trim with lace. Turn a narrow hem at the sleeve ends and trim with lace. Hem the lower edge. Thread white button thread through the neck and dress the doll in the shift. Pull up the button thread and tie ends in bow at centre front.

To make the stays, cut the pattern in fabric and in lawn for the lining (Fig 25). If the stomacher panel is used, centre this on the stays and stitch in place. With right sides facing stitch the two pieces together around the outside, leaving one back edge open to turn through. Clip the curves, turn through, slipstitch the opening closed and press. Try the stays on the doll to gauge the length of ribbon straps. Stitch straps in place. The stays may be laced by simply threading thin candle-

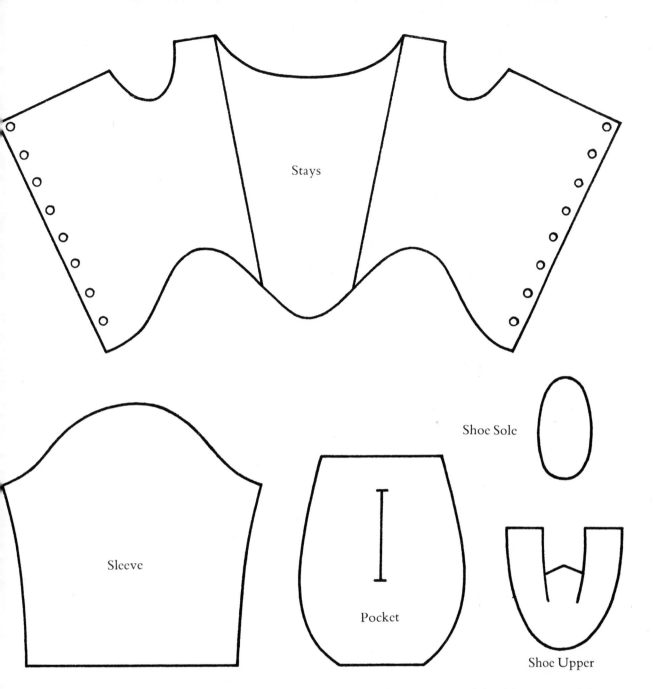

Figs 25 and 26 (overleaf) Clothes patterns for Georgian doll

wick or button thread with a darning needle, or you may prefer to make eyelet holes edged with buttonholestitch as shown on the pattern (metal eyelets were a later invention). Note that the stays are put onto the doll *after* the undercoats and petticoat.

For each undercoat, cut a piece of material 9×18in (this allows for a deep hem). Cut one in stiff cotton (eg calico) and one in fine cotton (eg lawn). Stitch the centre-back seam and turn a narrow casing at the top edge.

(Note: If the selvedge of the fabric is used for the top edge of the undercoat, the casing is less bulky.) Turn up and hem the lower edge. Thread thin candlewick through the casing, pull up and tie at the centre back of the doll. Allow the undercoats to fit loosely at the waist, so they sit below the waistband of the petticoat.

Cut the tubular gauze finger bandage in half to make two 4in lengths. Stitch across one cut end of each piece, turn through and pull up the doll's leg, tucking in the raw top edges. Secure above the knees with fine ribbon garters tied in bows.

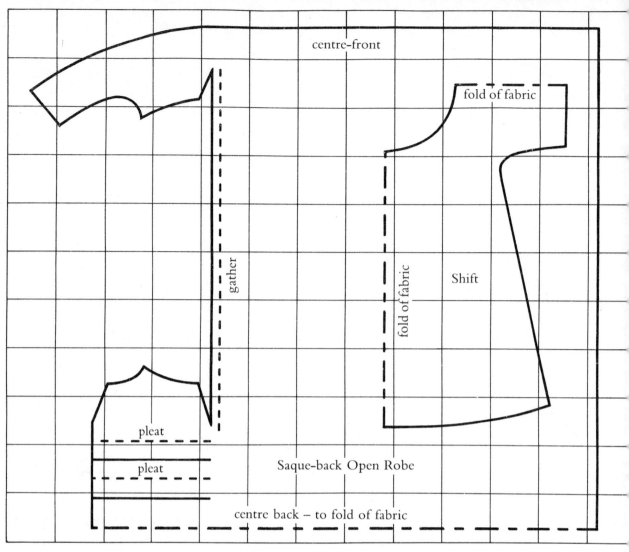

centre-front

fold of fabric

gather

fold of fabric

Shift

pleat

pleat

Saque-back Open Robe

centre back – to fold of fabric

Cut one sole and one upper for each shoe in thin leather (Fig 25). Stitch the back seam on each upper with oversewing stitches on the wrong side, then blanketstitch the upper to the sole on the right side. Slip buckles down the tongues, or glue them to the uppers.

For the pockets, cut four pieces from the pattern (Fig 25) and cut slits as shown in one of each pair. Buttonholestitch around the slits. With right sides facing stitch one slit piece to one un-slit piece around the outside edge. Turn through to the right side through the slit and press. Stitch the pockets to a piece of thin tape or candlewick to tie around the doll's waist with a pocket (slit side uppermost) over each hip (Fig 27). If you wish, make a tiny handkerchief and pin cushion to go in the pockets.

To make the petticoat, cut a piece of fabric 6×20in for the skirt, a piece 3×30in for the frill and a waistband to fit the doll's waist with a small hook and bar fastening. To give

access to the pockets, cut a slit approximately 1in long at either side of the skirt piece from the top edge. Buttonholestitch around the slits to prevent fraying. Stitch the centre-back seam in the skirt piece to 1½in below the

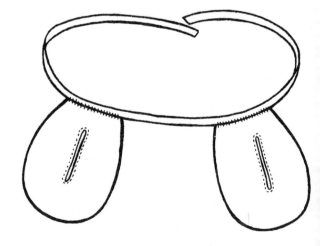

Fig 27 Pockets

waist. Turn and hem the remainder to form facings. Gather the top edge of the skirt to the waistband, concentrating the fullness to the sides and back and ensuring that the pocket slits are evenly placed over each hip. Stitch the short edges of the frill together, then fold and press the frill in half along its length. Gather the top (raw edges) of the frill evenly and stitch to the lower edge of the skirt. Stitch a small hook and bar to the centre back of the waistband.

To make the ruffled trimming (furbelow) for the petticoat, cut a strip of fabric 1in wide × 15in long with pinking shears. Run two gathering threads through the length of the piece and pull up evenly to form ruching. Stitch the furbelow to the petticoat through the lines of gathering across the front of the skirt above the frill, tucking in the ends to neaten. (On antique dolls, trimmings on the petticoat are confined to the front – the area which shows beneath the open robe.) Stitch tiny silk ribbon bows to the furbelow at either side of the centre front.

If the fabric you are using for the robe does not have sufficient weight to hang well, I recommend making up the robe in both fabric and a lining (eg silk or lawn) and stitching the two together right sides facing down the fronts and across the back, omitting the facings described below, and then turning through and completing with the ruched robings. For a fabric which has sufficient body to hang well, follow the method as given.

Cut the robe with the centre back to the fold of the fabric (Fig 26). Make two rows of small gathering stitches at the top edge of each side of the skirt as shown on the pattern. Fold, tack and press the pleats on the back of the robe – do not remove the tacking. Stitch the shoulder seams, noting that these seams are in fact on the back of the robe rather than on the shoulder. Gather the sleeve heads to ease and stitch them into the armholes. Stitch the sleeve seams through the underarm and down the side seams of the bodice. Pull up the gathered top edges of the skirt and stitch to the lower edges of the bodice. Make small hems on the sleeve ends. Face the top edge of the back with matching bias-binding, tape or a piece of dress fabric. Face the front edges of the robe with bias-cut dress fabric or matching bias-binding, hemmed in place (this hemming will be concealed by the robings).

Turn up and hem the lower edge of the robe (and the lining if you have used one).

To make the robings cut two strips of fabric 1in wide × 20in long for the fronts and two strips 1in wide × 3in long for the cuffs. Turn under and press the long edges on each piece. Run two gathering threads through the length of the pieces and pull up evenly to form ruching. Stitch in place to the fronts of the robe and the lower ends of the sleeves through the lines of gathering, turning in the ends to neaten. Stitch gathered lace frills to each sleeve end and a small silk ribbon bow to each cuff.

Pull out the tacking threads holding the pleats. The robe à la Française has pleats which hang loose from the top, but if you prefer to make the robe à l'Anglaise, stitch the pleats down to the waist.

Put the robe on the doll and pin the fronts to either side of the stomacher. If you prefer to lace the robe, work five small loops at either side of the front edges and thread narrow silk ribbon with a darning needle, lacing from the bottom up to the top and tying the ends in a bow at the front (Fig 28).

Fig 28 Ribbon-laced front bodice

To make the mob cap, cut a circle of organdie, muslin or fine lawn 7in in diameter (use a tea-plate as a guide). Roll a small hem around the edge and sew on two rows of narrow lace. Gather the cap above the lace with white button thread, pull up to fit the doll's head and tie in a bow. Trim the cap with a small silk ribbon bow at centre front.

Make a choker necklace by threading tiny pearl beads or use a length of ruched ribbon. To make a fan for your doll, see page 32.

4

EARLY VICTORIAN RAG DOLLS (c1830)

Rag dolls are among the oldest toys. They have been discovered among ancient Egyptian, Greek and Roman remains and in various forms they are found in most countries in the world. Sometimes they have religious significance, such as the voodoo dolls of Haiti, but most often they are simple playthings. As a child's toy, the rag doll has many advantages; it is soft and cuddly, unlike a wooden doll, easy to make from whatever scraps are available and relatively cheap to produce.

Before the nineteenth century there were no commercial rag dolls or patterns for them so these early dolls were very individual. They were the classic homemade doll, designed, made and dressed usually by the same person. Their beauty or otherwise depended upon the skill of the individual maker and the materials available. At this time, all fabrics were hand-spun and woven and therefore precious so it seems unlikely that rag dolls were a poor child's toy. The poor would have

Fig 29 Child rag doll

Fig 30 Lady rag doll

had little leisure-time for making dolls and the children of the poor had a very brief childhood, being set to work at simple tasks as young as five or six. It is more likely that the dolls owned by these children would have been simple wooden ones made by themselves or an indulgent parent from forked twigs and perhaps 'dressed' in leaves and grasses. The rag doll was therefore most probably the province of the middle-class child, whose mother had the time, the necessary sewing skills and the materials to make it.

Such early dolls are extremely rare (there are a few in museums), partly because of their perishable nature and their relatively low value but mainly, I believe, because few were in fact made. Before the end of the eighteenth century when attitudes to children and their needs changed quite radically, the child was regarded as a small adult, dressed as such and expected to grow up as quickly as possible. Toys were not considered essential to their well-being and were often regarded as 'status symbols' rather than playthings.

There was, however, a change in attitude towards the end of the eighteenth century, albeit slight. For the first time children had their own clothes – the 'skeleton suit' became fashionable for small boys, and little girls wore simple muslin dresses. Toys were considered to be 'a good thing' and dolls became popular and cheaper. By the middle of the nineteenth century children were once again dressed in layers of fussy uncomfortable clothes, but toys had become an established part of childhood (except on Sundays!). It was at this time that the homemade rag doll came into her own. Thanks to the Industrial Revolution, fabrics, especially cottons, had become available to all but the very poor. Thousands of middle-class women were now able to leave their housework to servants and thus had hours of empty time to fill with 'genteel' occupations. They had large families of daughters to be taught the 'ladylike' skills of needlework, and rag-doll-making offered a wholesome and educational pastime. By the middle of the century patterns were available for those lacking the skill to design their own dolls and commercial rag dolls were on sale, dressed or undressed.

A considerable number of Victorian rag dolls have survived, especially in America where, probably because of the shortage of manufactured goods, such things were more highly valued and passed on as heirlooms. These dolls, despite the similarities imposed by the medium, show an enormous variety of methods and standards of workmanship. Some are very crude; perhaps a flat two-sided doll without joints of any sort, the face simply painted on with vegetable colouring, the hair a hank of tow or wool and a very simple dress. Others show much ingenuity in design, with seated, gusseted bodies, stitched joints, beautifully embroidered faces, real hair wigs and elaborate wardrobes. It is hard to believe that a set of exquisitely hand-sewn underwear, on show at the Victoria and Albert Museum, is the work of a twelve-year-old, but such was the standard expected and often achieved by the 'young lady' of Queen Victoria's time.

During the 1880s cut-out-and-sew rag dolls printed onto a length of cotton cloth were available. These became very popular, so new designs and innovations were introduced. Shaped feet with flat soles, and faces printed from photographs and later heat-pressed to make fully shaped heads were all introduced in the early part of the twentieth century. The humble rag doll had come a long way from her simple beginnings. Today, whether homemade or commercial, she is still enormously popular. Most dollmakers begin with rag dolls; many of them make only rag dolls. They have a charm and appeal which is entirely their own and offer enormous scope for design, simple or very elaborate.

It is difficult to describe the 'typical' Victorian rag doll – being homemade, the variety is enormous – so I must generalise. The body is usually made of cotton, cambric, calico, or something similar. The simplest version would have a bag-shaped body cut in one with the head and perhaps the arms and legs as well. More complex bodies would have darts and gussets for shaping, and separate arms and legs with stitched joints at elbow and knee. Victorian dolls often have a very small waist as this was much admired, as were small hands and feet.

The stuffing might be sawdust, bran, hair or cotton waste, usually packed in firmly to make a rather hard stiff body. The face would be either painted, embroidered or appliqued, sometimes with beads or buttons sewn in for eyes. Wool was commonly used for wigs, but tow, hemp, embroidery yarn and occasionally real hair are sometimes found, the hairstyles usually making some attempt to follow the prevailing fashion. The clothes might be very simple (especially if made by a small child) or extremely elaborate, but they usually include a full set of white cotton underwear – chemise, drawers and petticoats – generally with little trimming. The dress would probably be a simple version of the current fashion and is usually made in printed cotton, again with little trimming. Rag dolls are rarely found dressed in silks or velvets or trimmed with expensive laces and ribbons, though of course there are exceptions. The dolls were usually hand-sewn, though domestic sewing machines were available in the 1850s. The fastenings were mostly tape drawstrings, hooks and eyes and buttons and buttonholes.

The dolls in this chapter are made in the style of the 1830s to represent mother and daughter. They both have bodies made in unbleached calico stuffed with terylene (you might use sawdust if you prefer) and wigs of mohair wool. The faces may be embroidered or painted. The child doll has a very simple 'bag' body without darts or shaping, with legs and arms sewn to the body at shoulder and hip to give some movement. The head is a rectangle of fabric, darted to give it some shape – a method which is not strictly authentic but which produces a more attractive result than the flat two-sided head. She is dressed in simple ankle-length pantaloons with an open crotch and a drawstring fastening, a petticoat on a waistband and a very simple dress with gigot-shaped sleeves. The patterns are very basic, can be adapted to make a doll of any period and are recommended for beginners.

The larger doll has a body which is darted to make a small waist and gusseted to shape the seat. The legs and arms are stitched at shoulder and hip to allow movement and the head is again a darted rectangle of fabric. She wears a chemise, open-crotch pantaloons on a buttoned waistband, a petticoat with tape drawstring ties, a simple dress with gigot sleeves, a pelerine (shoulder cape) and a mob cap. The patterns for this doll are also simple, though slightly more complex than for the child doll, and the beginner should have no trouble making it. The little doll carried by the child shown on page 50 is made from a bead and pipecleaners and instructions for it

can be found at the end of the chapter.

Choose only natural fabrics to make and dress these dolls, and any trimming should be silk or cotton. I recommend unbleached calico for the bodies – the flesh pink calico sold for dollmaking is much too strong a colour. Stuffing should be good-quality soft stuffing, kapok or sawdust. I recommend mohair wool for the hair because it does not separate on the head and therefore need not be applied thickly, making it easier to style. I have embroidered both dolls' eyes, painted the mouths and coloured the cheeks with powder blusher.

The underwear should be white linen, cotton lawn or bleached calico with white cotton tape for drawstrings and linen or mother-of-pearl buttons rather than plastic. I have used a narrow broderie anglaise for trimming, but you might prefer to use cotton lace or leave the underwear untrimmed.

The dresses should be in printed cotton, in soft muted colours. Flower-sprig patterns were popular at this time but be sure the pattern is small enough. The pelerine may be made in lace or fabric as you prefer, and fastens at the throat with ribbon ties or a small button and loop. The mob cap should be made in a fine cotton fabric, eg muslin or lawn (I have used a piece from an old cotton net curtain), and it is gathered on a fine ribbon drawstring. Both dolls have stockings made from tubular bandage (the size sold for lower-arm bandages) available from chemists and both wear black slippers with crossed ribbon ties, the mother doll's in leather, the child's in felt.

Child Rag Doll (c1830)
(15in tall)
Difficulty 1/Colour picture page 50
Body pattern: Fig 31
Clothes pattern: Fig 32

½yd unbleached calico (36in wide) for body
2oz mohair wool for hair
embroidery thread for features
stuffing

Cut two bodies, four legs, two soles, four arms and one head on the straight grain of the fabric (Fig 31).

Stitch the darts on the head, then seam the

Fig 31 Body pattern for child rag doll

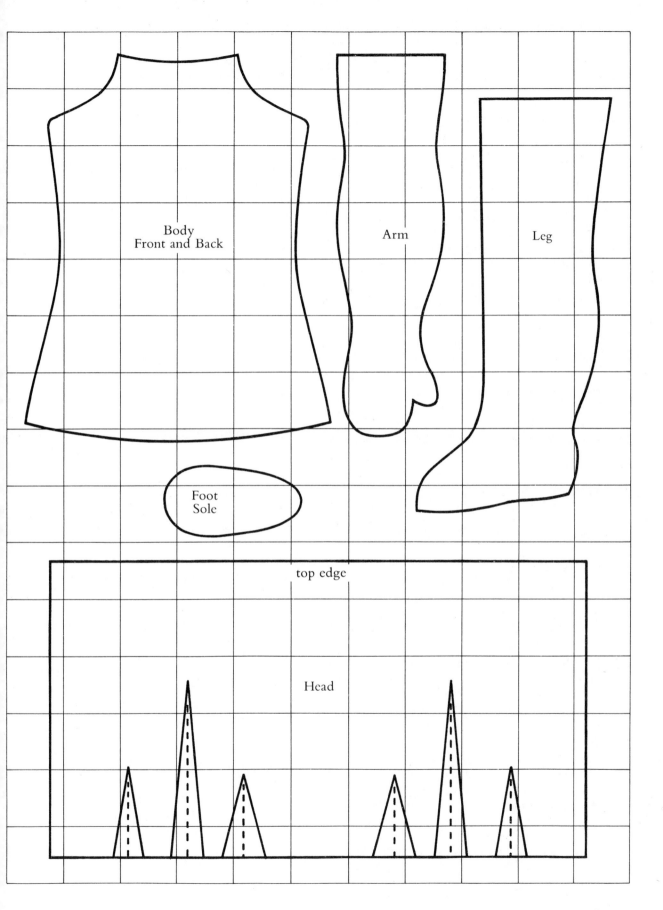

Body
Front and Back

Arm

Leg

Foot
Sole

top edge

Head

short edges together. Turn through, turn in the raw neck edge ½in and tack in place. Stitch the body pieces together to form a bag, leaving the neck edge open, and turn through. Seam the arms together in pairs, leaving the top edge open. Clip between the fingers and thumb and turn through. Stitch the legs together in pairs, leaving the top of the leg and the sole of the foot open. Stitch the sole into the foot on each leg and turn through.

Stuff the legs firmly and oversew the top closed, tucking the raw edges inside and matching front and back seams. Stuff the arms quite firmly to 1½in below the top, leaving this top part unstuffed. Oversew the top of the arms closed, tucking in the raw edges. Stuff the body firmly, working the stuffing well into the hips and shoulders and up into the neck.

Pull the neck edge of the head down over the neck, ensuring that the head seam is to the centre back. Oversew with small firm stitches. Continue stuffing through the top of the head into the neck so that it is very firm, then stuff the head, moulding and shaping it with your hands as you work. Run a gathering thread (strong button thread) around the top of the head, about 1in from the edge, pull it up tightly and fasten off. (If this thread pulls up easily, there is not enough stuffing in the head – release it and add more stuffing until it is an effort to pull up the gathers.) The gathering on the head will be completely concealed by the doll's hair.

Sew the tops of the arms over the shoulders with strong oversewing stitches, ensuring that both thumbs face forward and the arms hang naturally. Oversew the legs to the back lower edge of the body with strong thread.

To make the hair, cut sufficient 20in lengths of mohair wool to cover the head well without being too thick. Machine- or backstitch a centre parting in matching thread. Pin the hair to the doll's head and backstitch in place. Divide the hair into eight even bunches and secure each bunch to the lower edge of the doll's head with a few stitches. Twist each section of hair into a ringlet and secure the end of each ringlet by stitching in place. Turn up the ringlets and stitch to the doll's head. Use a few looped strands of wool to make a fringe on the forehead.

Draw the doll's features lightly on the face with pencil. The eyes are two circles of buttonholestitch – the inner circle black, the outer circle blue. The eye is outlined in stemstitch and the lashes are long straight stitches. The eyebrows are worked in stemstitch, and the mouth may be embroidered in satinstitch or coloured with felt pen. Rub in a little powder blusher to colour the doll's cheeks.

CHILD RAG DOLL'S CLOTHES
For the Underwear
½yd white cotton (36in wide)
1yd trimming (1in wide)
1yd cotton tape (⅛in wide)
1 small button
12in tubular bandage for stockings

For the Dress
½yd printed cotton (36in wide)
4 small hooks and eyes
½yd ribbon (½in wide) for sash
small buckle (optional)

For the Shoes
small piece black felt or leather
1yd black ribbon (⅛in wide)

Cut two pantaloon pieces from white cotton (Fig 32). Seam the legs, then roll narrow hems around the top part of each leg from the waist to the crotch. (The two legs are made quite separately and not joined, except by the drawstring.) Turn casings at the waist edge of each leg. Turn up the leg ends and hem and add trimming if required. Thread tape through the casings and tie at centre back.

Cut two 6in lengths of tubular gauze for stockings. Stitch through both thicknesses across one cut edge and turn through. Pull up the doll's legs, tucking in the raw top edge.

For the petticoat, cut a piece 25 × 7in and a waistband to fit the doll's waist with a button and buttonhole fastening in white cotton. Stitch the centre-back seam to 1½in below the top, then turn back the remainder and hem to form facings. Gather the top edge evenly and stitch to the waistband. Make buttonhole and sew on button. Turn up and hem the lower edge and trim.

For the dress, cut one bodice front, two bodice backs and two skirts on the straight grain of the fabric and two sleeves on the cross grain (Fig 32). (The skirt is cut with a fold to centre front and cut open at centre back.) Stitch the bodice front to backs at the

(right) The Georgian wooden doll; and the Dutch dolls or penny-woodens

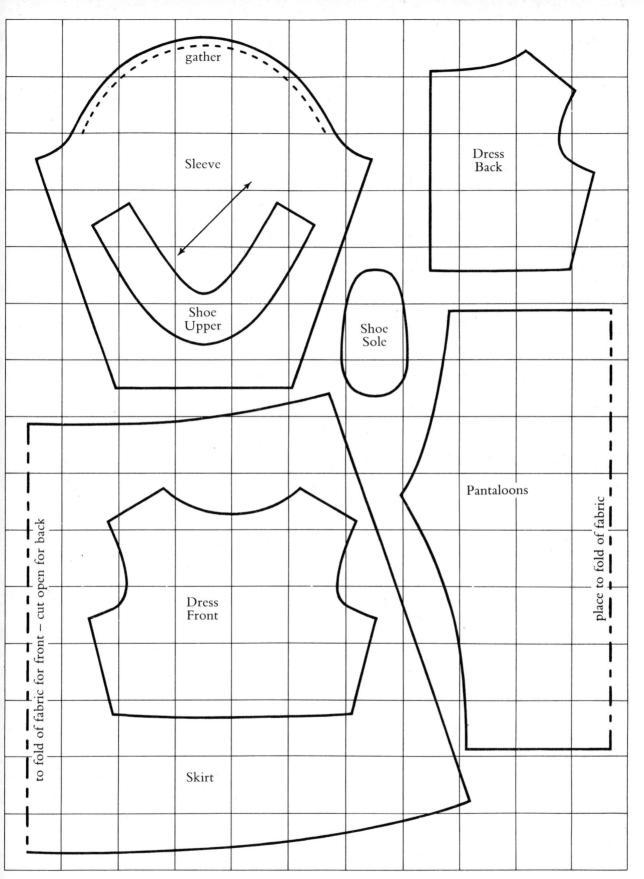

gather

Sleeve

Dress
Back

Shoe
Upper

Shoe
Sole

Pantaloons

to fold of fabric for front – cut open for back

place to fold of fabric

Dress
Front

Skirt

(*left*) The Victorian rag dolls with mini doll; and   Fig 32 Clothes patterns for child rag doll
the Victorian china doll

shoulder seams. Gather the sleeve heads and stitch the sleeves into the armholes. Stitch the side seams from the sleeve ends, through the underarms and down the bodice sides. Stitch the skirt side seams. Gather the top edge of the skirt evenly and stitch to the lower edge of the bodice. Stitch the centre-back skirt seam to 1½in below the waist then turn back the remainder of the back edges of the skirt and bodice to form facings and hem. Bind the neck edge with a bias-cut strip of fabric. Turn up sleeve ends and hem. Turn up lower edge of skirt and hem. Fasten the bodice with four small hooks and eyes at centre back. Tie a ribbon sash around the doll's waist with a bow at centre back and a small buckle at centre front if you wish.

To make the shoes, cut one upper and one sole for each shoe in black leather or felt (Fig 32). Stitch the centre-back seams in the uppers working on the inside, then blanket-stitch the upper to the sole (on the inside or outside as you prefer). Stitch ribbons to the uppers at the insteps and cross over the foot, tying at the ankle.

Tie a ribbon bow in the doll's hair if required. If you wish, this doll might also wear an apron made from a rectangle of cotton fabric hemmed and gathered to a waistband with ties, perhaps with pockets containing a tiny handkerchief. She might also wear a mob cap similar to her mother's or made in fabric to match her dress. A simple straw hat or bonnet trimmed with artificial flowers would also be appropriate for the period.

Lady Rag Doll (c1830)
(18in tall)
Difficulty 1/Colour picture page 50
Body pattern: Fig 33
Clothes pattern: Fig 35

½yd unbleached calico (36in wide) for body
2oz mohair wool and tape for hair
embroidery thread for features
stuffing

Cut one front, two upper backs, one lower back, four lower legs, four arms, two soles and one head on the straight grain of the fabric (Fig 33).

Stitch the darts in the front. Stitch the two upper backs together at the centre back. Stitch the upper back to the lower back at the curved

seam ABA. Stitch the body front to back down the sides then up one inside leg through the crotch and down the other inside leg. Clip the curves.

Stitch the lower legs together in pairs leaving the top edge and the sole of the foot open. Stitch the soles into the feet. With right sides facing, stitch the lower legs to the upper legs at the knee, ensuring that both feet face forward. (On the upper legs the seams are at each side, on the lower legs the seams are at centre front and back.) Turn the body through to the right side. Stitch the darts on the head, then seam the short edges together and turn through. Turn in the neck edge ½in and tack to hold in place. Stitch the arms together in pairs, leaving the top angled edge open. Clip between thumb and fingers and turn through.

Working from the neck, stuff the legs firmly up to the hips. To make the doll sit, stabstitch through the body at the dotted line shown on the pattern (Fig 33). Continue stuffing the body firmly up to the neck. Pull the neck edge of the head down over the neck, ensuring that the head seam is to centre back, and oversew firmly in place with small stitches. Continue stuffing through the top of the head into the neck so that it is very firm, then stuff the head, moulding and shaping the stuffing as you work. Gather the top of the head with strong button thread 1in from the edge and pull up the gathers. Ensure that the head is very firmly stuffed.

Stuff the arms fairly firmly, turn in the raw edges and oversew the openings closed. (If you wish, the arms may be stabstitched through at the elbow so that they bend.) Oversew the arms to the back of the body, working down from the shoulders.

To make the hair, measure around the doll's head at the hairline and cut a piece of tape to this length. Cut sufficient 24in lengths of wool to cover the tape evenly. Stitch the tape to the centre of the wool lengths, then stitch the hair to the doll's hairline with the tape uppermost (Fig 34). Draw all the hair up to the back of the head, twist into a bun and secure to the head. Make loops of wool for curls and stitch to either side of the face at the temples.

Either embroider or paint the doll's face in the same way as for the child doll, but make an 'older' face.

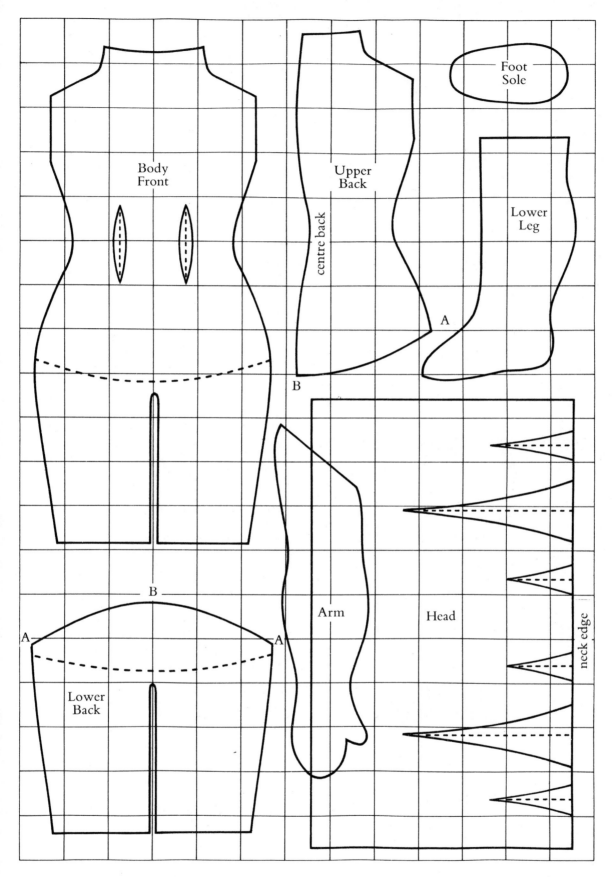

Fig 33 Body pattern for lady rag doll

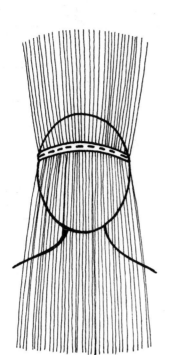

Fig 34 Lady rag doll's wig

LADY RAG DOLL'S CLOTHES

For the Underwear
¾yd white cotton (36in wide)
1½yd trimming (1in wide)
½yd cotton tape (⅛in wide)
1 small button
12in tubular bandage for stockings

For the Dress
¾yd printed cotton (36in wide)
2yd ricrac or braid for trimming
½yd narrow lace for sleeve frills
4 small hooks and eyes
¼yd lace or fabric (36in wide) for pelerine
12in square muslin for mob cap
1yd lace (1in wide) for mob cap
narrow silk ribbon for mob cap

For the Shoes
small piece black leather or felt
1yd black ribbon (⅛in wide)

To make the pantaloons, cut two pieces in white cotton (Fig 35). Seam the legs, then roll narrow hems around the top part of each leg from waist to crotch. (The two legs are quite separate and joined only by the waistband.) Cut a waistband to fit the doll with a button and buttonhole fastening. Gather the top edges of the legs and stitch them to the waistband. Make buttonhole and sew on button. Turn up and hem the leg ends and trim as required. Put the pantaloons on the doll to fasten at centre back. (The lady doll's pantaloons should not show below the hem of her dress.)

To make the chemise, use the pattern and instructions given on page 65 (Fig 44). Add ½in to the underarm and side seams. For the petticoat, cut a piece of white cotton 30×11in. Stitch the centre-back seam and make a ¼in casing along the top edge. Turn up and hem the lower edge and trim as required (pintucks are very appropriate for this petticoat). Thread tape through the casing and pull up to fit the doll, tying in a bow at centre back.

To make the dress, cut one bodice front, two bodice backs and two skirts in printed cotton on the straight grain of the fabric and two sleeves on the cross grain (Fig 35). Stitch the darts on the bodice front, then make up the dress in the same way as for the child doll. Add trimming to the skirt above the hem, and to the sleeve ends. The dress may also have a fabric or ribbon belt, with or without a buckle.

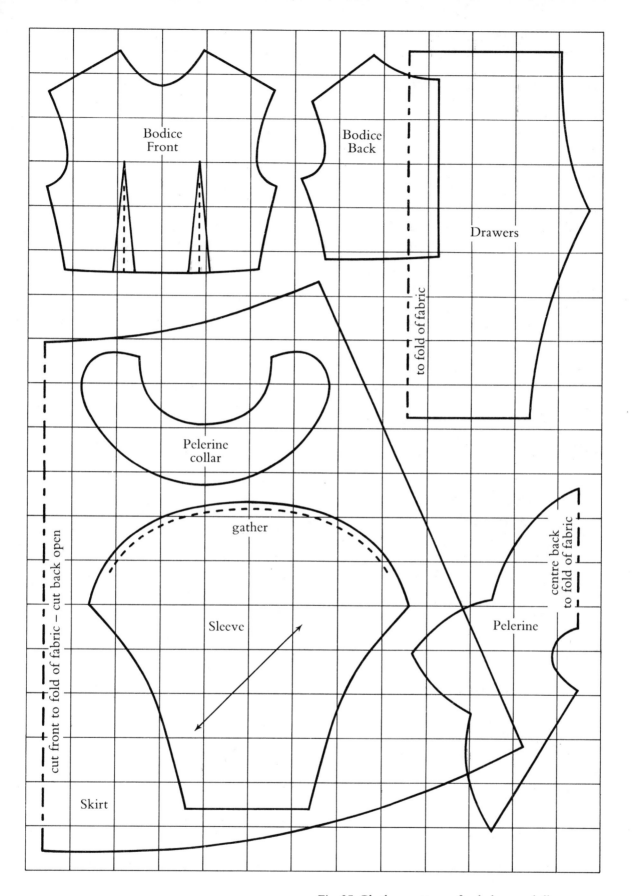

Fig 35 Clothes patterns for lady rag doll

Bodice Front

Bodice Back

Drawers

to fold of fabric

Pelerine collar

gather

cut front to fold of fabric – cut back open

Sleeve

centre back to fold of fabric

Pelerine

Skirt

For the pelerine, cut one cape and two collars in lace (Fig 35). (If you use fabric, cut a lining in lightweight fabric and stitch to the cape, right sides facing around the outside edges, turning through at the neck edge.) Whip the outside edges of the lace to neaten, or sew on a narrow lace edging. With right sides facing, stitch the collars together around the outside edge, turn through and press. Stitch the collar to the cape, enclosing the neck edge. Fasten the pelerine with narrow ribbon ties or a loop and button.

Make the stockings and shoes from the pattern and instructions given for the child doll. For the mob cap, cut a circle of fabric 12in in diameter. Roll a narrow hem around the outside edge and sew on lace. Thread narrow silk ribbon through a darning needle and work small running stitches through the fabric just inside the lace edge. Pull up the ribbon to fit the doll's head and tie the ends in a bow at the centre front.

This doll might also wear a cotton apron and carry a little drawstring bag (Fig 36). The straw basket shown in the colour illustration came from a local gift shop but a similar basket might be made from plaited raffia. (*See* instructions in Chapter 11.)

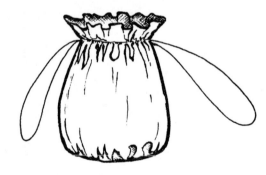

Fig 36 Drawstring bag

Miniature Doll

(5in tall)
Difficulty 1/Colour picture page 50
Body pattern: Fig 37
Clothes pattern: Fig 38

1 round wooden or plastic bead (1in diameter)
1 skein embroidery silk for hair
3×6in pipecleaners
1 pair pink or white shoelaces
about 4in tubular gauze finger bandage
a little cotton wool for padding
flesh-coloured paint
paints or felt pens (for features)

To make the doll, fold one pipecleaner in half and push the ends into a 2in length of shoe-lace. Glue the shoelace-covered pipecleaner firmly into the hole in the bead. For the arms, push the second pipecleaner into a length of shoelace so that it is completely enclosed. Tuck in the raw ends of the shoelace and oversew neatly to form the hands. Stitch the arms to the body ¼in below the head. For the legs, push the third pipecleaner into a length of shoelace and oversew the ends as for the arms. Take the looped lower end of the body and bend it up about 1in. Fold the leg length in half and hook it through the body, stitching through the legs and body to secure (Fig 37a).

Pad the body with cotton wool, the amount determined by whether you want a thin or fat doll. Hold the cotton wool in place by pulling a length of tubular gauze finger bandage up over the cotton wool. Tuck in the raw edges and oversew the bandage along each shoulder and under the crotch (Fig 37b). To define the doll's waist, run two gathering threads ¼in apart around the waistline, pull up and fasten off.

Using flesh-coloured paint, paint the head, neck, hands and any other part which will show when the doll is dressed. Leave the paint to dry thoroughly. For the hair, stitch a parting through the centre of the skein of embroidery silk and glue it to the doll's head. Draw the hair back into a pony tail and tie tightly with matching thread. Plait the pony tail, coil into a bun and glue to the back of the head to cover the 'bald patch'. Draw the features lightly in pencil and then paint in with a very fine brush, or felt pens.

MINIATURE DOLL'S CLOTHES
scraps of white lawn for underwear
1yd narrow lace for trimming
scrap of printed cotton for dress
scrap of thin leather or felt for boots
felt scrap or plaited raffia for bonnet
tiny flowers, feathers, ribbon etc for trimming

For the pantaloons, cut two pattern pieces (Fig 38), seam each leg, then seam together. Hem and trim the leg ends with narrow lace and turn in and gather the top edge, stitching to the doll's body. Cut an upper and sole for each boot (Fig 38). Fold the upper along the dotted line as shown on the pattern. Starting at the toe, blanketstitch the edges together

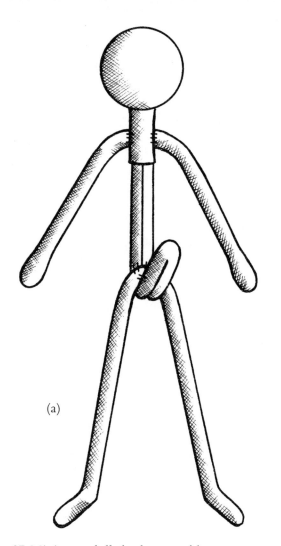

(a)

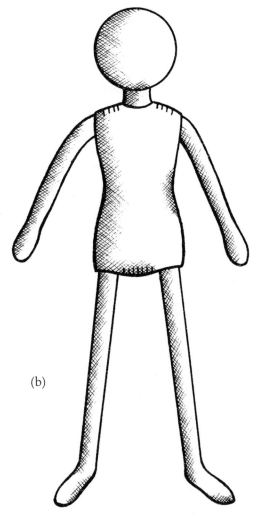

(b)

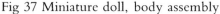
Fig 37 Miniature doll, body assembly

over the toe and up the leg. Slip the boot up the doll's leg and bend the doll's foot sharply forward into the foot of the boot. Holding the doll upside-down place the sole over the foot and blanketstitch it to the upper. If necessary, secure the top edge of the boot to the doll's leg with a few stitches. Cut a piece of lawn 9×3½in for the petticoat. Stitch the centre-back seam and hem and trim the lower edge with narrow lace. Turn in the top edge and gather to fit the doll, stitching to the body.

Cut the bodice (Fig 38) in printed cotton, neaten the neckline with oversewing, blanket-stitch or a tiny rolled hem, and stitch the side seams. Turn through and put on the doll. Turn in the raw back edges and oversew closed. Tuck in the raw edges of the sleeve ends and gather, pulling up to fit the doll's wrists. Fasten off. Cut the skirt (Fig 38) in matching printed cotton, stitch the centre-back seam and turn up and hem the lower

edge. Turn in the top edge and gather as close to the folded edge as possible to fit the doll's waist. Put the skirt on the doll over the bodice, and oversew to the body. Cover the seam with a narrow ribbon sash tied in a bow at the back. Trim the dress with lace as required. For the bonnet, cut one back and one brim in felt (Fig 38) or work these shapes in plaited raffia. Stitch the bonnet back to the brim and trim with ribbons to tie under the chin and tiny flowers or feathers.

These dolls make charming 'toys' for the larger dolls, but they are also properly scaled to be doll's-house dolls in their own right. To make doll's-house children, use a smaller bead for the head, shorten the arm and leg pipecleaners and bend the body pipecleaner higher up. For a male doll's-house doll, bend the body lower down to lengthen it.

The clothes patterns are easily adapted by lengthening or shortening. The pantaloon pattern will make trousers, and the bodice, fastened at the front, will make a shirt.

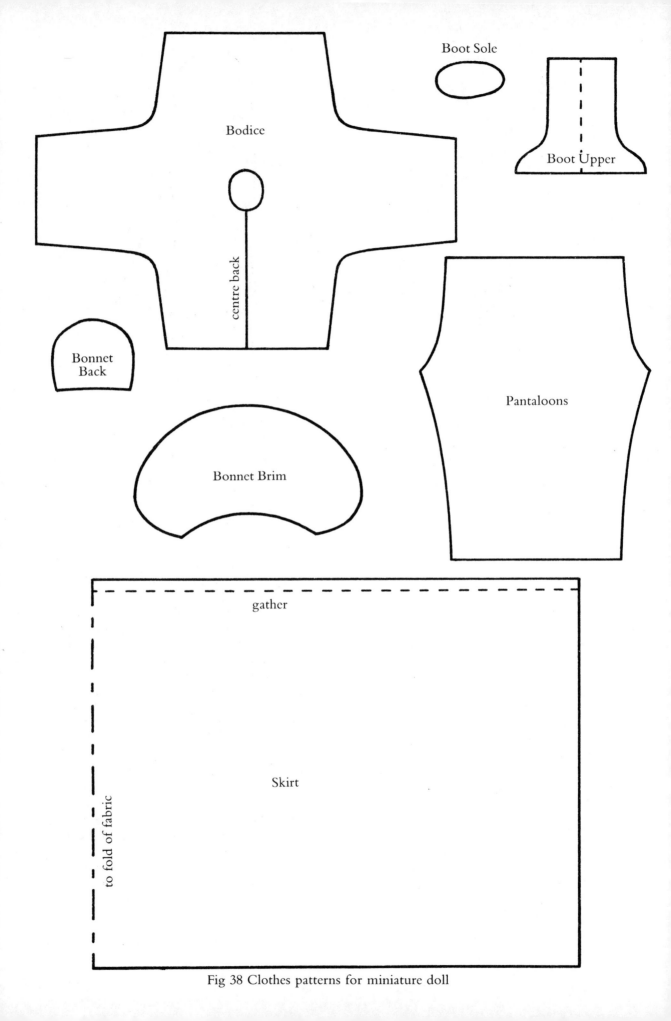

Fig 38 Clothes patterns for miniature doll

5
A VICTORIAN CHINA DOLL
(c1840)

Although a few porcelain dolls were produced during the eighteenth century, they were expensive and rare. It was not until the end of the 1830s that china dolls became popular. Mass-produced in Germany, they were imported into England in vast quantities and eventually sold so cheaply that every child, except the very poorest, might have one. Despite their German origins, these glazed white china dolls with their moulded hairstyles and prim faces evoke 'Victorian England' very strongly.

Originally, only the head of the doll was china. It was made up on a cloth body, usually with leather arms, and sold as a complete doll. The making up might be done in Germany, or by the English importer, who bought the heads, employed out-workers to make the bodies and sold the finished product. Some of these early commercial bodies are well made, with nicely shaped calico torsos and legs and neatly stitched leather arms, firmly filled with sawdust. Others are grotesquely crude. The quality of the body did not necessarily relate to the quality of the head. The china heads were also sold separately to be made up at home, and the variety of these homemade bodies is enormous, depending entirely on the skill of the individual maker as no patterns were available. Later, china lower arms and legs were made and sold on the same basis. The earlier dolls were usually made to represent ladies and it was not until the latter part of the nineteenth century that child dolls became popular, though often the lady heads were made up and dressed to represent children.

By the 1870s, however, china dolls were considered 'old fashioned' and the bisque dolls became generally more popular. However, the former were still made and sold at the end of the century though by then they had become rather crude and very cheap.

Despite the enormous variety of china heads, coming as they did from dozens of different manufacturers, they all have a pronounced similarity. The rather stark, shiny white china contrasts strongly with the almost invariable black hair. The faces are almost always painted (glass eyes are extremely rare) with blue eyes and bright red mouths. The face painting is very stylised and virtually the same on all the dolls of this type. The blue eyes (rarely brown) have a black pupil and a curved black line above them with neither upper nor lower lashes. The eyebrows are painted, with a single curved line, usually in black or brown, over each eye. A fine red line is painted above the eye to represent the crease of the eyelid. The lips are painted closed, the top lip bow-shaped, the lower a smooth curve, and the cheeks are usually coloured in a reddish pink. Occasionally the

Fig 39 China doll

59

nostrils are indicated with a red dot or circle and some of these dolls have a pale pink glaze rather than the more common white.

The moulded hairstyles are varied and tend to follow fashion, though often a style was still produced in doll-form long after it was démodé in the 'real' world, which makes it very difficult to date these dolls accurately. Popular hairstyles included the centre parting with hair drawn back over the ears to a bun at the back, or a centre parting with the hair in sausage curls around the head. Moulded hair ornaments such as flowers, ribbons and snoods were also popular. Most hairstyles showed the ears, and some examples have the ears pierced for earrings though this was the exception rather than the rule.

There is a popular myth that these dolls were made to represent Queen Victoria but one only has to look at a selection of them to realise that this was not the case. They represented the current ideal of feminine beauty – pale, placid and ladylike. The china hands and feet also followed this ideal and were usually very small and dainty. The legs had moulded boots (flat heeled before the 1870s, later with small heels) often decorated with laces and tassels as part of the moulding.

The heads themselves are on shoulder-plates, with a very pronounced sloping shoulder line. Often the top of the bosom is moulded into the shoulder-plate and some-times necklaces or collars are part of the moulding. There are two or three sewing holes pierced at the back and front of the shoulder-plate for attaching the head to the cloth body.

Though the cloth bodies vary a great deal in workmanship, they tend to be similar in shape. The pronounced sloping shoulder line dictated by the shoulder-plate is continued in the upper arms and makes a rather wide upper torso. The waist is usually very small and the hips large. The earlier bodies were mostly the simple 'bag' type with the shaping made by curved side seams, but later versions have more sophisticated shaping by means of darts and gussets with stitched joints at the knees. The leather arms were usually white or tan but red, blue and other colours are also found. They hang rather stiffly at the doll's sides with little movement and without stitched elbow joints. The later china limbs are tied on by means of grooves or sewing holes in the manner still used today, but the joint is

usually below the knee on the legs and at or above the elbow on the arms.

Cotton fabrics such as calico or a similar firmly woven cloth were almost invariably used for the bodies and the stuffing was usually sawdust, though hair, powdered cork and cotton waste were also used. Obviously, with a doll which was assembled at home, the materials would be dictated by whatever was to hand. A country-made doll might have a body of old home-spun fabric filled with sheep's wool from the hedgerow or sawdust from the local carpenter. The town doll might be made of newly bought calico stuffed with rag scraps.

The china doll's clothes were almost invari-ably homemade and most usually cotton. As with most homemade dolls, the underwear would be complete and well made, though usually rather plain. It would consist of a chemise, drawers and several petticoats in white cotton with drawstring fastenings and perhaps some tucks, featherstitching or a little lace for trimming. The dresses were generally simplified versions of the current styles in cotton prints, though fine wool and occasion-ally silk were also used. Trimming is usually rather restrained, perhaps a little braid or a few buttons particularly on the earlier dolls, though there are examples dressed in lavish ruffles, ribbons and lace. Taffeta was enormously popular in the mid-nineteenth century and sometimes one finds a china doll in a taffeta dress, but printed cotton was more customary. The dropped shoulder line was universal – one cannot make an 'authentic' Victorian dress without it – but styles of sleeve and the shape of skirts varied a great deal throughout the period. Waistlines were at the natural waist level, but they might be round or pointed at the front. The skirts were very full, with the fullness distributed evenly until the late 1860s when it moved to the back of the skirt and became a bustle. Necklines were very modest for daytime wear and low for evening dress.

The china doll in this chapter is in fact made in self-hardening clay (I have used Fimo). The head and shoulder-plate are modelled over a core-ball and a cleaning fluid bottle to give the correct sloping shoulder line. The hair is modelled onto the head in a centre-parted style with a braided bun at the back of the head, showing the ears. The lower arms with small hands are modelled to the elbow, and the lower legs with plump calves and small flat-heeled boots are modelled to just below the knee. The face is painted in the traditional manner as described. Several coats of gloss varnish give the doll its china effect. The simple body is made in calico stuffed with sawdust, and cut with a shaped seat so that the doll will sit.

The doll's underwear is all made in white cotton: a chemise with a ribbon drawstring at the neckline, and drawers, open at the back with a drawstring fastening and a lace trim at the leg ends, both made in bleached calico. There are two petticoats, one in untrimmed calico with a drawstring fastening and one in white lawn trimmed with pintucks and lace on a buttoned waistband. The dress is made in printed cotton with a high round neckline and pointed front waist. The bishop sleeves, gathered into cuffs, are set into dropped armholes. The dress is trimmed with a row of buttons down the front of the bodice and rows of écru cotton braid. It fastens at the back with hooks and eyes. Though I didn't plan it that way, my doll has turned out looking strangely like Queen Victoria!

I recommend Fimo for the modelled parts of the doll, using white Fimo for the head and shoulder-plate, arms and legs, and black for the hair and boots. Though the finished doll has to be painted, using the appropriate colours makes it easier to see the effect you are creating while you work. I suggest modelling a bald head on the shoulder-plate and baking this, then modelling the hairstyle and baking the head again. It is far easier to shape the hair on a hard-baked head than while the head is still soft. Likewise with the boots, I suggest modelling very small feet on the legs and baking these before modelling the boots over them. The limbs are tied onto the body by means of grooves cut in the upper ends, and the shoulder-plate has holes bored through either side at back and front for sewing it onto the body. I suggest un-bleached calico or linen for the body and saw-dust for the stuffing, though you might use a soft stuffing if you prefer.

The clothes should be in natural fabrics and any trimmings should also be made of natural materials. Tiny pearl buttons are the most suitable for the front of the dress, or if these are unavailable you might use glass beads. I have compromised with the fastenings and used small modern hooks and eyes. Whether you sew by hand or machine is a matter of personal preference – I use a machine for the seams, and hem and finish by hand.

China Doll (c1840)

(15in tall)
Difficulty 2/Colour picture page 50
Body pattern: Figs 40, 41, 42 and 43
Clothes pattern: Fig 44

large packet of white Fimo
small packet of black Fimo
core-ball (2in diameter)
black and white enamel paints (matt and gloss)
spray can of gloss varnish
paints for features
½yd calico (36in wide) for body
stuffing (sawdust or soft)

Full instructions for modelling are given in Chapter 1 and are repeated only briefly here.

Choose a bottle which has a small neck and sloping shoulders (many cleaning fluid bottles are this shape). Fill the bottle with sand or gravel to give it stability while you work. Centre the core-ball on the bottle. Cover the ball and the top part of the bottle with aluminium foil so that you can later remove the modelling easily. Cover the head, neck and shoulders with white Fimo. Build up the cheeks, forehead and chin and shape a plump face (*see* Fig 41 and colour illustration on page 50 as a guide). The face should be rather rounded, the nose small and the mouth shaped with a curved underlip. Make shallow sockets above the cheeks so that you will have a flat area on which to paint the eyes. Apply small ears (unless they will be covered by the proposed hairstyle). The neck should be short and rather plump. The shoulders will conform to the slope of the bottle, but cut a clean edge around the bottom (Fig 41). Bore holes through the shoulder-plate with a meat skewer or something similar. When the modelling is satisfactory, smooth the clay as thoroughly as possible and lift it gently off the bottle. Bake the head and allow to cool before modelling the hair.

To model the hair, work with pieces of black Fimo, rolled out thinly. Cover the head with a flat 'pancake' of clay then cut the hair-line to the required shape with a small sharp knife. Score the centre parting and 'pinch' slight waves with your fingers. Drag a comb lightly down either side of the fronts and push

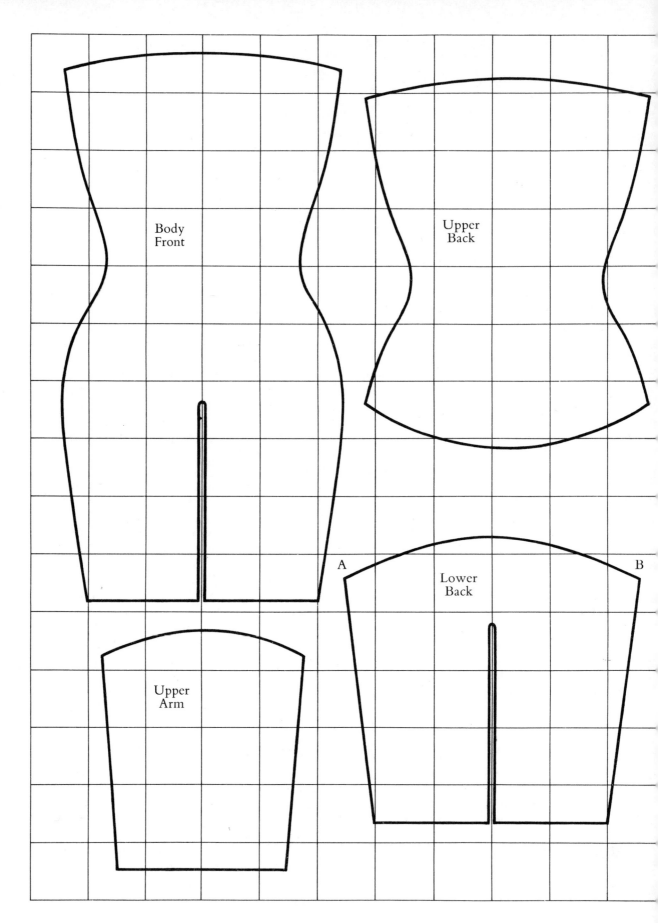

Body
Front

Upper
Back

A

Lower
Back

B

Upper
Arm

Fig 41 China doll's head

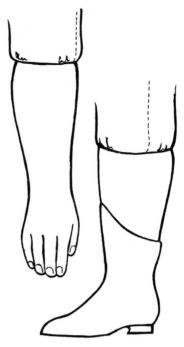

Fig 42 China doll's arm and leg

the clay slightly upwards to 'lift' it above the ears. Plait or twist a length of clay and coil it into a bun on the back of the head, ensuring that it adheres well to the main part of the hair. Clean away any specks of surplus black Fimo from the face before rebaking.

Modelling hairstyles is one of those procedures which is easier to do than to describe. When the head has been rebaked to harden the hair, leave it aside to cool and model the arms and legs. The arms are modelled to the elbow, and should be rather plump, tapering to small wrists and hands (Fig 42). For a doll of this scale it is wiser not to attempt to separate the fingers, rather to indicate them by scoring. The legs are modelled to just below the knee and should have plump calves tapering to narrow ankles and very small feet. Check that both arms and both legs are equal lengths and that both feet are the same size. Score grooves for tying on about ¼in below the ends. Bake the arms and legs. When the legs are cool, model the boots over the feet in black Fimo, rolled out thinly. Cut the shaped top edge (Fig 42) with a sharp knife and flatten the soles and heels. Rebake the legs to harden the boots. Remove the core-ball from the head. Allow all parts to cool completely before painting.

Paint the white Fimo with white enamel paint, and the black Fimo with black enamel paint. Use one coat of matt, allow it to dry thoroughly, then one coat of gloss. This may seem unnecessary as the Fimo is already black and white, but in fact Fimo, even when gloss-

Fig 40 Body pattern for china doll

varnished, simply doesn't look like china whereas enamel paint does.

Paint in the features using a fine brush (*see* page 50 for a detailed description of this type of face and use Fig 41 as a guide). The eyes should be a mid-blue, the mouth a clear crimson, and the cheeks should look 'rouged'. When the paint is thoroughly dry, spray all the modelled parts with gloss varnish (Humbrol is excellent). Leave for twenty-four hours, then spray again. (This gives the best results – you could make the body during this twenty-four-hour waiting period.) Leave the parts in a dust-free atmosphere while the varnish dries. The finished proportions of the modelled parts of this doll should be: length of head from forehead to chin, 2½in; length of arm from elbow to fingertips, 3in; and height of leg from top to heel, 3in. If your modelling is much larger or smaller than this, you may wish to alter the proportions of the body.

To make the body, cut one front, one upper back, one lower back and two upper arms from the pattern (Fig 40) on the straight grain of the fabric. Stitch the upper to lower back at the curved seam AB. Stitch the front to the back down each side, then up one inside leg, through the crotch and down the other inside leg. Clip the curves. Tie in the lower legs, ensuring that they face forward, and turn through. Stuff the legs to the top (stabstitching a knee joint if required) and stabstitch through the tops of the legs to allow the doll to sit. Continue stuffing to the top of the body, then turn in the raw edges and oversew closed. Fold down the corners at each side and sew down to the body (Fig 43). Stitch the seams in the upper arms to form tubes, tie in the lower arms and turn through. Stuff the arms loosely, and oversew the ends closed, turning in the raw edges. Pin the arms to the shoulders, check that they hang naturally with the hands level with the crotch, and stitch in place. Seat the shoulder-plate onto the body and sew in place using a darning needle and strong button thread or thin tape. If your finished doll is much taller or shorter than 15in, you may wish to alter the clothes patterns.

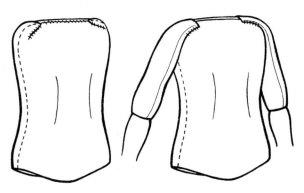

Fig 43 The top corners of the body sewn down and the arms stitched to the shoulders

CHINA DOLL'S CLOTHES
For the Underwear
1yd white cotton (36in wide)
1½yd white cotton lace
1yd tape (⅛in wide) for strings
½yd ribbon (⅛in wide) for drawstring
1 small button

For the Dress
½yd printed cotton (36in wide)
1½yd cotton braid for trimming
small buttons or beads for trimming
4 small hooks and eyes

To make the drawers, cut two pieces in white cotton (Fig 44). Stitch the inside leg seams, then stitch the two legs together from the centre-front waist to the crotch (the back is left open). Roll a narrow hem around the back edges. Make a casing at the top edge and turn up the leg ends and trim with lace. Thread tape through the casing and pull up to fit the doll, tying at the centre back.

For the chemise, cut two pieces in white cotton (Fig 44). Stitch the shoulder seams. Hem (or face with bias-binding) around the neckline to make a narrow casing. Stitch the side seams from the sleeve ends, through the underarm and down the sides. Hem the sleeve ends and trim with lace if required. Hem the lower edge. Thread narrow ribbon through the neckline, and pull up to fit the doll, tying in a bow at centre front.

For the first petticoat, cut a piece of white cotton 24×8in. Stitch the centre-back seam and make a ¼in casing at the top edge. Hem the lower edge. Thread tape through the casing and pull up to fit the doll, tying in a bow at centre back. For the second petticoat, cut a piece 26×9in and a waistband to fit the doll's waist with a button and buttonhole fastening. Stitch the centre-back seam to 1½in below the top, then turn back and hem the remainder to form facings. Gather the top edge evenly to the waistband, make buttonhole and sew on button. Turn up and hem the lower edge, work two or three pintucks above the hem and trim with lace.

To make the dress, cut one bodice front, two backs, two sleeves, two cuffs and a piece for the skirt 28×9in on the straight grain of the fabric (Fig 44). Fold the skirt piece in half and cut a shallow V shape at the centre-front waistline to correspond with the bodice. Stitch the bodice front to backs at the shoulder seams. Gather the lower ends of the sleeves and stitch to one edge of the cuffs. (Check that the cuffs fit easily over your doll's hands.) Gather the sleeve heads and stitch the sleeves into the armholes. Stitch the underarm seams from the cuff, up the sleeve through the underarm and down the bodice side. Hem the inside edge of the cuff over the gathering. Gather the top edge of the skirt evenly and stitch to the bodice. Stitch the centre-back skirt seam to 1½in below the waist, then turn back the remainder of the skirt and back-bodice edges and hem to form facings. Face the neckline with bias-binding. Hem the lower edge of the skirt. Fasten the dress with small hooks and eyes at centre back. Stitch an evenly spaced row of tiny buttons or beads down the centre front of the bodice and trim the dress with bands of cotton braid, above the skirt hem, around the cuffs and on the bodice front.

Fig 44 Clothes patterns for china doll

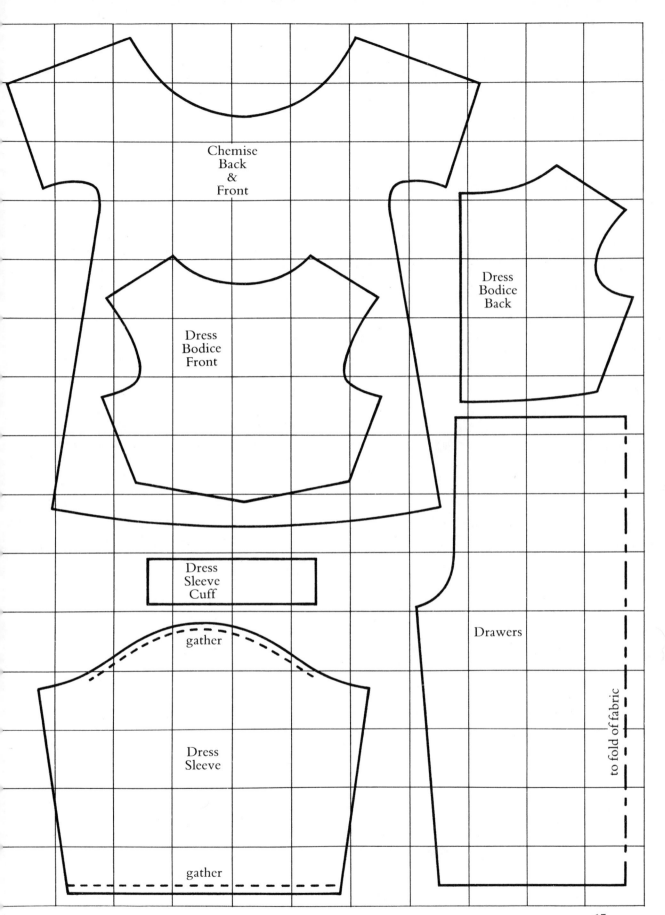

Chemise
Back
&
Front

Dress
Bodice
Back

Dress
Bodice
Front

Dress
Sleeve
Cuff

Drawers

gather

Dress
Sleeve

to fold of fabric

gather

6
WOODEN DUTCH DOLLS (c1850)

Simple carved wooden dolls were produced in several areas of Austria, Bavaria and Thuringia for centuries. Surrounded by pine forests, the people of these areas found a ready supply of materials for what started as a cottage industry but became, by the middle of the nineteenth century, big business. Originally, the dolls had been made during the winter by people forced to stay indoors for several months at a time when these remote areas were cut off from the rest of the world by bad weather. Carving wooden dolls and animals provided occupation and they could be exchanged for goods or sold when better weather came.

As with most types of doll, the earliest examples are the best; as demand and output increased, the doll became simpler, then finally quite crude. The name Dutch doll is a corruption of Deutch (German) doll – the merchants who exported the dolls were German firms working in the area. (They are also called peg-woodens, penny-woodens, wooden-bettys and various other regional and colloquial names.) Again, as with most types of doll, the Dutch doll developed gradually from a more elaborately carved and painted doll by a process of simplification. The Dutch doll's closest ancestor, produced in the early part of the nineteenth century, is usually called Grödnerthal by collectors, after the region in Austria in which it was made. The Grödnerthal dolls have more finely carved features, smaller heads (usually with a comb on the back) and properly shaped hands and feet. The face and hair are painted in some detail, with curls on the cheeks or forehead. The joints were pegged, although on some examples, especially the larger ones, ball-joints were used. These are the type of wooden dolls which Queen Victoria collected and dressed as a child. They were made in a wide range of sizes, from only half an inch, to three feet tall.

The Dutch doll as we know it emerged during the 1850s. By now, she had a larger head and had lost her comb. Her hands and feet were no longer properly carved but merely spade-shaped and the painting on her face was much simpler, sometimes just a few coloured dots. Her joints were still pegged at shoulder, elbow, hip and knee but she was a very simple little doll and incredibly cheap.

The simple little faces, with small wedge-shaped noses and bright dots of pink on the cheeks, lend themselves to a variety of charac-

Fig 45 Wooden Dutch dolls

(*right*) The fashion doll

ters and these dolls are often found in dolls' houses or dressed as pedlars, with red cloaks and trays of miniature wares for sale. The pedlar dolls were usually made for adults, but the vast majority of Dutch dolls were simply children's playthings and though many have survived, they are a very small percentage of those that were produced. A cheap doll, cheaply dressed, perhaps played with until it was broken or outgrown, would be thrown away – or used to light the kitchen stove!

Because of her pegged shoulders, the Dutch doll is not an easy doll to make clothes for and perhaps this explains why, when she is found in her original clothes, they are often very simple sewn-on garments or dresses made with gathers or drawstrings which can be pulled up to fit. The clumsy stitching seems to indicate a child's work, and the fabrics are usually cheap cottons with little or no trimming.

The two Dutch dolls in this chapter are made in the same way, with the same proportions, though the small doll is dressed to represent a 'baby' for the larger doll. They have heads and bodies turned on a lathe in one piece then shaped with a chisel. The legs and arms are peg-jointed at the shoulders, elbows, hips and knees. The hair, faces, stockings and shoes are painted in the traditional manner. The dolls have been copied from an old doll in my collection, though they are more carefully finished than the original. The large doll wears white cotton open drawers with a drawstring fastening and a white cotton petticoat also with a drawstring, both untrimmed. The printed cotton dress has a full skirt and bodice gathered to bands at the neckline and waist and full sleeves with lace frills gathered at the wrist. Her bonnet and cloak are both made in felt; the bonnet is trimmed with artificial flowers and has a lace frill inside the brim. The small doll wears a long white cotton baby gown, gathered at the neck and waist with ribbon strings, a gathered cap and wool wrapper. Both dolls have painted white stockings and red shoes.

If you are buying new wood, I recommend pine, which should have a straight grain and be free of knots. You might prefer to use old wood, such as the leg from a piece of furniture. A lathe and the appropriate wood-

(left) Little Women (conversation piece); and the Bye-lo baby and teddy

working tools are essential to make these dolls, though no great skill in woodwork is necessary.

You should use natural fabrics for the clothes. Cotton is recommended for the underwear and the dresses; felt or fine wool for the cloak and bonnet. Keep any trimmings simple as these dolls should not be overdressed.

If you wish to make the large doll up as a pedlar, I suggest using a dark cotton print for the dress and perhaps adding a white apron. The cloak should be cut longer to below the hips and made in red felt or wool and the bonnet should be black as these are the colours traditionally worn by pedlar dolls. The doll might have a tray, suspended from her neck, or a basket over her arm in which to carry her wares. A small doll stand will give sufficient stability to balance the added weight to display the pedlar properly.

The small doll is properly scaled to be a doll's-house lady doll in its own right, and the patterns may be lengthened or shortened slightly to make a family of Dutch dolls for the doll's house (*see* also the clothes patterns for the miniature doll on page 56).

(The dolls have been photographed against a view of Kirkgate, the Victorian street at the Castle Museum, York.)

Dutch Dolls (c1850)
(12in and 5in tall)
Difficulty 4/Colour picture page 67
Body: Figs 46, 47, 48, 49 and 50
Clothes patterns: Figs 51 and 52

TOOLS
lathe
woodworking chisel
woodturning chisels
fretsaw
small file
drill with 1/8 *and* 3/8in *bits (*1/12 *and* 3/16in *bits for small doll)*
vice
calipers
craft knife
sandpaper
white woodwork glue

MATERIALS FOR LARGE DOLL
1 piece of wood 6½in *long* × 2½×2½in
3ft length ¾in *square wood*
6in length ⅛in *dowelling for pegs*
3in length ⅜in *dowelling for pegs*

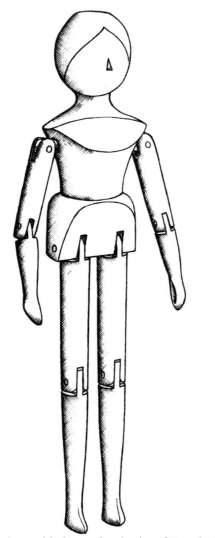

Fig 46 Assembled wooden body of Dutch doll

MATERIALS FOR SMALL DOLL
1 piece of wood 4in long × 1½×1½in
15in length ⅜in square wood
4in length 1/12in dowelling for pegs
2in length 3/16in dowelling for pegs

Instructions are given for the large doll but both dolls are made in exactly the same way.

Working with the drawings of the doll's body in front of you (Fig 47), centre the 6½in block of wood on the lathe and turn it until it becomes a 2½in diameter cylinder. Mark in pencil the positions of the neck, shoulders and hips. With the wood turning on the lathe use a parting tool or small gouge to reduce the wood at the neck and waist until the required dimensions are reached. (Use the calipers at frequent intervals to measure these dimensions as you work.) With a gouge reduce the head and hips to the required diameters. Con-

tinue with the gouge to shape the head, neck and torso. You should now have a round skittle-shaped piece which resembles Fig 47a. Check that the dimensions are correct and with the piece still turning on the lathe smooth with medium-grade sandpaper.

Clamp the hips of the piece horizontally into the vice and with a 1in woodworking chisel pare the flat planes on the back of the torso as shown in Fig 47b. Note that the angle of this plane changes slightly at the waist. To complete the back, smooth away the sharp edges at either side of these planes into the body. Turn the piece over in the vice and chisel away the slightly concave pelvis and the ridge above the chest. This ridge is smoothed away at back and front, the original shape remaining only at either side to form the doll's shoulders.

Mark in pencil and cut the slots for the legs in the lower torso with a fretsaw (Fig 47a). Clean these slots with a small file and check that they are parallel and uniform. Using a drill with ⅛in bit, drill through the hips from both sides. Do not drill right through the torso as the legs are pegged independently to ensure they both move freely. These holes are drilled towards the front of the torso, not through the centre (*see* Fig 47b).

From ⅜in dowelling, cut two shoulder pegs as shown (Fig 48) on which the arms will hinge. Carefully mark the centre points of the two holes below the shoulders and, clamping the body in the vice, use the drill and ⅜in bit to drill the holes to receive the pegs. Glue the pegs into the holes, ensuring that the tenon is vertical (Fig 49a). For the doll's nose, glue a small wedge-shaped piece of wood to the centre of the face with white woodwork glue.

Cut two 4in lengths of ¾in square wood for the upper legs, and two for the lower legs. Turn these pieces to the shapes shown (Fig 48). Turn the lower legs to the ankle, then remove from the lathe and shape the feet with a craft knife. Cut tenons at the top of both upper and lower legs (in Fig 48). Work gradually until the tenon on the upper leg fits snugly into the slot in the lower torso. Cut the slots in the lower ends of the upper legs with a fretsaw and refine them with a file until the tenons on the lower legs fit snugly into the slots. (Note that before the joints are pegged, the tenons and the bottom of the upper leg are rounded as shown in Fig 48.) To ensure free movement of the joints, the

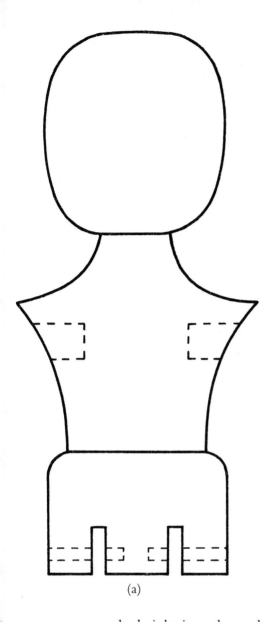

(a)

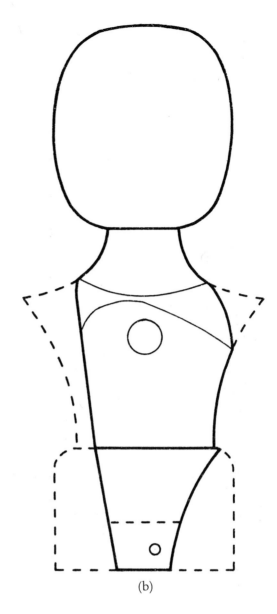

(b)

Fig 47 (a) Actual size pattern for turning head and torso of Dutch doll
(b) Side view showing areas to be pared from torso

tenons are not pushed right into the sockets, but a small gap is left (Fig 49).

Position the lower leg tenon in the upper leg and, holding it firmly in place, use the ⅛in bit to drill through the knee joint from side to side. Insert a ⅛in dowelling peg and trim to size. Repeat for the other leg. Similarly, insert the completed leg into the body socket, drill through the tenon and peg in place. (If any pegs do not fit tightly, glue them in place, ensuring that the glue does not touch the tenons.)

Cut two 3in lengths of ¾in square wood for the upper arms and two for the lower arms. Turn these pieces to the shapes shown (Fig 48). Turn the lower arms to the wrist, then remove from the lathe and model the hands to simple spoon shapes with a craft

knife. Cut tenons at the top of the lower arms and sockets at both top and bottom of the upper arms. (Note: These sockets are at right-angles to one another – see Figs 48 and 49.) Before the joints are pegged, the tenons in the lower arm and top and bottom of the upper arm are rounded (Fig 48). The shoulder and elbow joints are assembled in the same way as the leg joints. Smooth the doll thoroughly with fine-grade sandpaper.

Paint the head, neck, shoulders and lower arms with pale flesh-coloured paint. I recommend Humbrol matt enamel paint, mixing

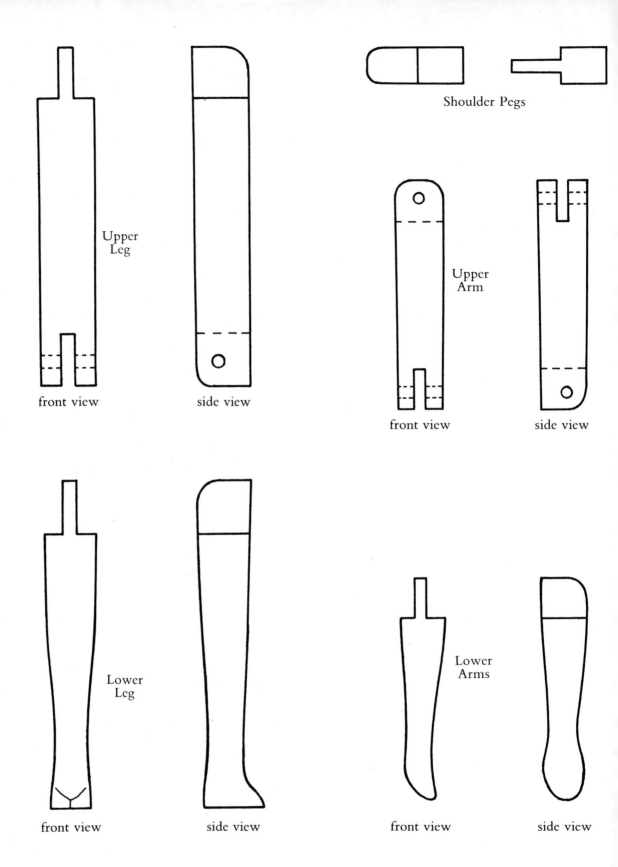

Shoulder Pegs

Upper Leg

front view   side view

Upper Arm

front view   side view

Lower Leg

front view   side view

Lower Arms

front view   side view

Fig 48 Actual size patterns for arms, legs and pegs for Dutch doll

flesh and white to the required shade. Two or three coats should be applied, allowing each coat to dry thoroughly. Paint the lower legs white. The shoes may be any colour you wish, though red is the colour most often found on old dolls.

As the colours will be sealed with varnish, the features may be painted with any type of paint (use Fig 45 and the colour illustration as a guide). The eyes and eyebrows are black and the mouth and cheeks a clear bright red. The hair is painted onto the head – invariably black – with a centre parting and I have added curls on the cheeks though these were more typical of the earlier Grödnerthals than Dutch dolls. When the paint is dry, spray the head, shoulders, lower legs and arms with varnish. I recommend Humbrol satin finish as it is not too shiny. Apply a second coat of varnish twenty-four hours after the first and leave the doll in a dust-free place until the varnish is thoroughly dry.

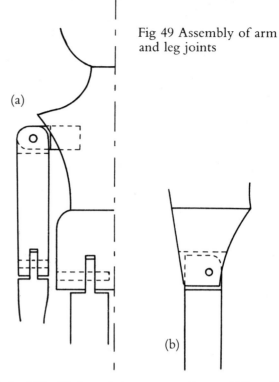

Fig 49 Assembly of arm and leg joints

(a)

(b)

(*below*) Fig 50 Actual size patterns for small Dutch doll

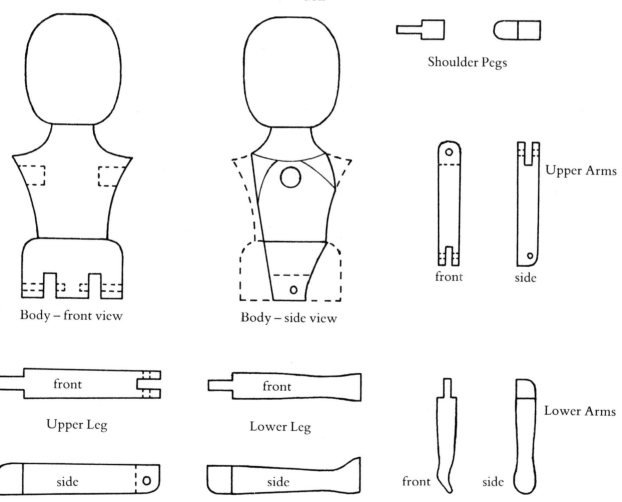

Shoulder Pegs

Upper Arms

front   side

Body – front view

Body – side view

Upper Leg

Lower Leg

Lower Arms

front   side

side   side

front   side

73

LARGE DUTCH DOLL'S CLOTHES

½yd white cotton (36in wide) for underwear
½yd printed cotton (36in wide) for dress
12in square of felt for bonnet
12in square of felt for cloak
scraps of lining for cloak and bonnet
½yd cotton lace (1in wide) for bonnet frill
½yd cotton lace (¼in wide) for sleeve frills
½yd cotton tape (¼in wide) for drawstrings
shirring elastic
4 tiny hooks and eyes
scraps of ribbon, flowers etc for trimming

To make the drawers, cut two pieces in white cotton (Fig 51). Seam the legs, then roll fine hems around the upper parts of each leg. (The two legs are quite separate and only joined by the drawstring.) Turn a narrow casing at the waist edge of each leg and a narrow hem at the leg ends. Thread tape through the casings and pull up to fit the doll's waist, tying in a bow at the centre back.

For the petticoat, cut a piece of white cotton 18×8in (this allows for a deep hem) and stitch the centre-back seam. Make a narrow casing at the waist edge, and hem the lower edge. Thread tape through the casing and pull up to fit the doll's waist tying in a bow at centre back.

For the dress, cut two bodice pieces and two sleeves (Fig 51), a piece 20×9in for the skirt and a 1in wide waistband to fit the doll's waist with a 1in overlap. Fold one bodice piece in half and cut open for the centre back.

Stitch the sleeves to the backs and front at the armhole. Stitch the side seams from the sleeve ends, through the underarm and down the bodice sides. Gather the lower edge of the bodice and stitch to one edge of the waistband. Gather the top of the skirt and stitch to the lower edge of the waistband. Stitch the centre-back seam in the skirt to 1½in below the waist. Turn back and hem the remainder of the skirt and the centre-back edges of the waistband and bodice to form facings, checking that the waistband meets around the doll's waist to fasten with a hook and eye. Gather the neckline and pull up the gathers to fit around the doll's shoulders (or higher if you prefer). Fasten off the gathers and bind the neckline with a narrow bias-cut strip of dress fabric, or if you prefer, make a casing around the neckline and gather with a drawstring. Hem the sleeve ends, trim with ¼in lace and gather with shirring elastic to fit the wrists.

Make a deep hem on the lower edge of the skirt and fasten the back bodice and waistband with small hooks and eyes.

For the cloak, cut one cape and one collar in felt and one each in lining (Fig 51). With right sides facing, stitch the cape lining to the cape around the outside, turn through at the neck edge and press. With right sides facing, stitch the collar lining to the collar around the outside, turn through and press. Stitch the collar to the cape, enclosing the raw neck edges. Stitch ribbon ties to the fronts or make a small button and loop fastening.

To make the bonnet, cut two brims, one crown and one back in felt and one crown and one back in lining (Fig 51). Stitch the two brims together around the outside, turn through and press. Stitch the brim to the crown and the crown to the back around the curved edge. Stitch the crown lining to the back lining around the curved edge. With right sides facing, stitch the lining to the bonnet across the back edge and the sides of the crown. Turn the lining to the inside and hem over the brim seam to neaten. Sew a gathered frill of 1in wide lace to the inside of the bonnet brim, and ribbon ties to either side. Trim the bonnet with ribbon, flowers or feathers.

SMALL DUTCH DOLL'S CLOTHES

¼yd white cotton (36in wide) for dress and cap
small piece of fine wool for wrapper
scraps of lace, ribbons for trimming
1yd narrow silk ribbon for strings

To make the dress, cut the pattern in white cotton and slash the back opening (Fig 52). Roll a fine hem around the opening. Hem or bind the neckline to make a narrow casing. Stitch the side seams from the sleeve ends through the underarm and down the sides. Hem the sleeve ends. Working on the inside, stitch a length of narrow ribbon or tape around the dress at the high waistline shown on the pattern to make a casing. Hem the bottom edge of the skirt. Trim the dress with lace as required – I suggest a frill at the neckline, wrists and hem. Thread narrow ribbon strings through the casings at the neckline and waist and pull up to fit the doll, tying in bows at the back.

Fig 51 Clothes patterns for large Dutch doll

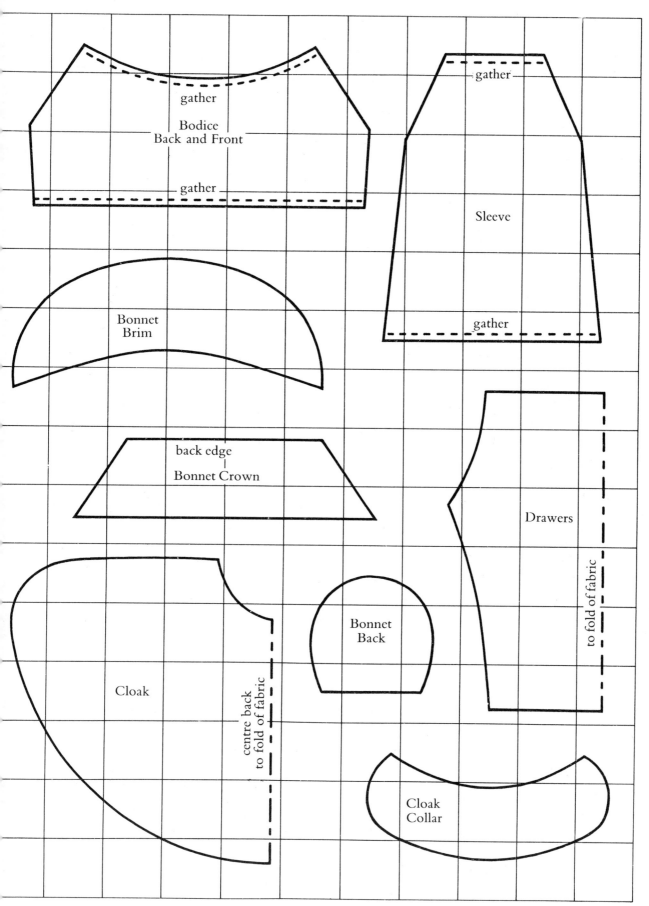

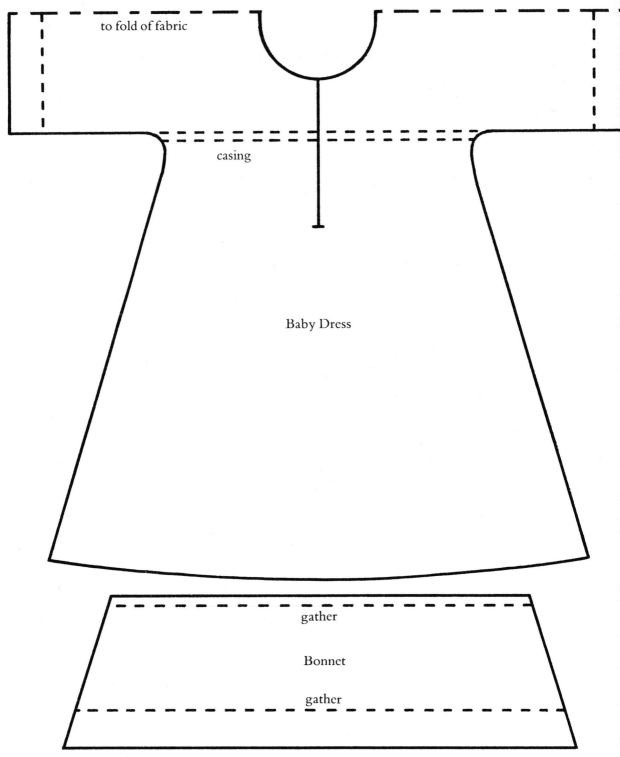

to fold of fabric

casing

Baby Dress

gather

Bonnet

gather

Fig 52 Clothes patterns for small Dutch doll

For the bonnet, cut the pattern in cotton, or wide lace or broderie anglaise edging (Fig 52). Neaten the short edges, and if necessary the front edge. Gather the back edge and pull the gathers up tightly so that the piece forms a cap shape. Gather behind the front edge, and pull up the gathers to fit the doll's head, making a frill around the face. Stitch ribbon ties to either side.

For the wrapper, cut a semi-circle of fine wool fabric (use a tea-plate as a guide), using a selvedge for the straight edge. Stitch narrow lace to the outside edge of the piece to neaten and ribbon ties at the neck.

7

A CONVERSATION PIECE (c1860)

The conversation piece was a quaint Victorian piece of interior decoration. This display of dolls, birds, animals or 'curiosities' was usually encased in a glass dome in a prominent position in the parlour, to give the visitor a topic of conversation.

The pedlar dolls (Chapter 6) were popular subjects for this treatment, or grander ladies with bazaar stalls full of miniature items. A group of small dolls might be dressed to represent a wedding party or musical ensemble, or a scene from a book or play. I have chosen *Little Women* for the subject of the conversation piece in this chapter though the dolls might easily be adapted to make other groups. *Little Women*, written by Louisa May Alcott and published in 1868, tells the story of four sisters, Meg, Jo, Beth and Amy, and is full of the 'proper' Victorian sentiments. The characters are described in the opening chapter of the book and I have used these

descriptions and my own interpretations of them to make the four dolls.

I preferred to make proper dolls rather than the simple padded wire figures more usually found in groups of this type, so the patterns and instructions in this chapter can be used to make a variety of dolls, male or female, and would be particularly suitable for use as costume dolls. Each doll is made in the same way, though Amy and Beth are a little shorter than Meg and Jo. The heads are modelled in self-hardening clay on shoulder-plates and the lower arms are modelled to the elbow. (You may also model the lower legs if you wish.) The bodies are a simple bag shape, made in calico, with a soft stuffing, and the arms and legs are wired with pipecleaners so that the dolls may be posed to look as life-like as possible. All the dolls have painted faces, each

Fig 53 Little Women

one with her own character, and mohair wigs. They wear drawers, petticoats and dresses made from the same simple basic patterns with variations for each doll. Full instructions are given for all props – chair, table, vase, books etc.

I recommend Fimo for modelling the heads and hands of the dolls and mohair or embroidery silks for the wigs. The bodies should be made in a closely woven cotton fabric (eg calico) and stuffed with good-quality soft stuffing. Pipecleaners are very effective for wiring these small limbs. The clothes should be made in natural fabrics; the March family was poor so I felt that printed cotton was most appropriate though you might prefer something more elaborate. I have made the clothes removable, though they might equally well be sewn onto the dolls. The base is a 13in-diameter round cakeboard covered in velvet and I have used the same velvet for the chair cover. In this group, Jo and Amy are both supported by small doll stands under their skirts and Meg and Beth are seated, so none of the dolls is permanently fixed in place.

Little Women (c1860)
(9½in and 10in tall)
Difficulty 3/Colour picture page 68
Body pattern: Fig 54
Clothes pattern: Fig 55

FOR EACH DOLL
small packet Fimo
mohair or embroidery silk and tape for wig
12in square of calico for body
4 pipecleaners
stuffing (soft)
paints
brushes
glue

Full instructions for modelling are given in Chapter 1 and are repeated only briefly here.

Model the doll's head in a solid piece of Fimo without a core-ball. Begin by rolling an egg shape, approximately 1½in long. Build up the cheeks, chin and forehead and shape the nose. Smooth the areas above the cheeks so that you will have a flat plane to paint the eyes and, if you wish, define the shape of the eyes with a small pointed tool. Shape the mouth and add ears if desired. At this stage, it is difficult to vary the faces a great deal, so it is better to model them simply and then paint

on the individual characteristics. Add the neck and shoulder-plate. Model the lower arm to the elbow (about 2½in long), with simply shaped small hands. Score to indicate the fingers, and score grooves at the upper ends of the arm for tying on to the body. (If you wish, model the lower legs to the knee with shoes.) Bake the modelled pieces.

When thoroughly cool, paint with two or three coats of flesh-coloured paint. Paint modelled shoes as realistically as possible. With very fine, good-quality brushes, paint the features. I have given Meg dark brown eyes with painted upper and lower lashes and a fine pink line to indicate the crease of the eyelid. Her dark brown eyebrows are fine and arched and the mouth is well shaped and painted dark pink. Jo has blue eyes, with neither upper nor lower lashes painted in; just a mid-brown outline around the eye. The eyebrows are straighter and thicker than Meg's and also mid brown. Jo's mouth is wide, painted in a light rusty red and she has light brown freckles dotted over her nose and cheeks. Amy's eyes are green, outlined and lashed with dark brown. Her eyebrows are small and slightly arched in mid brown and the mouth is small and pouting in dark pink. She has a 'mole' on her left cheek below the eye. Beth has light brown eyes, outlined but not lashed in dark brown. The eyebrows are also dark brown and rather heavy. Her wide mouth is a light rusty red. Each doll's cheeks are coloured with a little powder blusher rubbed in with the finger, Beth rather paler than the others.

I have used mohair for the wigs, glued onto the heads with UHU. (Embroidery silk would be an effective alternative.) Meg has brown hair, styled with a centre parting and two long ringlets at either side. The rest of the hair is drawn up to the back of the head and twisted into a small bun. Jo's tawny hair is applied on a piece of tape around the hairline then lifted to fall straight down her back. It is held by a small ribbon, tied at the back of her head. Beth has dark brown hair, styled with a centre parting and left to fall in waves to just below her shoulders. Amy's blonde hair is styled with a centre parting and plaits tied with fine ribbons. A little hairspray will help to keep the mohair in shape.

To make each doll's body, cut two bodies,

Fig 54 Body pattern for Little Women

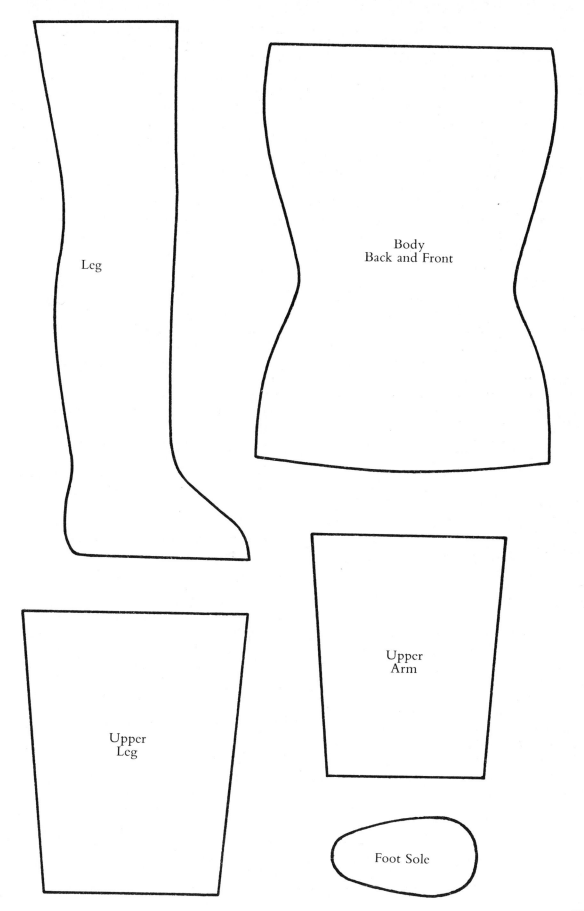

Leg

Body
Back and Front

Upper
Arm

Upper
Leg

Foot Sole

two upper arms and four legs (or two upper legs) and two soles in calico (Fig 54). Stitch the body pieces together to form a bag, leaving the top edge open. Clip the curves, turn through and stuff firmly. Oversew the top edge closed, then turn down the corners at each side and sew down to the body. Seam the upper arms into tubes and tie in the lower arms. Turn through, stuff the upper arms loosely around a pipecleaner (bent in half) and oversew closed. If you have used modelled lower legs, make up in the same way as the arms. Seam fabric legs together in pairs, sew in the soles, turn through and stuff around pipecleaners, pinching the feet to flatten and shape the soles. Oversew the top ends closed. (Note that for Amy and Beth the leg pattern should be shortened by ½in at the top end, and the completed arm should be ¼in shorter than for Meg and Jo.)

Stitch the legs to the back lower edge of the body with firm oversewing stitches and strong thread. Stitch the arms to the shoulders, ensuring that they are the correct length and hang naturally. Glue the underside of the shoulder-plate liberally (UHU) and seat it firmly onto the body, holding it in place until the glue is dry.

LITTLE WOMEN'S CLOTHES
For each Doll
¼yd white lawn (36in wide) for underwear
1yd narrow lace for trimming
¼yd printed cotton (36in wide) for dress
scraps of ribbon, lace etc for trimming
3 tiny press studs
shirring elastic

To make the drawers, cut two pieces in white lawn (Fig 55), then hem and trim the leg ends with lace. Seam each leg, then seam the legs together and hem the top edge to form a narrow casing. Thread doubled shirring elastic through the casing and pull up to fit the doll. For the petticoat, cut a piece of lawn 6½×14in (for Meg and Jo) or 5½×14in (for Amy and Beth). Stitch the centre-back seam, hem and trim the lower edge with lace. Turn a narrow casing on the top edge and thread doubled shirring elastic, pulled up to fit the doll's waist.

For each dress, cut one bodice front, two bodice backs and two sleeves (Fig 55) and one skirt piece 7×16in (for Meg and Jo) or 6×16in (for Amy and Beth). Stitch the bodice front to

backs at the shoulder seams. Gather the sleeve heads and stitch the sleeves into the armholes. Stitch the side seams from the sleeve ends, through the underarms and down the bodice sides. Gather the top edge of the skirt and stitch to the lower edge of the bodice. Stitch the centre-back seam in the skirt to 1in below the waist, then turn in and hem the remainder of the skirt and the back bodice edges to form facings. Roll a fine hem around the neckline and hem the lower ends of the sleeves. Hem the lower edge of the skirt and fasten the back bodice with tiny press studs.

For Meg: Cut the sleeve a little narrower than the pattern; trim the dress with bands of narrow ribbon down the centre front of the bodice and above the skirt hem and the sleeve ends. Add a collar made from a scrap of scalloped lace trimming and a small brooch (broken earring, bead etc) at the throat.

For Jo: Cut the sleeve a little narrower than the pattern. Trim the dress with a band of narrow lace at the neckline and sleeve ends. Make a V-shaped lace trim on the front of the bodice, mitring the corner above the waist. Add a ribbon sash, tied in a bow at the back, and a small brooch at the throat.

For Beth: Gather the sleeve ends at the wrists. Make collars from folded white bias-binding and add a ribbon bow to the centre of the neckline.

For Amy: Cut the neckline a little lower and roll a fine casing. Thread shirring elastic through the casing to pull up the neckline. Gather the sleeves above the hems to form frills. For the pinafore, cut a skirt 5×10in in hemmed white lawn or broderie anglaise and a waistband to fit the doll's waist with tape or ribbon ties. Gather the skirt and stitch to the waistband. Make shoulder frills from gathered broderie-anglaise edging stitched to the waistband at back and front on either side of a small bib. Add ties to the waistband and tie in a bow at centre back.

If the dolls have fabric legs, stockings can be made from tubular gauze finger bandage, and shoes in felt or thin leather. (Use the Georgian doll's shoe pattern on page 42 as a guide, adapting to fit as required.)

To complete the group, make the base, chair, footstool, table and 'props' as follows. You will need ½yd of velvet (36in wide) to cover the base and chair. To make the base use a 13in-diameter round cakeboard. Cut an 18in-

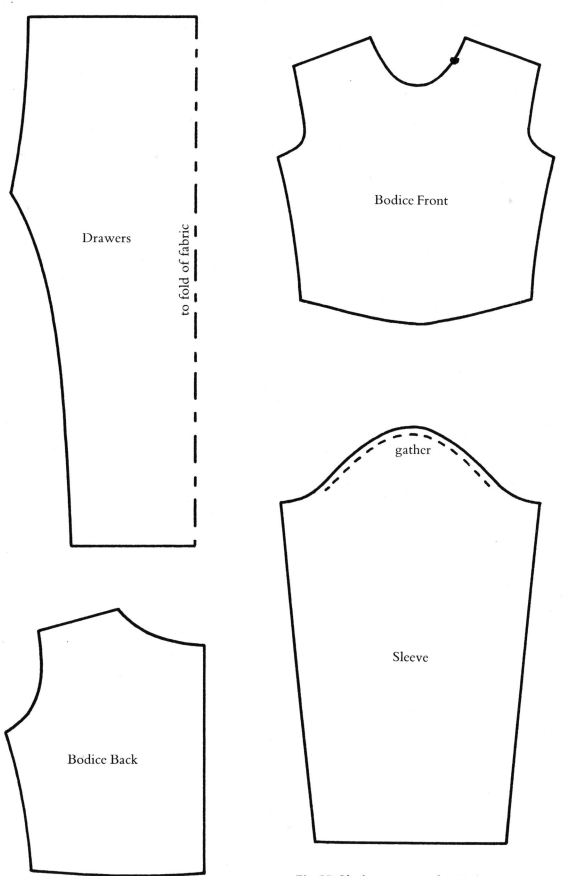

Drawers

to fold of fabric

Bodice Front

gather

Sleeve

Bodice Back

Fig 55 Clothes patterns for Little Women

diameter circle of velvet and run a strong gathering thread around the edge. Pull up the gathers on the underside of the cakeboard as evenly and tightly as possible so that the velvet is stretched taut, and fasten off. (You could cover raw edges with a Fablon circle.)

To make the chair, cut the pattern in stiff cardboard (Fig 56). (The type used for the back of writing and drawing pads is ideal – cardboard boxes or cereal packets are too flimsy.) Score the two dotted lines marked on the pattern to bend the arms of the chair forward. The padding may be ¼in thick foam or terylene wadding and should be cut to the same shape as the pattern but ½in larger all round. Glue the padding to the inside of the chair (with UHU), rolling the ½in overlap over the edges and gluing to the back all the way round (Fig 57). Cut two covers for the chair, using the pattern as a guide. Cut one on the straight grain of the fabric and one on the bias grain, ½in larger than the pattern, using the outline of the pattern as the sewing line. Stitch the fabric covers together, right sides facing, around the arms and back of the chair, leaving the lower edge open. Clip the curves and corners and turn through. With the bias-cut side of the cover to the inside of the chair and the straight grain to the outside, gently stretch the cover over the padded cardboard. Pull the cover

down as tightly as possible and, turning in the raw edges, slipstitch closed.

The seat of the chair is made by cutting a block of balsa wood to fit inside the back and arms to the required height. The block is padded and covered in fabric like a parcel, with the ends glued firmly in place (Fig 57). The back and sides of the seat are glued and put in place inside the chair. Pins pushed through from the outside will hold everything in place until the glue is dry. Make a small stuffed cushion, perhaps in miniature patchwork, and an antimacassar made from a scrap of lace for the back of the chair. To neaten the underside of the chair, glue a square of felt to cover the raw edges and make 'feet' from round wooden beads glued under each corner.

The footstool is made from a large cotton reel, sliced in half through the centre. Pad the top with a circle of foam or wadding and cover the whole piece in a circle of velvet, gathered around the outside edge and pulled up underneath. Finish the underside with a circle of felt to cover the raw edges. (If Beth will not 'sit' on the stool without support, push a large darning needle up into the body and down into the centre of the stool.)

The table is made from a chess piece with the top sawn off for the pedestal and a 2½in-diameter circle of thin wood glued on for the top. The top is stained with woodstain (or painted) to match the base.

Fig 56 Little Women – chair pattern

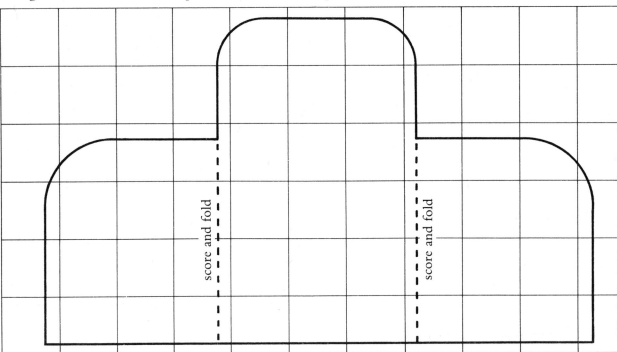

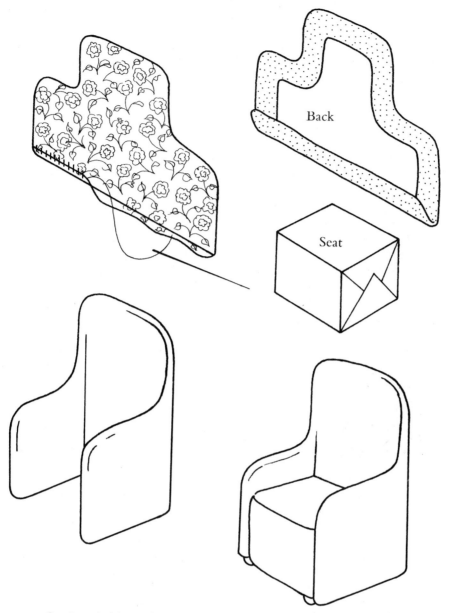

Fig 57 Assembly of chair

Use a square of printed fabric for the rug and model a small flower vase in self-hardening clay. Fill with a few artificial flowers. Beth's music is drawn onto small sheets of paper with a fine-nibbed pen (eg, a Rotring drawing pen). Amy's pencils are made from wooden toothpicks, cut to size and coloured with felt pens. Jo's book is made from sheets of thin paper, glued into the folded spine of a cardboard cover. Meg's workbasket is plaited raffia, coiled and stitched to shape, with tiny balls of wool and knitting worked on glass-headed pins. The tiny scissors are a bracelet charm. Arrange the furniture, dolls and accessories on the base, as you please, bending the dolls' arms so that they look as life-like as possible.

8

THE FASHION DOLL (c1870)

The 1860s and 1870s were the 'golden age' of the beautifully dressed lady dolls known as French Fashion or Parisienne. Though some of the heads were in fact made in Germany, the dolls were made and dressed by a large number of French firms, most of them based in Paris. They were luxury dolls made for the growing rich middle class, and reflected the prevalent social attitudes to material possessions. In France especially, young girls were encouraged to pay as much attention to their toilettes as their fashionable mamas, and the fashion doll with her trousseau of clothes for every occasion offered an example for the child to follow.

Tens of thousands of these dolls were produced, and perhaps the fact that a fair percentage has survived, often with their original clothes, is a reflection of the value that was placed on them, either for the sake of their beauty, or their cost. The survivors are much prized by modern collectors, and examples in good condition sell for thousands of pounds. They not only reflect an age of luxury and ostentation which is past, but they are perhaps one of the finest examples of the doll-maker's art.

The earlier Parisiennes had bisque heads with shoulder-plates on gusseted kid bodies. The arms were usually kid with a gusset at the elbow and had separate fingers. Most of the firms which produced this type of doll during this period experimented with other materials and methods in an attempt to produce more life-like dolls. Gutta-percha, rubber and fabric bodies were used, but some of the best fashion dolls have jointed wooden bodies, often covered with a leather 'skin'. The articulation of these ball-jointed wooden bodies was similar to that of the artist's lay figure, with movement at the shoulder, elbow, hip, knee and waist, enabling the doll to hold very natural poses. The kid body, with or without gusset joints, remained popular throughout the period and is probably the type most commonly associated with the fashion doll. The swivel head with socket neck and bisque lower arms superseded earlier types, with lower legs often carved in wood or moulded in bisque instead of the leather legs made as part of the body.

Fixed glass eyes were customary (a few very rare examples have sleeping eyes worked by a lever) and the faces were modelled and painted to represent plump, gentle, beautiful ladies, though a thinner, more elegant face

Fig 58 Fashion doll

became fashionable in the 1870s. The elaborately coiffured wigs, styled in the current fashion, were usually of real hair, though mohair was also used.

Though the dolls themselves were usually very well made, it was their clothes which accounted for the larger part of their cost. Professionally made by departments of the firms which produced the dolls or by other firms making only dolls' clothes and accessories, the standard of workmanship on these tiny garments was extremely high. They were miniature versions of real clothes, complete to the smallest detail. Encouraged by the interest of the Empress Eugenie, doll and dolls' clothes manufacturers produced ever more exquisite examples of their art. Competitions were held for doll's dress designers and a large industry grew up devoted to equipping the fashion doll with everything which was modish. The dresses were often made of silk, in the latest styles and elaborately trimmed with lace, ribbons, braid, fringe and beads. Most of the sewing was done by hand at first, though towards the end of the period many commercial dolls' clothes were machine-sewn. Although sets of underwear would be supplied as part of the doll's trousseau, it was on the dress that most attention was lavished.

The dolls of the 1860s wore the full-skirted dresses of the period and when bustles became the fashion in the 1870s, dolls too wore them. Their clothes were rivalled by their accessories. Everything that the fashionable lady required could be bought in miniature, from perfectly made boots and shoes, jewellery and parasols, to writing cases, handbags and gloves; even tiny spectacles were available for short-sighted dolls! There were dolls' corset-makers, milliners, glovemakers, shoemakers and jewellers all producing tiny items which rich little girls were encouraged to buy for their dolls.

As the popularity of the fashion doll grew, cheaper versions were produced, especially in Germany, for those who could not afford the fabulous French dolls. These dolls had bisque shoulder heads on cloth or kid bodies, or socket heads on composition bodies. Their clothes were designed to be eye-catching but were usually poorly made with the minimum of underwear, and often glued in place. Though cheaper than the luxury dolls, even these fashion dolls were comparatively expensive. A china head doll with a cloth body could be bought for a fraction of the price. Despite their popularity, the fashion dolls had many critics who regarded them as over-priced, over-dressed and unsuitable for children and, by the early 1880s, their popularity had waned in favour of the simpler French bébés.

During the early 1900s, the fashion doll enjoyed a brief revival. Made in France and Germany and dressed in the latest styles, these dolls were popular as a change from the, by then, more usual child and baby dolls. They were still quite expensive and lavishly dressed in Edwardian fashions. They had bisque heads and bisque or composition limbs on cloth or composition bodies. The wigs were usually mohair, and the faces often had 'sleep eyes' and open mouths with teeth, both new developments since the 1870s. Though many of these later fashion dolls are attractive, they do not have the quality and style of the earlier Parisiennes and the First World War saw the end of the revival.

It was not until the 1960s when the Sindy doll came into vogue that the fashion doll again became really popular, though it is a subject which has always interested most home dollmakers. (However, few people today dress dolls in the current fashion, preferring to make costume dolls.)

The fashion doll in this chapter is dressed in the style of the 1870s. The head and shoulderplate and the lower arms are modelled in self-hardening clay and painted to represent bisque. A pattern for leather arms is also included. The inset eyes are acrylic and the wig, styled in ringlets, is real hair. The kid body, stuffed with sawdust, is a copy of the type of body often found on antique dolls. For simplicity, I have made a version without gussets, and as the doll looks most attractive displayed standing, I felt that the gusset joints enabling her to sit were unnecessary. The arms are wired, so they may be posed.

The costume is that of a bride (though it could also be made in another fabric for everyday wear), made in white moire taffeta lavishly trimmed with pleated ribbon and lace. The lined basque jacket fastens down the centre front with hooks and eyes covered by a lace frill and pearl buttons. The skirt is demi-trained and worn over a small bustle pad. Under the costume the doll wears lawn combinations and petticoats.

I have simplified the cutting for the clothes patterns a little, inasmuch as the shaping of the jacket is made by one dart on either side of the front rather than two, and the sleeves are cut in one piece rather than the more usual two-seamed coat sleeve. I have done this mainly to avoid unnecessary darts and seams, although still retaining the correct shape, and partly to make the patterns a little simpler. The back of the skirt is cut in two panels, and as I have used a very stiff fabric, is not very full. If you use a lightweight fabric I would recommend cutting the back skirts wider by up to half as much again, and this will also allow for the back of the skirt to be looped up to form a bustle as an alternative to the demi-train.

I have modelled the doll's head, shoulder-plate and lower arms in Fimo, but Das or any other self-hardening clay would be suitable. The eyes are the usual flat-backed acrylic type. The wig is a matter of individual preference, but I would recommend real hair or mohair in a style with long curls. Hairstyles of this period tended to echo the shape of the dress, with most of the interest focused at the back. A curled fringe was fashionable as was a small bun on the back of the head with the remainder of the hair falling in long ringlets. The wig I have used is a simple style parted in the centre with a small fringe and ringlets which allows the headdress and veil to sit well – a point worth considering if you are making a bride.

While experimenting with leather bodies I experienced some frustration with the stretchy quality of new leather. I found that however much I stretched it before cutting, when I stuffed the doll, the body still 'grew', often quite alarmingly. As the proportions of this type of doll are all important, this was most unsatisfactory! I eventually solved the problem by cutting the body from Edwardian kid gloves which, having been worn, were already fully stretched, and found that it worked extremely well. These long white kid gloves can be found in junk shops, jumble sales and antique markets. As the hands are usually very small, they are of little interest and are usually sold quite cheaply. You will need two elbow-length pairs to make the fashion doll's body. Cut off the hand part of the glove and cut along the seam to open the piece out flat. If necessary iron on the wrong side with a cool iron to remove creases. If the gloves are grubby, use the inner side as the outside.

If you choose to use new leather, stretch it as thoroughly as possible before use and back it with lightweight iron-on Vilene to prevent further stretching. (Note that leather skins should be very fine and either pink or white.) Roll the skin in a damp towel and leave overnight. With another person, pull and stretch the dampened skin, turning it constantly. Pull firmly but gently. Any very thin areas might tear and will have to be avoided when laying out the pattern.

You can also make this body in unbleached calico, but I do not recommend it, as calico will not 'give' to make the curved chest and well-shaped legs as leather does. It will however produce an adequate body.

If you have never seen this type of body pattern before, you may find it a little confusing. The doll is made in two pieces from the waist downwards, with a seam at the centre back of each leg and another seam from the waist, through the crotch from back to front, to join the two legs together. The feet are sewn into slits in the lower ends of the legs. The upper body is made in two layers – with a lining of muslin or lawn which has darts to shape the bust and seams at either side. This is sewn to the lower body at the waist and the body is stuffed in the usual way, and oversewn closed at the top. When the shoulder-plate is seated onto the body (and the top of the arms attached), the leather body cover, cut in two pieces (back and front), is glued on separately over the body lining. (I recommend UHU for gluing leather.) The back piece, glued around the edges, covers the waist seam and the lower edges of the shoulder-plate; the front piece also covers the waist seam and the lower edges of the shoulder-plate and overlaps the back piece down the sides and across the shoulders.

I strongly recommend that you do not cut these body cover pieces until the rest of the doll is completed. Cut the pattern pieces in paper kitchen-towels first to check that they fit the individual doll. (Variations in shoulder-plate and stuffing etc will affect shape and size to some extent.) Make any necessary adjustments and use the paper-towel patterns to cut the leather.

Though not designed for the beginner, this doll should present no problems to the experienced dollmaker – even one unfamiliar with this type of body. It is in fact easier than it looks! It is however necessary to get the size and proportions of the modelled parts right as it is very difficult to change the proportions of the body pattern (especially the lower half) as all the shaping is governed by one seam. I would suggest that if you do model the head too large or small you model another head rather than trying to alter the body pattern. The scalloped edges on the body cover pieces are easily cut with pinking shears. Sew the leather by machine with a new small sharp needle. The doll is stuffed with sawdust packed in very firmly.

Use natural fabrics for the clothes – silks, satins, velvet or silk and wool mixtures are usually more appropriate for this type of doll than cotton, though a well-chosen plain colour or soft print in fine cotton can look very effective (see the Bru kit from Creations Past in Chapter 14). Most colours were fashionable, and often two or three toning or contrasting colours would be used on a cos-tume. Costume reference books are very useful as fashion dolls' clothes wore the latest fashions in miniature (see Bibliography).

Trimmings popular at this time included velvet and silk ribbons, silk braids and fringes, black, cream and white lace, beads and pleating. Though evening dresses had low necklines and short sleeves, day wear almost invariably had a high neckline, round, square or V-shaped, and elbow-length or long sleeves. The most popular hat styles were small, lavishly trimmed, and worn tilted to the front of the head. Fashionable acces-sories included parasols, fans, small handbags and gloves. Pearl necklaces and earrings and cameo brooches were worn, though there was little display of jewellery except for evening wear.

Underwear was still generally white and was by now elaborately trimmed with frills, tucks and lace. Combinations had come into fashion in the late 1860s and were a popular alternative to chemise and drawers. The bustle might be a stuffed pad tied around the waist (as used here) or a complex structure of wire or whalebone (the latter are rarely found on dolls). Many of the original fashion dolls wore laced corsets, heavily boned like the real thing and usually fastening down the front. White stockings were still the norm, though black or brown might be worn in the country. Boots or shoes were in fine leather or fabric and in doll-size were often made to match the costume.

To complete the bridal costume the doll has a tulle veil with a lace edging, an artificial flower headdress and a bouquet of artificial flowers.

Fashion Doll (c1870)

(18in tall)
Difficulty 5/Colour picture page 67
Body pattern: Figs 59 and 60
Clothes patterns: Figs 61 and 62

1 large packet Fimo (head, shoulder-plate and lower arms)
4 white kid gloves (long)
core-ball (2½in diameter) for head
small piece muslin or lawn for body lining
1 pair acrylic eyes (14mm)
stuffing (sawdust and soft)
wire
paints
brushes
glue
wig

Full modelling instructions are given in Chapter 1 and are repeated only briefly here.

Model the head to resemble the head of the original French fashion doll as closely as

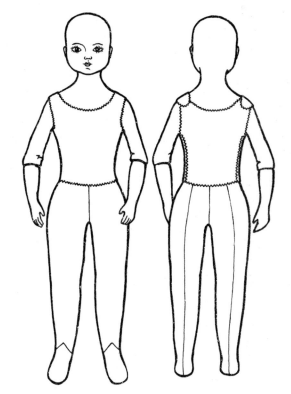

Fig 59 Fashion doll's body

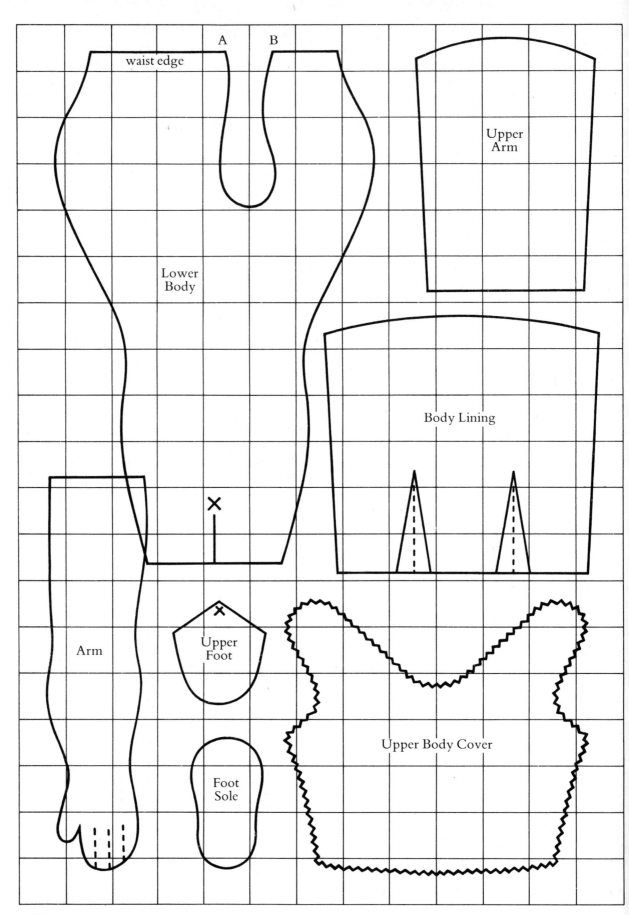

waist edge

A B

Upper
Arm

Lower
Body

Body Lining

Arm

Upper
Foot

Upper Body Cover

Foot
Sole

possible (*see* Fig 58 as a guide). The face is fairly heavy, with full cheeks and a well-pronounced chin. The eyes are deep set and almond-shaped. The nose is well defined, and the mouth has full well-shaped lips. Model the ears and pierce them for earrings. The neck should be slightly plump and not too long, and the shoulders slightly sloping with a fairly deep shoulder-plate. Set the head onto the shoulders at an angle, so that the doll looks to one side. (As it is not possible to model a swivel neck, this will achieve a similar, though fixed, effect). Ensure that the shoulder-plate is fairly wide from front to back as the doll has a full bosom. Model the lower arms to the elbow with a plump fore-arm tapering to a small wrist and hand. Curve the fingers to a natural position and score grooves for tying on. The dimensions of the modelled parts should be as follows: head from forehead (hairline) to chin, 3in; circumference of head, 9in; arm from elbow to fingertips, 4in (maximum). If the proportions of your doll are very different from these, I suggest re-modelling as it is difficult to alter the proportions of the body pattern.

When the modelling is satisfactory, bake and leave to cool thoroughly. Remove the core-ball from the head. Paint the modelled parts with several coats of pale flesh-coloured paint. I recommend Humbrol matt enamel, mixing white and flesh to the required shade. Usually, the more coats of paint the smoother the finished piece will be, so apply as many coats as necessary (at least three) and allow each coat to dry thoroughly before applying the next.

Paint the features with a very fine, good-quality brush (using Fig 58 and the colour illustration on page 67 as a guide). The eyes should be outlined with a very fine black line, and straight lashes painted all around the eye. The brows should be fairly heavy, painted in feathery strokes in brown. The mouth is a soft rusty red and the cheeks are coloured slightly with a little powder blusher, rubbed in with the finger. If you wish, fingernails may be defined (not painted) with the same rusty red as the mouth.

To make the body, cut two lower bodies (remember to reverse the pattern), two upper feet and two soles in leather (Fig 60). Cut two body linings in thin cotton. (Do not cut the

Fig 60 Body pattern for fashion doll

body covers at this stage.) With small over-sewing stitches, sew the upper feet into the slits in the front lower ends of the legs (the Xs correspond). Fold each lower body piece in half lengthwise (right side to the inside) and machine-stitch down the centre-back seams. Stitch the soles into the feet (this is more easily done by hand with small firm over-sewing stitches). Stitch the two legs together (right sides facing) from the front waist (A), around the crotch to the back waist (B). Turn through to the right side. Stitch the darts in the front body lining, and stitch front to back at the side seams. Adjust the side seams if necessary so that the waist edge of the body lining fits the waist edge of the lower body. With right sides facing stitch the body lining to the lower body around the waist.

Stuff the body very firmly with sawdust, paying particular attention to shaping the feet. Be patient with the stuffing – it takes time to do it properly, but it is important. When the body is filled, tuck in the raw top edges of the body lining and oversew closed. Turn down the corners at each side and stitch to the body. The doll should have a very firmly stuffed body, with the feet and legs well shaped and the bosom full and rounded. Seam the upper arms to form tubes and tie in the lower arms. Stuff the upper arms fairly loosely with soft stuffing around a wire. (If you drill a small hole into the lower arm and insert and glue in the end of the wire before tying on then the elbow will be flexible and the arms will hold any position.) Oversew the tops of the arms closed. Pin the arms to the shoulders ensuring that they hang naturally. (The arms on antique fashion dolls seem just a little too long to the modern eye in relation to their legs.) Stitch the arms firmly in place. Glue the underside of the shoulder-plate liberally and seat it onto the body, holding it firmly in place until the glue is dry.

Using kitchen paper, cut two upper body covers from the pattern (Fig 60). Make any necessary adjustments and ensure that the pattern is a good fit. Use the paper-towel patterns to cut the pieces in leather with pinking shears. Glue all around the edge of the back body cover and lay it onto the back of the doll to cover the waist seam and the lower edges of the shoulder-plate. Press firmly in place, stretching and moulding it around the body. Glue around the outside of the front body cover and lay it onto the front of the doll, lining up the waist with the back body cover, overlapping at the side seams, covering the lower edges of the shoulder-plate and overlapping at the shoulders. Press the edges firmly in place, stretching the leather and moulding it over the doll's bosom and around the body (Fig 59). Check that all edges are thoroughly glued.

If you prefer to make the doll with leather arms you will need extra leather; a pale colour such as white, cream, pink or beige would be most suitable. Cut two pairs of arms from the pattern and stitch each pair together (right sides facing) leaving the top edges open. Stuff loosely with soft stuffing and close the top edges. Stabstitch in matching thread to indicate the fingers. Stitch the arms to the shoulders before seating the shoulder-plate onto the body, then proceed as before.

I suggest that you do not glue the doll's wig in place until she is dressed. If your finished doll is taller or shorter than 18in you will need to alter the length of the skirt pattern.

FASHION DOLL'S CLOTHES

For the Underwear
½yd stiff white cotton (36in wide)
1yd white cotton lawn (36in wide)
1yd lace (½in wide)
1yd lace (1in wide)
1yd fine silk ribbon
5 tiny buttons
½yd cotton tape (¼in wide)

For the Dress
1yd fabric (36in wide)
matching bias-binding
scraps of lawn (or silk) for lining
2yd pleated lace and ribbon trimming
2yd narrow gathered lace trimming
½yd satin ribbon (½in wide)
½yd satin ribbon (1in wide)
½yd tulle (36in wide)
1½yd narrow lace edging
artificial flowers for headdress and bouquet
fuse-wire
5 pearl beads or buttons
tiny hooks and eyes

To make the combinations, cut two pieces in white lawn (Fig 61) and check that the shoulder to crotch measurement is long enough for your doll. Stitch the two pieces together down the centre back. Stitch the centre-front seam for 2in from the crotch, then turn back the remainder of the front edges and hem to form facings. Stitch the leg seams from one leg end, through the crotch to the other leg end. Stitch the shoulder seams. Roll a narrow hem around the neckline to make a casing. Roll fine hems around the armholes and trim neckline and armholes with ½in wide lace. Hem the leg ends and also trim with ½in wide lace. Make four buttonholes and sew on buttons down the fronts. Thread narrow silk ribbon through the neckline casing and pull up to fit the doll, tying in a bow at the front.

Use stiff white cotton, eg calico, for the under-petticoat. Cut a piece 26×12in, and stitch the centre-back seam. Turn a ¼in casing at the top edge and a deep hem at the lower edge. Thread tape through the casing and pull up to fit the doll's waist, concentrating the fullness to the back. Allow the under-petticoat to sit loosely at the doll's waist, beneath the waistband of the top petticoat.

For the top petticoat, cut a piece of lawn 28×12in and a waistband to fit the doll's waist with button and buttonhole fastening. Stitch the centre-back seam to 2in below the waist, then turn back and hem the remainder to form facings. Gather the top edge and stitch to the waistband, concentrating the fullness to the sides and back. Make buttonhole and sew on button. Hem the lower edge and trim with lace. Make three or four pintucks above hem.

To make the bustle pad, cut two pieces in white lawn (Fig 61). Stitch together around the edge, turn through and stuff lightly with soft stuffing. Turn in the top edges and oversew closed. Stitch the pad to a length of tape and tie around the doll's waist over the top petticoat.

For the skirt, cut one front, two backs and a waistband (Fig 62) to fit the doll's waist with hook and eye fastening. Stitch three rows of pleated lace and ribbon trim to the skirt front, the bottom row 1in above the edge. Stitch the skirt front to backs down the side seams. Stitch the centre-back seam to 2in below the waist, then turn back and hem the remainder to form facings. Face the hem of the skirt with matching bias-binding, then stitch a row of pleated ribbon and lace trimming all the way around the lower edge of the skirt. Gather the top edges of the skirt backs and

Figs 61 and 62 (overleaf) Clothes patterns for fashion doll

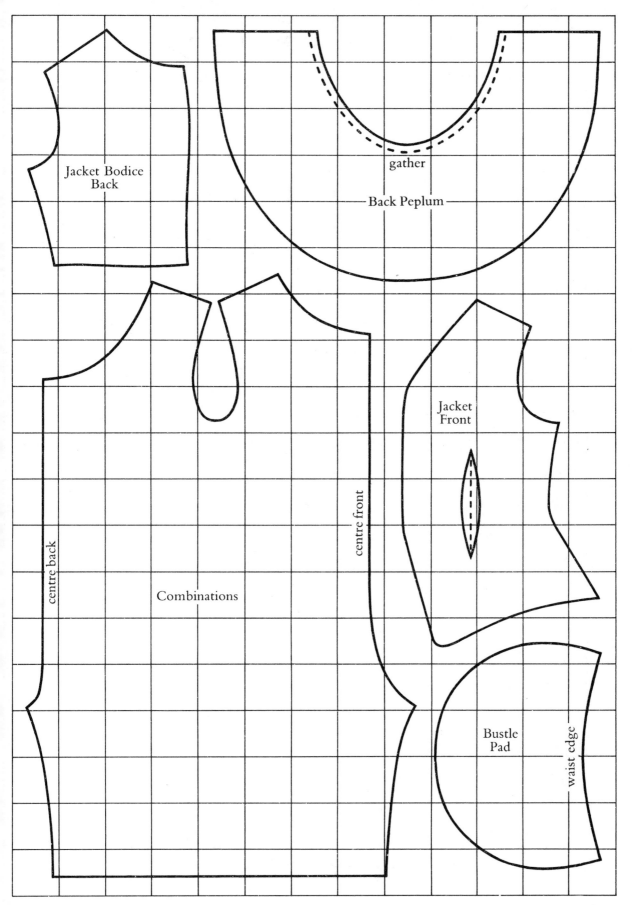

Jacket Bodice
Back

gather

Back Peplum

centre back

Combinations

centre front

Jacket
Front

Bustle
Pad

waist edge

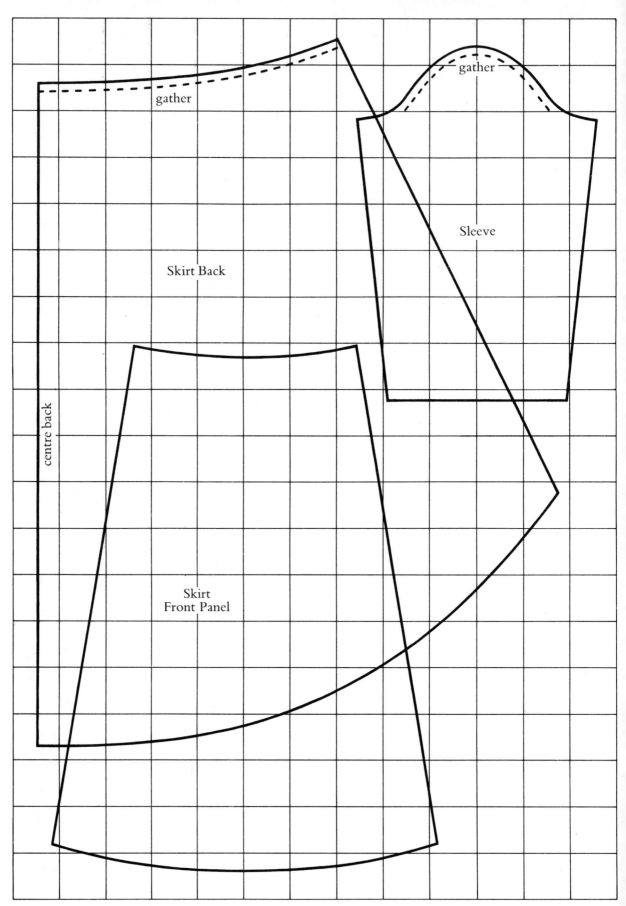

gather

gather

Sleeve

Skirt Back

centre back

Skirt
Front Panel

stitch the skirt to the waistband. Fasten with small hooks and eyes at centre back.

To make the jacket, cut two fronts, two backs, one back peplum and two sleeves in fabric and the same in lining (Fig 61). Make up one jacket in fabric, and one in lining as follows. Stitch the darts on the fronts. Stitch the centre-back seam. Gather the back peplum and stitch to the lower edge of the back. Stitch fronts to back at shoulder and side seams. Stitch the sleeve seams, gather the sleeve heads to ease and set the sleeves into the armholes.

With right sides together, stitch the jacket to the lining all the way around the outside edges, leaving a small gap at the centre back (lower edge of the peplum) to turn through. Clip curves and corners, turn through, slip-stitch the opening closed and press. Pull the lining sleeves into the sleeves and hem the sleeve ends to the lining. Stitch gathered lace trimming all around the edges of the jacket and to the sleeve ends. Stitch hooks and eyes to the fronts to fasten and sew on pearl beads or buttons. Make four bows of ½in wide satin ribbon and sew one to each cuff, one to the skirt and one to the centre front of the bodice. Make a bow of 1in wide satin ribbon and stitch to the centre-back waistline.

For the veil, cut an oval in tulle, 18in long × 12in wide. Cut straight across the top edge. Stitch lace edging all the way around the tulle. Gather the straight edge to fit across the top of the doll's head. (If you have not previously fitted the wig do so now.) Twist and wire (fuse-wire) the stems of the artificial flowers to shape a crescent headdress to fit over the doll's head and stitch the top edge of the veil to the crescent of flowers. Arrange the bouquet, and wire to hold in shape. (The bouquet may be attached invisibly to the hand with a small piece of surgical tape.)

The doll wears pearl bead earrings in her pierced ears (see Chapter 2) and bought white cotton stockings and leather buttoned boots (see Stockists).

For the more adventurous dollmaker, the patterns given here may be adapted to make a trousseau for the fashion doll. Consider making the skirt and jacket in velveteen trimmed with silky fringed braid (the type sold for trimming lampshades is very suitable) or velvet ribbon in a toning colour. The jacket might be fastened with buttons and loops or buttonholes and the neckline and sleeve ends trimmed with frills of lace. The shape of the skirt may be altered by cutting the front twice as wide on the fold of the fabric, thus making the skirt fuller and pushing the train further back. Made up in a lightweight fabric, the skirt backs might also be cut wider and looped up into a bustle, the extra length of the train allowing the looped-up back skirt to fall to the same length as the front. This style was popular for walking costumes, where a train was impractical.

To adapt the pattern to make a princess-line dress (named after Princess Alexandra, then Princess of Wales), extend the lines of the front and side edges of the jacket to full length for the front of the dress, and extend the top edge of the back skirt to meet the lower edge of the back bodice, omitting the peplum. The princess dress usually buttons all the way down the centre front.

The sleeve pattern may be altered to make the more authentic two-piece coat sleeve, shortened to elbow length, or flared slightly and turned back to make a deep cuff.

A little straw hat may be made from plaited raffia and lavishly trimmed with ribbons and flowers or feathers. A small drawstring reticule (handbag), complete with a tiny handkerchief, purse and perfume bottle, would make a charming accessory for a doll dressed in walking costume. Parasols may be made by covering commercial wire frames (see Stockists) or furling a cover around a whittled or paintbrush-handle stick (see Chapter 2).

You might also consider adapting other patterns from the book to enlarge the fashion doll's wardrobe.

Fig 62 Clothes patterns for fashion doll

9

THE FRENCH BÉBÉS
(c1880 and 1890)

The French bébé dolls were made to represent young girls, aged between four and twelve years. Although some bébés were produced during the 1870s and earlier, it was during the 1880s and 1890s that they became most popular and this popularity continued well into the twentieth century. The early French bébés are the most coveted among collectors and examples in good condition command very high prices. The earliest bébés have bisque heads and lower arms on kid bodies stuffed with sawdust, hair or cork. The leather bodies might have gussets at hips, knees and elbows to give the doll some movement, but apart from the modelling of the head, the first bébés were similar in con-

struction to the lady dolls of the 1870s. The doll manufacturers, including the two best-known firms of Bru and Jumeau, experimented to produce more realistic bodies. Various materials were tried – kid bodies with wooden limbs, wooden bodies and limbs, and hard rubber bodies – but eventually the jointed composition body, firstly strung with cord, and later elastic, was developed and proved the most popular. The majority of bébés are to be found on jointed composition bodies though kid bodies were still produced until the 1920s.

France and Germany were in fierce competition in the dollmaking industry at the end of the nineteenth century. Germany had led

Figs 63 and 64 French bébés

the field for some time with its cheaper mass-produced dolls, the French dolls being too expensive for all but the rich. The popularity of the bébés grew rapidly as they were considerably cheaper than the fashionable lady dolls and more and more of the middle classes both wanted them and could afford them. By the 1890s, the French firms were selling bébés in millions. Obviously, with the enormous popularity of this type of doll, the German manufacturers soon began to copy the French. The German dolls were generally cheaper and did not have the beauty of the best French dolls but the lower prices meant that everyone but the poor could afford them and they were extremely popular.

The bébés vary a great deal, as does any type of doll, but they share the same appeal. At a time when society generally took an interest in children, these 'little girl' dolls appealed not only to the little girls who would own them but also to their parents who would buy them. They are idealised children with the type of beauty which was fashionable at the time. Their large eyes, heavy brows and full faces seem very unchildlike to the modern eye but their charm is timeless. The first bébés had bisque shoulder or socket heads, with fixed glass eyes and closed or open/closed mouths. The open head had a cork pate and the wigs were of sheepskin, mohair or real hair. Later, the bébé was provided with sleeping eyes and an open mouth with teeth. The cheaper German dolls were sold undressed wearing just a chemise, socks and shoes and they were usually dressed in simple homemade clothes. The most expensive French dolls were very beautifully dressed in silks, satins and laces – the professionally made clothes often costing three or four times as much as the doll. The lucky owner could choose from an enormous range of 'ready-made' clothes and accessories which included everything a doll could ever need.

Our two bébés are made and dressed to represent the styles which were popular in the 1880s and 1890s. The small bébé is a child of about six years old; she has a head and shoulder-plate, lower arms and lower legs modelled in self-hardening clay and a plump, childish body with a shaped seat made in calico stuffed with soft filling. The face is plump, with a small nose and heavy cheeks. The acrylic eyes are inset, the eyebrows heavy and the open/closed mouth pouts childishly.

The real hair wig is styled with a fringe and long ringlets. She wears drawers with straight legs which show below the skirt, a full-length petticoat and the low-waisted French dress so typical of the 1880s. The dress has a shirred front panel and is trimmed with lace. The little bandeau bonnet is tied under the chin with ribbons to match the sash and is lavishly trimmed with lace, feathers and flowers. The kid shoes are made from the pattern on page 31.

The clothes are not difficult to make, the style is simple, but the choice of fabric and trimmings is important. The underwear should be in white cotton lawn trimmed with white cotton lace, and mother-of-pearl buttons are preferable to plastic. The dress should be in a soft natural fabric (I have used lawn, but silk or silk satin would be suitable) in a plain colour, or a small pattern woven into the fabric rather than a print, and a soft colour to suit the 'age' of the doll. The lace should, of course, be cotton not nylon and again, mother-of-pearl buttons look better than plastic. The ribbon for the sash and bonnet ties should be soft satin, not the stiff sort which does not make good bows. If your doll has dark eyes and colouring and a darker wig, you might consider using cotton velveteen for the dress and bonnet in a rich crimson, green, brown or blue. Bébés were often dressed in colours and fabrics which we would consider too 'adult' for children these days, but it is better to choose the fabric and colour to suit the individual doll than to have definite ideas before you start.

The miniature doll carried by the small bébé is a pipecleaner lady doll with a modelled clay head and painted features. Her wig is mohair and she wears a satin and lace dress.

The large bébé represents a girl of about twelve years. She has a head and shoulder-plate and lower arms modelled in self-hardening clay, and a slimmer body, including the legs, in calico stuffed with sawdust. The face is still plump but is more sophisticated than the smaller doll. The nose is longer and more shapely, the mouth less pouting and closed. The inset acrylic eyes have both painted and 'real' eyelashes, and the eyebrows are typically heavy. The real hair wig has a fringe and ringlets. She wears white lawn combinations which button up the front, trimmed with white lace, and a full half-length petticoat gathered to a waistband. The dress has a coloured underslip, the frill of which shows at the hemline. The simple dress with full sleeves and a slightly high waistline relies for its impact on the choice of fabric. The shirred bonnet with its wired brim is trimmed with feathers and ties under the chin with satin ribbons.

White cotton lawn and lace are again best for the underwear, with mother-of-pearl buttons. The slip might be in lawn, silk or satin in virtually any colour you please but should match the sash and the feathers on the hat and complement the dress fabric. For the dress I have used an embroidered Swiss lawn, utilising the scalloped edge for the hem of the dress. This is an expensive fabric but a similar effect can be achieved more cheaply with broderie anglaise, or as an alternative, consider spotted muslin, lawn or organdie. Any fine fabric which is semi-transparent so that the colour of the slip shows through will look attractive. The bonnet looks very elaborate but is in fact straightforward to make. The brim is wired with millinery wire (or thin cane) to stand away from the doll's face and can be fairly modest as shown, or much larger if you prefer by using a longer length of wire. The shoe pattern can be found on page 31. I have cut the straps a little longer to fasten with a button and buttonhole and trimmed the fronts with gilt buckles and ribbon bows.

As with the small bébé, I suggest that you leave the choice of colours and fabrics until the doll is made, then select those which best suit the individual doll's colouring. By the 1890s, the range of fabrics and styles in which dolls' clothes were made was enormous: fabrics ranged from white cotton lawn to deep shades of velvet and wool; skirts were ankle- or knee-length, high, low or natural waisted, full or straight; and sleeves were long or short. As you can see, the possibilities are endless.

Small Bébé (c1880)

(16in tall)
Difficulty 5/Colour picture page 101
Body pattern: Fig 66
Clothes patterns: Figs 68 and 69

½yd unbleached calico (36in wide) for body
large packet self-hardening clay for head,
*   shoulder-plate, arms and legs*
core-ball for head (2¼in diameter)
sandpaper
1 pair oval acrylic eyes (14mm)
wig
stuffing (soft or sawdust)
paints

Full instructions for modelling are given in Chapter 1 and are repeated only briefly here.

Model the head to resemble, as closely as possible, the shape and proportions of the original French bébé heads. Fig 67 shows the shape to aim for, with heavy cheeks, rounded chin and large, fairly wide-set eyes. (As always, pictures or a doll to copy will be helpful.) As this is a child doll, ensure that the neck is not too long, or the shoulders too wide. If you model ears, they can be pierced for earrings – most French bébés wore them. Check your modelling very carefully to ensure that the head is symmetrical, and when satisfactory bake or leave aside to dry.

The finished proportions of the head should be: length from forehead to chin, 3in; circumference of head (at hairline), 9½in. If your head has turned out much larger or smaller than this you may wish to alter the proportions of the rest of the body.

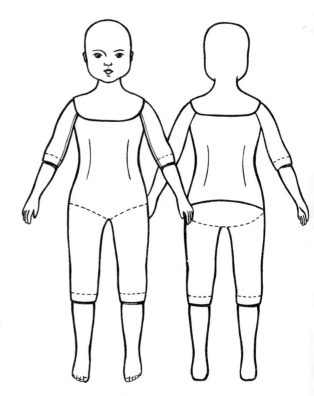

Fig 65 Small bébé's body
Fig 66 Body pattern for small bébé

96

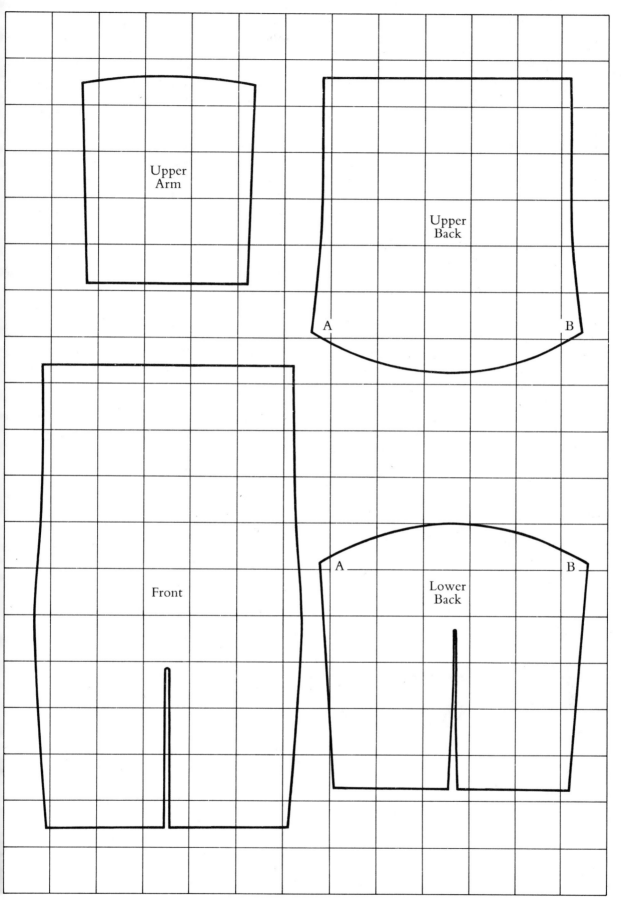

Upper
Arm

Upper
Back

A   B

Front

A _____ B

Lower
Back

The lower arms are modelled to the elbow and the finished length from fingertips to elbow should be no more than 4in to allow for a natural bend level with the doll's waist. Shape small, childish hands with the fingers slightly curved and score a groove for tying on the upper arms. The legs and feet are modelled in one piece to the knee. When the foot has been shaped, with a flat sole, the height of the finished leg should be 3in. Score a groove for tying on the upper leg. When the limbs are satisfactory, bake or leave aside to dry.

When the modelled pieces are thoroughly dry, remove the core-ball from the head, either through the neck, or by slicing off the back of the head and replacing it with a cardboard pate (see Chapter 1). Sand the head and shoulder-plate and the limbs with fine-grade abrasive paper, taking particular care not to scratch the eyes. Paint the pieces in a pale flesh colour to represent bisque, or, if you prefer, the head may be painted to represent bisque and the arms and legs a slightly darker colour for composition.

To paint the features, see Fig 67 as a guide and refer to the colour picture of the doll. The eyes should be outlined with a very fine black line and the upper and lower lashes painted in small slightly curving lines around the eye. The brows should be fairly heavy, in light and dark brown, painted with small feathery

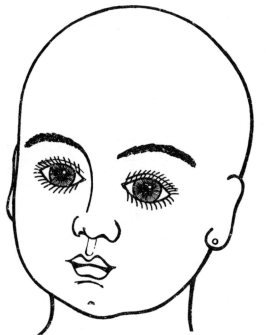

Fig 67 Modelling and face-painting guide for bébés

strokes. The mouth should be full, and rather pouting, in a soft rusty red. (Mix flesh, a little red and a little brown for the right colour – not pink!) I suggest powder blusher in a tawny pink shade rubbed into the cheeks with the finger rather than paint, as it blends into the face more subtly. Make a small pink cornea at the inner corner of each eye, and if you wish, outline the fingernails in the same light pink. Leave the paint to dry thoroughly.

To make the body, cut one front, one upper back, one lower back and two arms in calico (Fig 66). Seam the upper back to the lower back at AB (this curved seam will give the doll a 'seat'). Stitch the front and back together down each side and up one inside leg through the crotch and down the other inside leg. Clip the seam at the crotch and turn through. Turn in the top edge of the body ½in and tack. Check the lower legs against the body, ensuring they match and the feet face forward, then turn the body inside out and tie on the lower legs. Turn through and check again. Stuff the body firmly from the legs upward, using a good-quality soft stuffing or, if you prefer, sawdust. When the body is filled, oversew the top edges together, then turn down the corners at each side and sew these to the body.

Fold the upper arms in half lengthwise and seam into tubes, leaving the top and bottom open. Tie in the lower arms and turn through. Stuff the upper arms with soft stuffing, fairly loosely to allow for easy movement. Pin the upper arms to the shoulders and check the length. The elbows should be level with the doll's waist, the hands level with the crotch. Stitch the upper arms to the shoulders. Glue the underside of the shoulder-plate and seat it firmly onto the body, holding it in place until the glue is dry.

The completed doll should be 16in tall; if you have altered the proportions, you may need to adjust the clothes patterns.

SMALL BÉBÉ'S CLOTHES
For the Underwear
½yd white lawn (36in wide)
2yd narrow white lace
4 small white buttons

For the Dress
½yd lightweight fabric (36in wide)
2yd lace (1in wide)
4 small buttons
1yd satin ribbon (2in wide) for sash

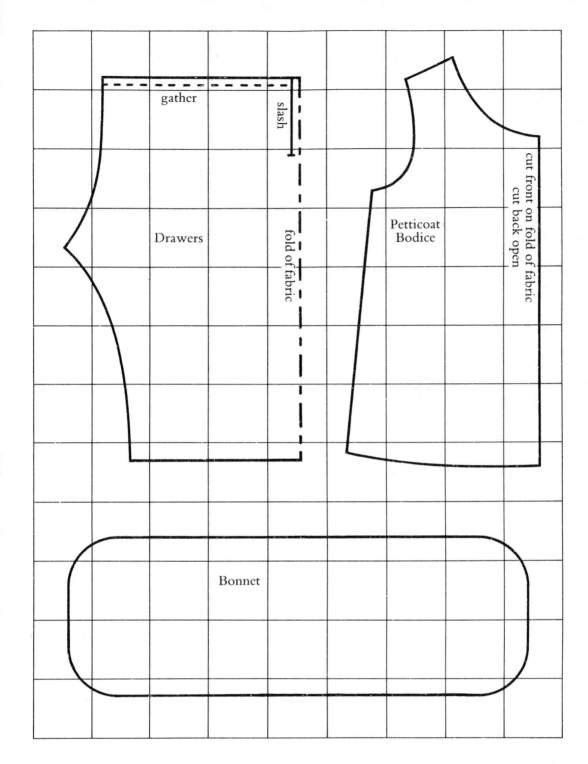

gather

slash

Drawers

fold of fabric

Petticoat Bodice

cut front on fold of fabric
cut back open

Bonnet

Fig 68 Clothes patterns for small bébé (part)

For the Bonnet
½yd satin or ribbon (3in wide)
scrap of lawn for lining
1yd lace (1in wide)
1yd satin ribbon (1in wide)
artificial flowers, feathers for trimming

For the drawers, cut two pieces (Fig 68) in white lawn and slash one side. Roll a fine hem around the slashed opening. Seam each leg, then seam together. Cut a waistband to fit the doll's waist allowing for button and buttonhole fastening. Gather the top edge of the drawers and stitch to the waistband. Work a buttonhole and sew on a button. Turn up and hem the leg ends and trim with lace.

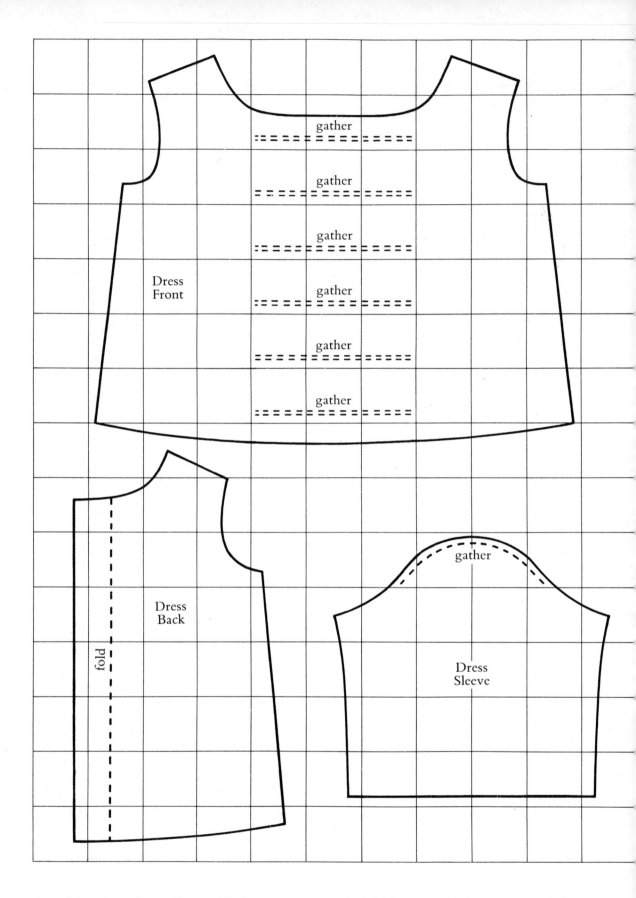

gather

gather

gather

gather

gather

gather

Dress
Front

Dress
Back

fold

Dress
Sleeve

gather

Fig 69 Clothes patterns for small bébé   (*right*) The French bébés and mini doll

For the petticoat, cut the bodice pieces, the front on the fold of the fabric, the back in two pieces (Fig 68). Stitch the shoulder and side seams and roll fine hems around the neck and armholes. Cut a piece 5×24in for the petticoat skirt. Gather the skirt evenly to fit the bodice and stitch. Sew the centre-back seam up to 1in below the waist. Turn under the open back edges of the bodice and skirt to make facings and hem. Make two or three pintucks parallel with the bottom edge of the skirt, and turn up the hem behind the lowest pintuck. Sew lace to the hem to match the drawers. Work three buttonholes down the back of the bodice and sew on buttons.

For the dress, cut one front, two backs, two sleeves (Fig 69) and a piece for the skirt 5×26in. Work rows of tiny gathering stitches as marked on the dress front. Seam the front to backs at shoulder and side seams. Put the bodice on the doll, pull up the gathering to form a shirred panel down the centre front, checking that the bodice fits well, and fasten off the gathers. Stitch lace trimming to the bodice on either side of the shirred panel. Stitch the sleeve seams and gather the sleeve heads to ease. Set in the sleeves. Turn up the sleeve hems and trim with lace. Turn under the centre-back edges and hem to form facings. Lap the left side over the right side by ½in and tack the lower edges together. Stitch the centre-back seam in the skirt and gather the upper edge evenly to the lower edge of the bodice. Turn up the skirt hem, and sew on a band of lace trimming above the hemline. Bind the neck edge of the dress with a bias-cut strip of dress fabric, and add a lace frill if you wish. Work four buttonholes down the left back of the dress and sew on buttons. Work a vertical row of gathering on either side of the sash, and tie in a large bow at the back.

To make the bandeau bonnet, cut the pattern (Fig 68) in wide satin ribbon, and in lawn for lining. With right sides facing, stitch the two pieces together around the outside edge, leaving a gap to turn through, and sandwiching a gathered lace frill all around. Turn through, slipstitch the opening closed and press. Stitch ribbon ties to either side of the bonnet and trim lavishly with artificial flowers and feathers.

(*left*) Edwardian child and mini Bye-lo baby; and the Chad Valley Bambina

This doll wears blue glass-bead earrings (*see* Chapter 2), bought white socks and blue kid shoes made from the pattern on page 31 (size 2).

Miniature Doll

small piece of self-hardening clay for head
3×6in pipecleaners
a little cotton wool for padding
small piece of gauze finger bandage
mohair for wig
scraps of lawn, lace and satin for clothes

The miniature doll is made in basically the same way as the bead and pipecleaner doll on page 56, but instead of using a bead, the head is modelled onto the neck in self-hardening clay. In such a tiny scale, only very simple modelling is required – a good oval shape for the head with a clearly defined nose, chin, cheeks and forehead, and slight sockets for the eyes. Smooth a little clay around the pipe-cleaner for the neck and if you wish, model clay hands on the ends of the arms and clay feet (with shoes) on the legs. When the clay is thoroughly dry, smooth and paint it as for the

Fig 70 Miniature doll

103

larger dolls. Paint the features with a very fine brush, putting in as much detail as you can (Fig 71).

The doll is dressed in lace-trimmed drawers, petticoat and a satin dress using the patterns on page 58. She also has a lace over-skirt and a narrow satin ribbon sash. The hair (mohair) is glued onto the head – three ring-lets at either side of the face, a wispy fringe, and a plaited bun on the back of the head (*see* Wigs, Chapter 1). This doll is properly scaled to be a lady doll's-house doll. To adapt to other sizes for doll's-house men and children see the notes on page 57.

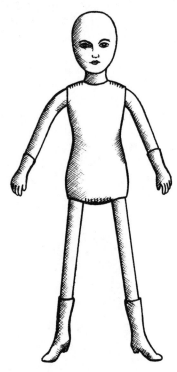

Fig 71 Miniature doll, body assembly

Large Bébé (c1890)

(18in tall)
Difficulty 5/Colour picture page 101
Body pattern: Fig 72
Clothes patterns: Figs 73 and 74

½yd unbleached calico (36in wide) for body
large packet self-hardening clay for head, shoulder-plate and arms
core-ball for head (2½in diameter)
1 pair oval acrylic eyes (16mm)
eyelashes
wig
stuffing (sawdust or soft)
paints

Full instructions for modelling are given in Chapter 1 so are repeated only briefly here.

This doll is modelled to resemble an older child. The head is still shaped with full cheeks, a rounded chin and large eyes, but the nose is a little longer and more shapely, the neck a little longer and the shoulders a little wider. She is generally more 'sophisticated' than her younger sister. The head is set at a slight angle on the shoulders. Again use Fig 67 as a guide, and pictures or a doll to copy. Check your modelling carefully to ensure that it is symmetrical. The finished proportions of this head should be: length from forehead to chin, 3½in; circumference of head (at hair-line), 11in. The lower arms are modelled to the elbow, with larger hands than the pre-vious doll and the finger and thumb are curved to hold a costume accessory. The finished length of the arm from finger tips to elbow should be 4½in. Do not forget to score grooves for tying on the upper arms.

When the modelling is satisfactory, bake or leave aside to dry. Smooth thoroughly, then paint the head and arms a pale flesh colour to resemble bisque. The features are painted in the same way as the previous doll: the eyes outlined with very fine black lines, the lashes painted in fine curved lines around the eyes, the rather heavy brows in two shades of brown with feathery brush strokes, and the lips a soft rusty red. I would again recom-mend powder blusher rather than paint for the cheeks. Add the cornea and fingernail detail. This large bébé also has 'real' eye-lashes. You can use either ordinary false eye-lashes, sold in chemists, or those made specially for dolls. Cut a length for each eye to fit the lower edge of the top lid and trim them roughly to shape. Spread a thin line of glue (eyelash fixative or UHU) along the edge of the lashes using a pin or toothpick, then carefully press the lashes to the ridge where the clay eyelid meets the eye. Gently push the eyelashes in place with a toothpick and leave them alone until the glue is dry. Then curl them upwards with your finger and trim them to shape with small scissors (this is a fiddly procedure but not as difficult as it sounds!).

To make the body, cut one front, one upper back, one lower back, two upper arms, four lower legs and two soles in calico (Fig

Fig 72 Body pattern for large bébé

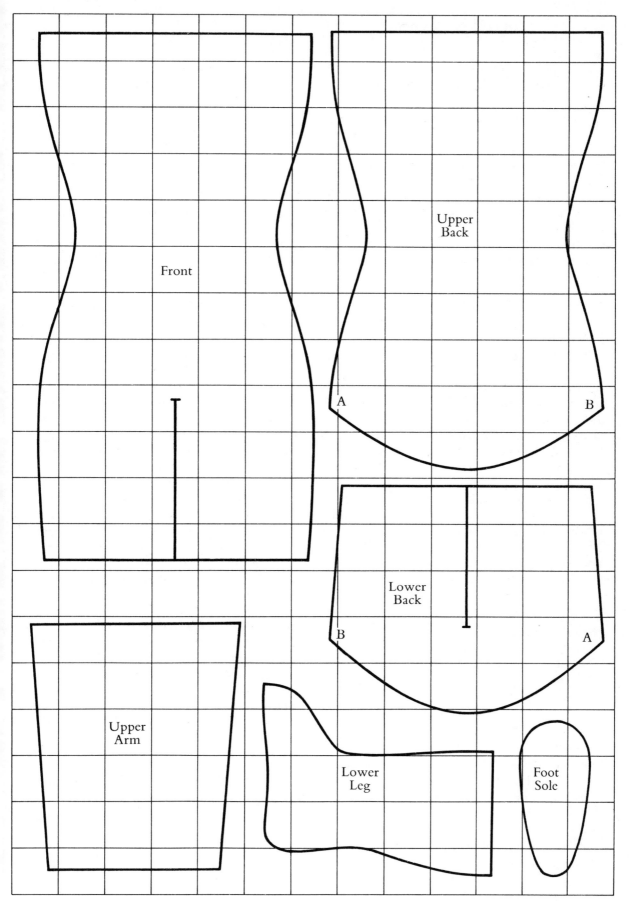

Front

Upper Back

A   B

Lower Back

B   A

Upper Arm

Lower Leg

Foot Sole

72). Stitch the upper back to the lower back at AB. Stitch the front and back together down each side and up one inside leg, through the crotch and down the other inside leg. Clip the seam at the crotch. Stitch the lower legs together in pairs, leaving the top edge and the sole of the foot open. Stitch the soles into the feet. With right sides facing, stitch the lower legs to the upper legs at the knee, ensuring that the feet face forward. (On the upper legs the seams are at each side; on the lower legs the seams are centre back and front.) Turn the body through to the right side and stuff very firmly with sawdust (or soft stuffing). Shape the feet carefully as you stuff, and, especially if using sawdust, ensure that every part is packed as firmly as possible before adding more. When the body is filled, turn in the top edges ½in and oversew closed. Then turn down the corners at each side and sew these to the body.

Fold the upper arms in half lengthwise and seam into tubes. Tie in the lower arms and turn through. Stuff the upper arms loosely with soft stuffing to allow for easy movement and pin them to the shoulders. Check that the arms hang naturally and are the right length – the elbows level with the doll's waist, the hands with the crotch. Sew the arms to the shoulders.

Glue the underside of the shoulder-plate liberally and seat it firmly onto the body, holding it in place until the glue is dry. The completed doll should be 18in tall; if you have altered the proportions, you may need to adjust the clothes patterns.

LARGE BÉBÉ'S CLOTHES

For the Underwear
1yd white lawn (36in wide)
2yd white lace (1in wide)
1yd lace (½in wide)
5 small white buttons
½yd coloured lawn or satin (36in wide) for slip
1½yd satin ribbon (2in wide) for slip frill
3 small buttons

For the Dress
1yd sheer fabric with scalloped border (36in wide)
½yd matching lace (1in wide)
3 small buttons
shirring elastic
1yd satin ribbon (2in wide) to match slip for sash

For the Bonnet
remnants of fabric (used for dress)

1yd lace (1in wide)
1yd ribbon (1in wide)
flowers or feathers for trimming
approx 12in millinery wire

To make the combinations, cut two pieces in white lawn (Fig 73). Before proceeding, check the shoulder-to-crotch measurement in case the body of your doll is longer than the original; if so, amend the pattern, then proceed.

Stitch the centre-back seam from neck to crotch. Stitch the centre fronts together for 1in from the crotch, then turn back the remainder of the centre fronts to form facings, and hem. Stitch the inside leg seams, up one leg, through the crotch and down the other leg. Turn a hem on each leg. Stitch the shoulder seams, then roll a narrow hem around the neck and armholes. Trim neck, armholes and leg ends with ½in wide lace. Make four buttonholes and sew buttons down centre fronts.

To make the petticoat, cut a piece of lawn 9×28in and a waistband to fit the doll's waist with button and buttonhole fastening. Stitch the centre-back seam, leaving the top 2in open, then turn under the hem to form facings. Gather the top edge evenly and stitch to the waistband. Make three or four pintucks at the lower edge and turn up the hem behind lowest pintuck. Trim hem with lace, make buttonhole and sew button to the waistband.

For the slip, cut one front bodice and two back bodices from the pattern (Fig 73) and a skirt 7×30in in coloured lawn or satin. Stitch the front to back bodice at shoulder and side seams and roll narrow hems around the neck and armholes. Gather the top edge of the skirt and stitch to the lower edge of the bodice, distributing the gathers evenly. Stitch the centre-back seam in the skirt to 2in below the waist then turn under and hem the remainder of the centre-back skirt and bodice to form facings. Gather the satin ribbon to a frill and stitch to the lower edge of the skirt. Make buttonholes and sew buttons to the back bodice.

For the dress, cut one bodice front, two bodice backs, two sleeves (Fig 74) and a piece 9×32in for the skirt. Stitch the bodice front to back at shoulder and side seams. Stitch the

Figs 73 and 74 (overleaf) Clothes patterns for large bébé

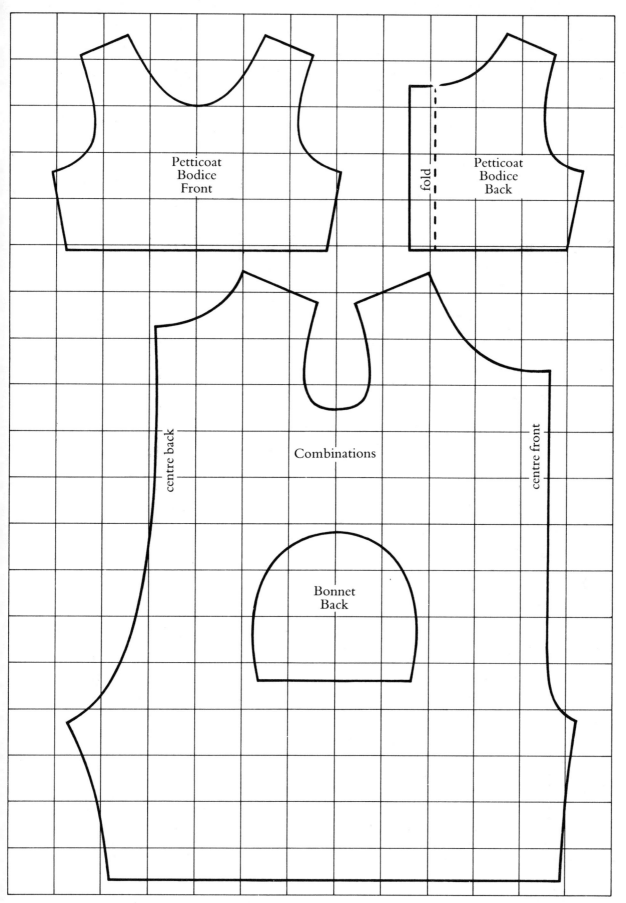

Petticoat
Bodice
Front

Petticoat
Bodice
Back

fold

centre back

Combinations

centre front

Bonnet
Back

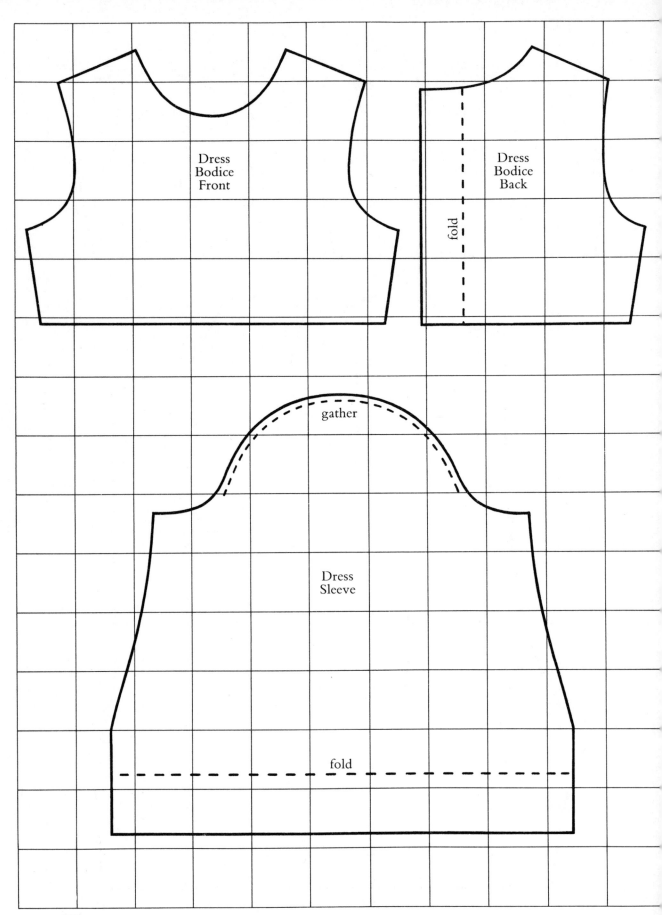

Dress
Bodice
Front

Dress
Bodice
Back

fold

gather

Dress
Sleeve

fold

sleeve seams, gather the sleeve heads and set in the sleeves. Turn up and hem the sleeve ends. Gather the top edge of the skirt to the lower edge of the bodice and stitch. Sew the centre-back seam in the skirt to 2in below the waist, then turn under and hem the remainder of the skirt and the bodice to form facings. Bind the neckline with a bias-cut strip of dress fabric. Stitch lace trimming to the sleeve ends and gather with shirring elastic to make frills. Make buttonholes and sew buttons to bodice back. Tie a ribbon sash around the doll's waist in a large bow at the back.

To make the bonnet, cut a piece 8×36in and two bonnet backs from remnants of the dress fabric. Hem the two short edges of the brim. Fold under the hem at the front long edge to form a narrow casing 1in from the edge. Work two rows of small gathering stitches 2in from the back edge along the length of the piece (Fig 75). Work two more rows of gathering along the back edge. Put the piece onto the doll's head, pull up the gathering to fit and fasten off securely. With right sides together stitch one bonnet back to

the gathered back edge of the brim. With right sides together sew the second bonnet back to the first along the lower edge, then turn it to the inside and oversew to cover the raw edges.

Oversew lace to the edge of the front hem of the brim, neatening the ends. Thread millinery wire (or fine cane) through the casing to hold the brim away from the doll's face and form a frilled front edge to the bonnet. Secure both ends of the wire. Stitch ribbons to either side of the bonnet brim and trim with flowers or feathers as required.

The doll wears bought white cotton stockings and cream kid shoes (size 4) made from the pattern on page 31 and trimmed with ribbon bows and small fancy-gilt buckles. She has a necklace and bracelet made from tiny pearl beads and carries a handkerchief made from a 2in square of lawn, hemmed and edged with lace and a small posy of artificial flowers.

Fig 75 Bonnet brim showing casing and gatherings

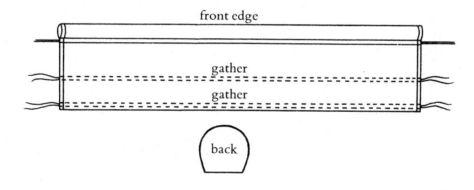

Fig 74 Clothes patterns for large bébé

10
A CHARACTER DOLL (c1910)

During the early decades of the twentieth century, taste turned against the idealised and lavishly dressed bébés and a simpler and more realistic type of doll became popular. The character dolls, made mostly in Germany, were designed to represent real children, and were often modelled from life. Firms such as Kammer and Reinhardt, Simon and Halbig, and Heubach made many different dolls in the new style. Interest in the early teaching and development of children was growing and it was felt that these more realistic dolls were of more educational benefit to a child than the

Fig 76 Edwardian girl

elaborate bébés. At first the general public was not enthusiastic; sales of the first character baby, Kammer and Reinhardt's 'Kaiser' (popularly but erroneously believed to have been modelled on the Kaiser) were slow, but gradually the new type of doll caught on and most of the German manufacturers produced their own character children.

Kathë Kruse and Marion Kaulitz, both doll artists, helped to popularise the character doll, Kathë Kruse working in cloth and Marion Kaulitz in composition. Both ladies felt strongly that children's play dolls should be realistic and simply dressed, so that the child would identify with the doll and use its imagination in devising games around the doll. Kathë Kruse experimented for several years before she devised the stuffed cloth dolls which are now so popular with collectors. She produced a sand-weighted baby (weighing seven pounds) in both sleeping and awake versions, which feels very real when held in the arms, with the intention that little girls should 'practise' for the future through play. Her child dolls, also made in cloth with painted features, were charming portraits of small children, dressed in the sort of clothes which ordinary children wore. Though they were regarded as 'art' dolls, and were comparatively expensive, the Kruse dolls were very popular with the wealthier middle-class parents who were keen to give their children 'educational' toys. Most of the character dolls were made in bisque or composition, some of the earlier ones on kid or cloth bodies, but the majority on jointed composition bodies.

There is, of course, a large variety of character dolls; most of the German dollmakers produced a range and the French cooperative, the SFBJ, also produced a few. They represent boys, girls and babies, their faces modelled with different expressions to look as life-like as possible, to the extent that some of them are quite ugly. Some of the dolls were given names and this proved a popular sales ploy. Most character dolls had painted eyes and wigs of real hair or mohair, their bodies were realistically proportioned and their clothes, though usually simple styles, were well made. The majority were sold ready dressed, though few are now found in their original clothing and many collectors re-dress them in more elaborate styles. The original factory-made clothes were usually cotton or wool, with simple socks and leather shoes.

As the popularity of character dolls grew, sleeping eyes were used and oriental and negro variations were introduced. Sometimes these were simply the standard models made in coloured bisque, but others have well-modelled faces with proper oriental or negro features. The simpler bent-limb body super-seded the ball-jointed body as it was cheaper and easier to produce and it became almost universal for baby dolls, though jointed types were still customary for boys and girls. By now, though, bisque was largely used for heads, and the cheaper composition was used for most bodies and some heads.

The fashion for character dolls continued until the 1920s, when taste changed again and little girl dolls and babies became popular. However, they have never quite died out and the modern Sasha dolls have much in common with their early twentieth-century predecessors.

The character doll in this chapter is a young girl of about fourteen dressed in the style of 1910. The young girls of this period were the original 'flappers' (young birds trying out their wings), although by the 1920s it became the common term for young women who wore the fashionable short skirt. They were aged between fourteen and eighteen – that is before they reached the age when skirts must be lengthened and hair put up – and as a generation experienced a previously undreamed-of freedom. Though their clothes and lifestyle seem very restrictive by modern standards, they were benefiting from a revolution in attitude to children's clothes. Instead of corsets and very elaborate dresses in heavy fabrics and fussy styles they wore liberty bodices and simple smock-shaped dresses. The badge of the Edwardian flapper was her hair ribbon – usually black and made of wired ribbon, the enormous bow was worn either to one side or on the back of the head.

The doll has a head and shoulder-plate and lower arms and legs modelled in self-hardening clay. The eyes are incised with a pointed tool and painted. The simple seated calico body is stuffed with soft stuffing. She wears a liberty bodice with suspenders to hold up her black stockings, and buttoned drawers and petticoats. The simple cotton dress is covered by a broderie anglaise pinafore.

I suggest Das or Fimo for the modelled parts of the doll, and unbleached calico for the body. I have painted the doll a slightly darker flesh shade to represent composition, but a paler shade to represent bisque would be equally appropriate. As usual, Humbrol matt enamel paint is recommended. The face painting is a matter of taste; on most antique character dolls the eyes are quite simply painted with a coloured iris and black pupil on the white, outlined with a curved dark line above the eye. I have painted the eyes in rather more detail, and painted lashes above and below them.

The wig on this doll is mohair, styled with a wispy fringe around the hairline and left to fall over the doll's shoulders. The large fashionable ribbon bow holds the hair back from the face. This wig is particularly appropriate for an Edwardian doll, both in material and style (see Stockists [Kinloch and Sellers]).

The clothes should be made in natural fabrics. I suggest white winceyette lined with lawn for the liberty bodice, stiffened with cotton tape and buttoned with small mother-of-pearl or old cotton buttons. The suspenders are made from the small ribbon shoulder-strap clips which are sold in haberdashery departments. The doll's stockings should be black cotton (white stockings were worn only on Sundays). The doll's drawers, which have a side-buttoned waistband, and petticoat are made in white cotton trimmed with lace. I have used a piece of broderie anglaise for the pinafore, cut from an old torn baby dress. Similar baby dresses can be found in junk shops, jumble sales and antique markets and though examples in good condition can be expensive, torn ones are usually very cheap. New broderie anglaise would be perfectly suitable as an alternative or you might make the pinafore in white lawn and trim it with lace and pintucks. This doll's shoes are made in black leather from the pattern on page 31 but, if you prefer, black button boots would be equally appropriate (see Stockists).

The patterns and instructions are simple and will adapt easily to make a variety of dolls. By shortening the body, arms and legs the proportions can be changed to make a younger child, or you can lengthen the arms and legs to make an adult. The modelling of the head is very basic, and any type of character face may be painted. I suggest that you model and paint the head before finally deciding on the type and 'age' of the doll, then adapt the body patterns as necessary.

The clothes patterns are equally simple: a waisted dress which can be made up in a variety of fabrics and trimmed to suit any period, and the pinafore pattern which can also be used to make a smock dress. This is the ideal doll on which to experiment.

The miniature doll in the photograph is a tiny version of the Bye-lo baby doll (*see* Chapter 11).

Edwardian Girl (c1910)
(15in tall)
Difficulty 2/Colour picture page 102
Body pattern: Fig 77
Clothes patterns: Figs 78 and 79

small packet Das or large packet Fimo
½yd unbleached calico (36in wide)
core-ball for head (2½in diameter)
wig
stuffing (soft)
paints

Full modelling instructions are given in Chapter 1 so are repeated only briefly here.

Model the doll's head to represent that of a real child. The Edwardian girl has fairly full cheeks and a small chin with a slightly square jawline. Her nose is small but well shaped. The mouth has fully shaped lips, the upper lip bow-shaped, the lower smoothly curved. The area above the cheeks is smoothed, then the upper eyelids and the shape of the eye are incised with a small pointed tool, eg a wooden toothpick. Check that the eyes are level and both the same shape and size. This simple modelling is all that is necessary, but if you wish the face may be modelled in greater detail. Many antique character dolls have very well-formed features; the eyelids are shaped, the lips curved to smile and there are dimples on the cheeks or chin. I suggest using a child or good photograph as a model and experimenting. The essence of the character doll is

that it looks like a real child, so if you have the ability, the more detail you model into the face the more life-like your doll will look. However, much can be achieved with paint, so if you find modelling difficult, shape the face simply and paint in the detail. Model small ears, set close to the head, and a small neck and shoulder-plate.

The lower arms are modelled to the elbow, and the lower legs, with bare feet, are modelled to the knee. The doll has small hands (the fingers not separated, merely scored) and small feet. Don't forget to cut grooves for tying on the lower limbs. When the modelled pieces are satisfactory, bake or leave to harden. Remove the core-ball from the head.

Paint the modelled pieces in either a pale flesh colour to represent bisque or a slightly darker shade for composition. For a good smooth surface use several coats of paint, and allow each coat to dry thoroughly before applying the next. Paint the features with a very fine, good-quality brush. Paint the whole of the eye areas white, then paint the iris, shading the colour from darker at the top to lighter at the bottom. This gives the eye 'depth' and creates the illusion that the eye is shaded by the eyelid. Outline the eye in brown rather than black for a youthful effect and paint in 'eyelashes if you wish. A touch of white paint in each eye gives them a highlight and makes them look more realistic, though this is a method which was not always used on the original dolls. The eyebrows and mouth should both be painted in soft colours, the eyebrows brown and the mouth a natural pink. Colour the cheeks with powder blusher, rubbed in with the finger.

The finished proportions of the Edwardian girl should be: length of head from hairline to chin, 2½in; circumference of head, 8½in; length of arm from elbow to fingertips, 3in; height of leg from heel to knee, 3½in. If the proportions of your doll are very different from these, or if you have made a different type of doll, you may wish to alter the proportions of the body.

For the body, cut one front, one upper back, one lower back and two upper arms in calico (Fig 77). Stitch the upper back to the lower back at the curved seam AB. Stitch the front to the back down each side, then up one inside leg, through the crotch and down the

Fig 77 Body pattern for Edwardian girl

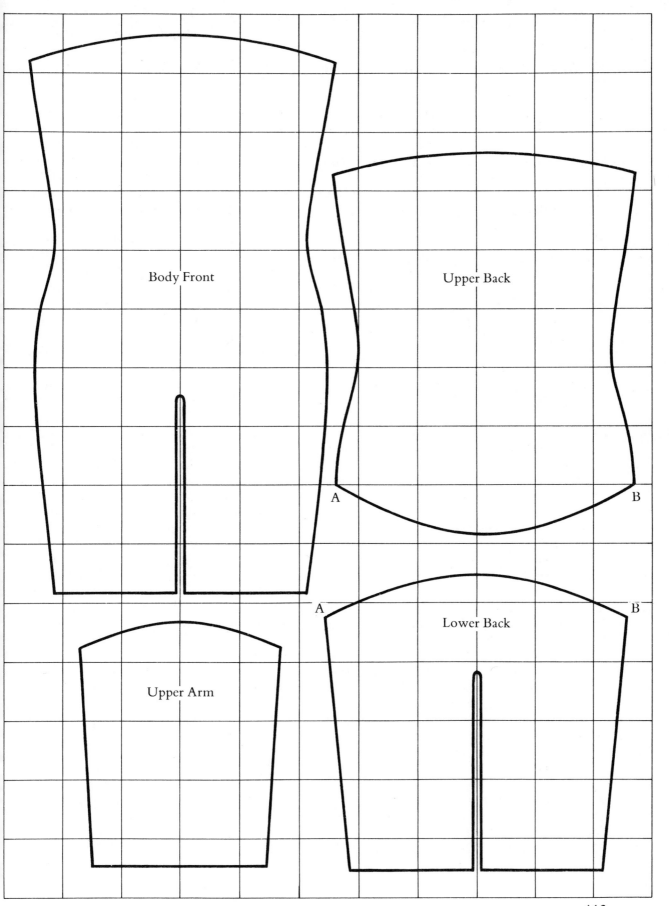

Body Front

Upper Back

A

B

A

B

Upper Arm

Lower Back

other inside leg. Clip the curves and turn through. Tie in the lower legs, ensuring that they both face forward. Stuff the upper legs, then stabstitch through the body at the top of the legs to enable the doll to sit. Continue stuffing firmly to the top of the body, turn in the raw edges and oversew closed. Turn down the corners at each side and stitch to the body. Seam the upper arms to form tubes and tie in the lower arms. Stuff the upper arms loosely, turn in the top edges and oversew closed. Stitch the arms to the shoulders, ensuring that they hang naturally and are the correct length, the hands level with the crotch.

Glue the underside of the shoulder-plate liberally and seat it onto the body, holding it firmly in place until the glue is dry. The finished height of the Edwardian girl is 15in; if you have altered the body pattern, you may need to alter the clothes patterns.

EDWARDIAN GIRL'S CLOTHES
½yd white lawn (36in wide) for underwear
1yd lace (½in wide) for trimming
elastic
½yd fabric (36in wide) for dress
1yd broderie anglaise (8in wide) for pinafore
6 small buttons
½yd stiff black ribbon (2in wide) for hair ribbon
scraps of winceyette and lawn for liberty bodice
1yd cotton tape (¼in wide)
white cotton bias-binding
7 tiny buttons
1 pair white strap clips
black cotton stockings

To make the drawers, cut two pieces (Fig 79) in white lawn and slash an opening on one side. Cut a waistband to fit the doll's waist with a button and buttonhole fastening. Seam each leg and then stitch the two legs together. Roll a fine hem around the slashed opening. Gather the top edge to the waistband, make buttonhole and sew on button. The leg ends may be hemmed and trimmed with lace, or gathered to bands above the knee – both types of drawers were worn by girls at this time.

To make the liberty bodice, cut two backs and two fronts in winceyette (or similar fleecy cotton fabric) and in lawn for lining (Fig 79). Stitch the darts in the fronts in both fabric and lining. Stitch the backs together down the centre-back seams. Stitch backs to fronts at shoulder and side seams. With right sides

facing, stitch fabric to lining all the way around the outside edge, leaving a small gap at the centre-back lower edge to turn through. Clip the curves and corners, and turn through. Slipstitch the opening closed and press. Bind (or face) the armholes with white cotton bias-binding. Stitch cotton tape to the outside of the bodice back and front as shown on the pattern. Make seven buttonholes and sew on buttons down centre fronts. Stitch lingerie strap clips to the lower front edges – and clip to the tops of the stockings (I have used bought black cotton stockings).

For the petticoat, cut a piece of lawn 7×18in. Stitch the centre-back seam and make a casing at the top edge. Hem the lower edge and trim with lace. Thread elastic through the casing to fit the doll's waist.

For the dress, cut one bodice front, two bodice backs, two sleeves (Fig 78), a piece 9×20in for the skirt and two cuffs wide enough to slip over the doll's hands. Stitch the bodice front to backs at the shoulder seams. Gather the sleeve ends and stitch to the cuffs. Gather the sleeve heads and stitch the sleeves into the armholes. Stitch the side seams from the cuff, up the sleeve, through the underarm and down the bodice sides. Hem the other edge of the cuff to the inside of the sleeve. Gather the top of the skirt and stitch to the bodice. Stitch the centre-back seam in the bodice to 2in below the waistline. Turn back the remainder of the back skirt and bodice edges and hem to form facings. Bind the neckline with a bias-cut strip of dress fabric. Hem the lower edge of the skirt. Make three buttonholes and sew on buttons down centre-back bodice.

To make the pinafore, cut two yoke fronts and four yoke backs in cotton lawn (Fig 78), and two sleeve frills and a skirt piece 8×20in in broderie anglaise. Stitch the yoke fronts to backs at the shoulder seams. Gather the sleeve frills and stitch into the armholes of one yoke. Hem the back edges of the skirt, gather the top edge and stitch to the lower edge of the yoke. With right sides facing, stitch the yokes together at the centre backs and around the neckline. Clip the curves and corners, turn the second yoke to the inside and press. Hem the lining yoke to the inside, around the armholes and over the skirt seam. Make two

Figs 78 and 79 (overleaf) Clothes patterns for Edwardian girl

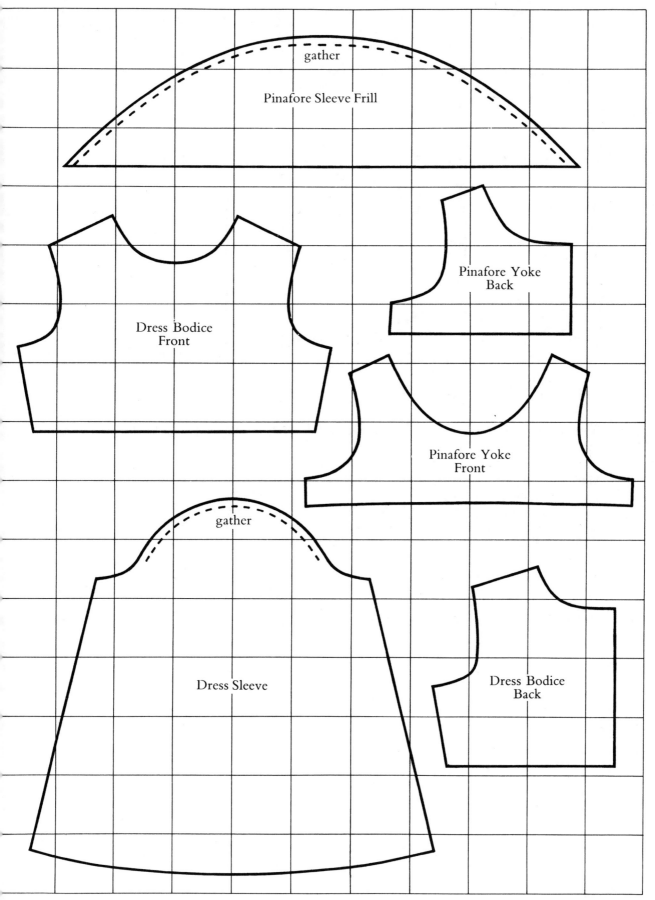

gather

Pinafore Sleeve Frill

Dress Bodice
Front

Pinafore Yoke
Back

Pinafore Yoke
Front

gather

Dress Sleeve

Dress Bodice
Back

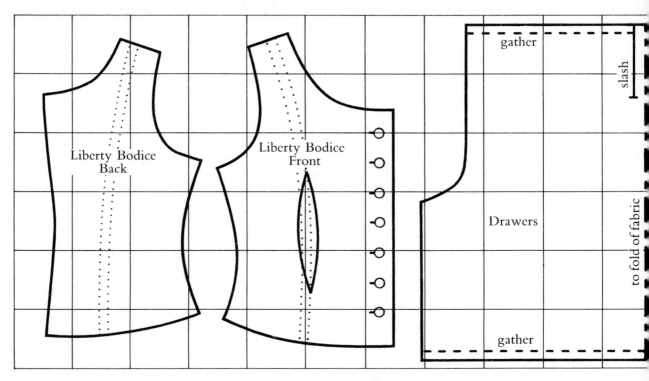

Fig 79 Clothes patterns for Edwardian girl

buttonholes and sew on two buttons to fasten the back yoke.

Tie a large black ribbon bow in the doll's hair. Make leather shoes from the pattern on page 31. The Edwardian girl holds a small piece of knitting worked on needles whittled from thin dowelling (wooden toothpicks with small beads glued to the ends would make a simpler alternative).

To adapt the patterns to make different dolls, gauge the proportions by the age and type of doll. For a younger child whose head is the same size as described, model the lower limbs a little shorter. Shorten the upper limbs and the body (at the top edge) to give a plump, child-shaped body. The clothes patterns will need to be shortened, but otherwise will fit.

This method for modelling and painting faces can also be used for lady dolls. The face should be more adult-shaped and darker colours used for the eyes and mouth. The Edwardian child's body pattern can be given more shape by making darts in the front body and lengthening the arms and legs. The clothes patterns can also be adapted by putting darts in the front bodice and lengthening the skirt, or other patterns in the book might be used as a guide for different styles.

11

THE 'BYE-LO' BABY (c1925)

Baby dolls have always been popular, though before the twentieth century the design and proportions of dolls supposed to represent babies left a great deal to the imagination and in many cases it is only the clothing which suggests that the doll is a baby. Early wooden dolls and white china-head dolls with adult proportions are found dressed in baby clothes, although it is generally accepted that the latter type of head with short curly hair and a short neck was intended to represent a baby or child rather than an adult. During the middle of the nineteenth century, many wax baby dolls were made. Their faces and lower limbs were beautifully modelled in great detail with plump cheeks and rolls of fat at the neck and wrists, but no attempt was made to proportion the body correctly, and, as a result, these dolls do not look at all realistic undressed. They were however sold dressed, in lavishly trimmed long baby clothes which disguised the proportions completely.

This method of making baby dolls continued throughout the nineteenth century; bisque heads, intended to represent babies, are found on gusseted kid bodies of the same type used for girl and lady dolls. It is only the short neck and relatively short arms which show that the doll was intended to be a baby and many of these dolls lose their original identity as babies if they have lost their baby clothes.

It was not until the beginning of the twentieth century that an attempt was made to produce realistic baby dolls with properly proportioned bodies. In 1909, Kammer and Reinhardt produced their character baby mould 100 on a composition bent-limb baby body and this began the trend for more life-like dolls, both children and babies.

In 1922, Grace Storey Putnam, an American artist, first patented her Bye-lo Baby. The original life-size wax model was copied from a three-day-old baby in a Los Angeles hospital. The doll, made in Germany, and con-

Fig 80 Bye-lo baby

siderably altered from the original model, was distributed by the Borgfeldt Doll Company, in America. The original Bye-lo baby had a bisque head with glass sleeping eyes, a flange neck, and celluloid hands on a cloth body. The two-piece cloth body which was designed for this doll has a casing at the top to tie in the flange neck; it is quite plump with bent legs and the arms flop at the doll's sides which makes an oddly attractive and very life-like baby body.

The timing was right, and the marketing was good; the Bye-lo baby became the 'Million Dollar Baby' and sold in tens of thousands. Later versions had bisque or composition heads on cloth, composition, bisque or celluloid bodies. By 1926 the dolls were available in seven sizes, from 9 to 20in, and separate heads could be bought. Bisque

Bye-lo babies with pink or blue moulded shoes were produced by Kestner and eventually the doll was produced in rubber and celluloid.

Other firms were quick to copy the Bye-lo baby. Armand Marseilles produced 'My Dream Baby' in 1924–5 with a bisque head on a cloth or composition body, and this doll rivalled the popularity of the Bye-lo in Europe. For a while, baby dolls were almost as popular as the chubby little girls which were the current favourites.

Most of the baby dolls were sold commercially dressed in cotton. The dresses had high necklines and long sleeves and were usually trimmed with lace and satin ribbon bows. Baby bonnets were more popular in Europe than America and were usually simple caps with ruffles around the face.

Patterns were available for homemade layettes for baby dolls and included garments that real babies were wearing at this time, such as buttoned nappies, binders, long petticoats and nightdresses. Shorter baby dresses which just covered the feet were popular for bent-limb babies and these were usually worn with matching frilly bonnets. Most baby dolls had shawls or blankets and home-knitted bootees, and jackets were very popular. Accessories such as bibs, rattles and feeding bottles could be bought and some dolls were sold with complete layettes. Many antique dolls are found in beautifully made christening gowns, the original simple cotton dress having been replaced by the more elaborate homemade one, or, occasionally, the commercial dress serves as a petticoat under the homemade one.

The baby doll in this chapter has a head with inset acrylic eyes, and a flange neck and hands modelled in self-hardening clay. The cloth body is the Bye-lo type with bent legs, filled with soft stuffing. The face is modelled to represent a real baby, though I have made no attempt to copy the Bye-lo. I have added a fringe of mohair, which is sewn inside the doll's bonnet and styled into a curl on the forehead. Most of the original baby dolls had modelled and/or painted hair; very few had wigs, but I prefer the softer effect that a little hair gives the face. The head is also painted to represent hair so that the doll is not 'bald' when the bonnet is removed. The yoked dress and matching bonnet are made in ivory silk trimmed with lace, and worn over a but-

toned nappy, petticoat and knitted bootees. Instructions are also given for the crocheted shawl and lace-covered pillow. Teddy bears were not 'invented' until the first decade of the twentieth century, so though they are not appropriate to nineteenth-century dolls, miniature teddies make charming accessories for child dolls made in this century. The pattern and instructions for the teddy bear are given in Chapter 13. Patterns and instructions are also given for a miniature version of the Bye-lo baby, dressed in the simple long cotton dress usually found on the originals. The miniature doll has its own Moses basket.

I recommend Fimo for the modelled parts of the doll, though if you prefer, another type of self-hardening clay would be perfectly suitable. The acrylic eyes are the usual flat-backed type, and you should ensure that they are not too large. The body may be made in any closely woven cotton fabric, eg calico, stuffed with a good-quality soft stuffing.

The clothes are best made in natural fabrics, though some man-made fibres such as rayon were in use by the 1920s. Cotton, lawn or silk would be most appropriate for the dress and bonnet, trimmed with cotton lace and satin ribbons. I have used white winceyette for the buttoned nappy and the petticoat, and ivory pure wool for the bootees and shawl. I have found that this body reclines rather than sits, so the pillow is an attractive way of supporting the doll. I have used a piece of old lace for the cover but you might also consider using fine cotton with a tiny print, trimmed with a self-fabric frill. If you use new lace, it should be cotton rather than nylon.

Bye-lo Baby (c1925)

(12in tall)
Difficulty 4/Colour picture page 68
Body pattern: Figs 81 and 82
Clothes pattern: Fig 84

large packet Fimo
core-ball for head (2¼in diameter)
1 pair eyes (12mm)
½yd calico (36in wide) for body
stuffing (soft)
½yd cotton tape (¼in wide) for tying on head
paints
mohair for hair (optional)

(*right*) The four felt children

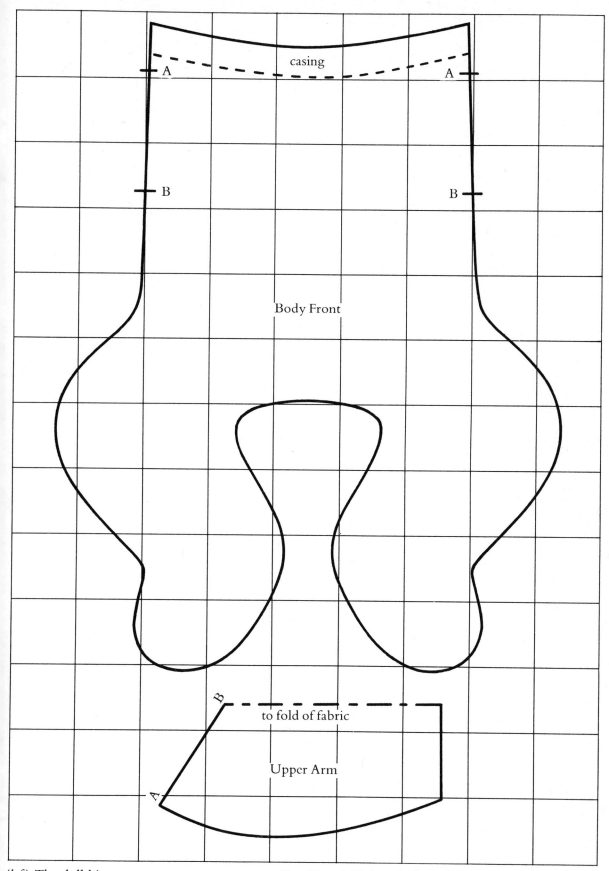

casing

A   A

B   B

Body Front

B

to fold of fabric

Upper Arm

A

(*left*) The doll kits   Figs 81 and 82 (overleaf) Body pattern for Bye-lo baby

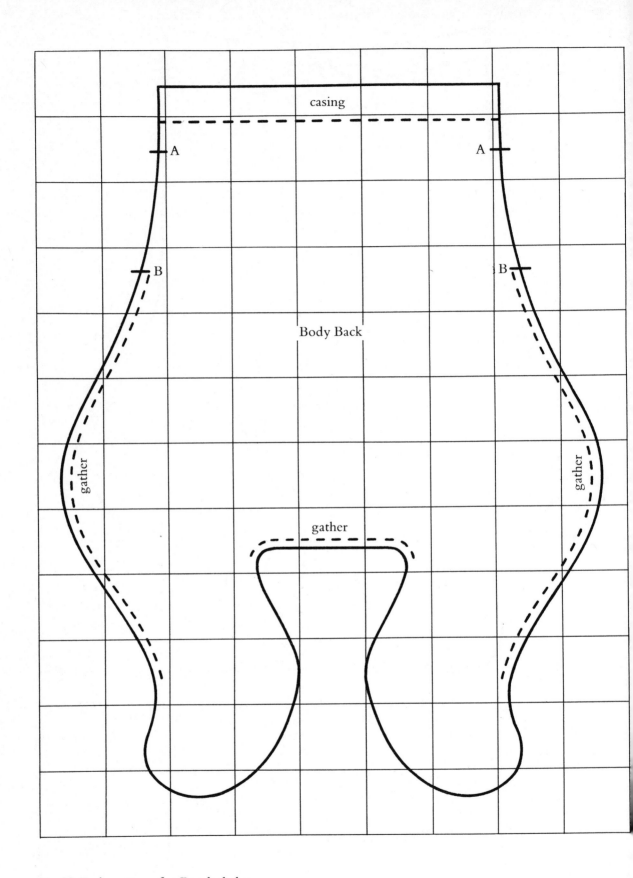

Fig 82 Body pattern for Bye-lo baby

Full instructions for modelling are given in Chapter 1 so are repeated only briefly here.

Model the head and neck over the core-ball and the neck of a bottle. Cover the ball and bottle with aluminium foil so that the modelling may be removed easily.

Shape the head to resemble the head of a real baby. As this doll does not have a wig, it is important that the shape of the whole head, front and back, is accurate and attractive (use Fig 83 and the picture on page 123 as guides). Shape a well-rounded back to the head, full cheeks and a small chin. The nose should be very small with virtually no bridge. The eyes should be set quite deeply without shaped eyelids. Check that the eyes are set well down the face, and that the distance between the nose and mouth is very short. Shape the mouth with a full upper lip and well-rounded lower lip. The expression on the baby's face is a matter of taste, but it should be 'real' rather than idealised.

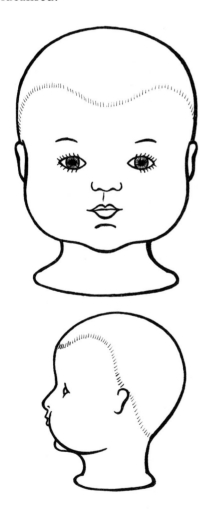

Fig 83 Modelling guide for Bye-lo baby's head

Model a short neck with a flange at the lower end and small ears set close to the head. Check the modelling very carefully from all angles – above, below and both sides – and smooth it as thoroughly as possible. Remove the head carefully from the bottle and bake. Model the hands to the wrists, making the hands small and chubby with curled fingers and the wrists plump. Score grooves or make flanges for tying on at the wrists. Bake the modelled parts and, when cool, remove the core-ball from the head.

Paint the head and hands with pale flesh-coloured paint. I recommend several coats of Humbrol matt enamel. Paint the features with a fine brush. The eyes are outlined with brown and fine straight lashes are painted in brown around them. The small eyebrows are painted lightly with single curved strokes. The mouth should be a natural soft rusty red rather than pink. The hair is painted onto the head in one light coat, using the flesh shade with a little brown added to it. Colour the cheeks with a little powder blusher. The finished proportions of the modelled parts should be: head circumference, 10in; length from hairline to chin, 3in; hand from wrists to fingertips, 1in. Minor differences in size will not affect the proportions of the finished doll, but if your head and hands are much larger or smaller than this you may wish to adjust the body patterns.

To make the body, cut one back (Fig 81), one front and two upper arms (Fig 82) in calico on the straight grain of the fabric. Gather the back body on the outer sides of each leg and across the crotch and pull up the gathers so that the back body fits the front body. Pin and tack the two pieces together. Stitch the back to the front around the outside, leaving openings AB at each side for the arms and leaving the top edge open. Reinforce this seam and clip the curves. Turn a ½in casing around the top of the body.

Seam the upper arms, and tie in the hands, with the fold in the upper arm above the thumb and the seam to the outside of the hand. Stuff the arms loosely and tack the top edges closed. Insert the arms in the sides of the body AB and stitch the side seams of the body through the tops of the arms. Turn the body through to the right side and stuff fairly firmly. Take care to shape the feet and ease the legs into a sitting position as you stuff. Cover the end of the flange neck with a disc of

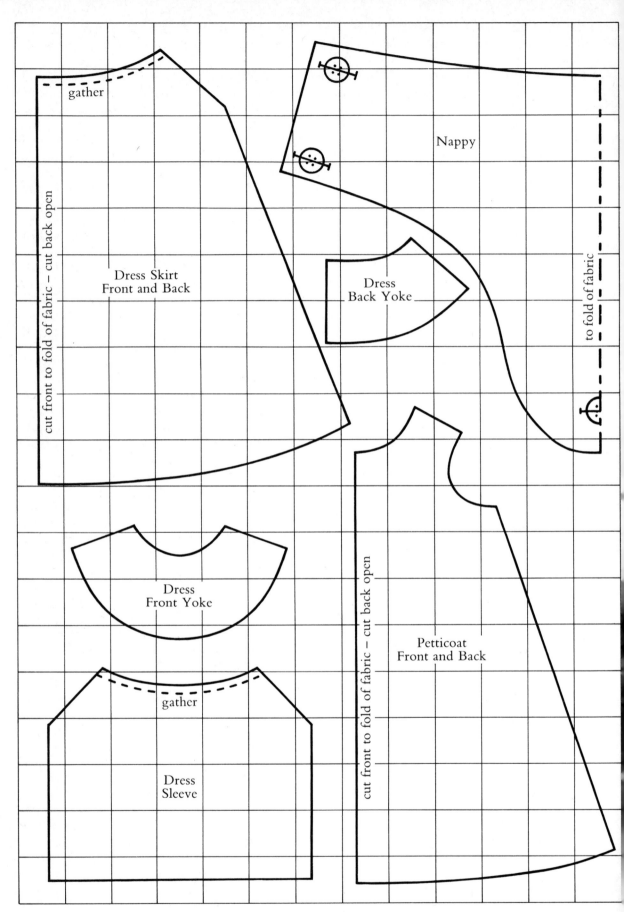

gather

Nappy

Dress Skirt
Front and Back

cut front to fold of fabric – cut back open

to fold of fabric

Dress
Back Yoke

Dress
Front Yoke

Petticoat
Front and Back

cut front to fold of fabric – cut back open

gather

Dress
Sleeve

cardboard, glued in place, to prevent the body stuffing shifting up into the head. Thread tape through the casing at the neckline and tie in the flange neck, as tightly as possible, knotting the tape firmly at centre back.

BYE-LO BABY'S CLOTHES

½yd white winceyette (36in wide) for underwear
¾yd white lace (1in wide) for trimming
½yd fabric (36in wide) for dress and bonnet
2yd lace (1½in wide) for trimming
1yd satin ribbon (½in wide)
3×½in buttons
4 small buttons
shirring elastic
2×25g balls of wool (2-ply) for shawl and bootees
no 14 (2mm) knitting needles
size 12 (2.50mm) crochet hook

To make the nappy, cut one piece (on the fold of the fabric) in winceyette (Fig 84). Make a small hem all the way around. Work two buttonholes on one front edge and one buttonhole on the lower curved edge. Stitch ½in buttons to the other front edge. Wrap the nappy around the doll and button the front edges. Draw the lower curved edge up through the legs and button onto the front.

For the petticoat, cut one front on the fold of the fabric and two backs in winceyette (Fig 84). Stitch the front to backs at shoulder and side seams. Roll narrow hems around the neckline and armholes. Stitch the centre-back seam to 2in below the neckline, then turn back and hem the remainder of the back edges to form facings. Hem the lower edge and trim with lace. Make thread loops and sew on buttons to fasten the back.

To make the dress, cut two sleeves, two front yokes and four back yokes (one yoke is used as lining). Cut the skirt front on the fold of the fabric and two back skirts, all on the straight grain of the fabric (Fig 84). Stitch the shoulder seams on both yokes, then stitch the yokes together, with right sides facing, down the back edges and around the neck. Clip the curves, turn through and press. Stitch the skirt front to backs. Stitch the sleeve seams, then stitch the sleeves to the skirt at the armholes. Stitch the centre-back skirt seam to 1in below the top edge then turn back and hem

Fig 84 Clothes patterns for Bye-lo baby

the remainder to form facings. Place a length of 1½in wide lace to the top edge of the skirt and gather skirt and lace evenly to fit the yoke. Stitch to the yoke, then oversew the yoke lining to the inside to cover the seam. Hem the sleeve ends, trim with lace and gather to frills with shirring elastic. Stitch the skirt hem and trim with lace and a satin ribbon bow. Make buttonholes and sew on buttons to fasten the back yoke.

To make the bonnet, measure over the doll's head from the jawline, and from the forehead to the centre back of the head. Add a ½in seam allowance to both measurements, and cut two pieces. With right sides facing, stitch the two pieces together and press. Gather the back (raw) edge and pull up the gathers so that the cap fits the doll's head. Cut a semi-circular back for the bonnet to fit the gathered edge of the crown, and a second piece for lining. Stitch the gathered edge of the crown to the curved edge of the back piece. With right sides facing, stitch the two back pieces together across the straight edge, then turn the lining to the inside and oversew over the crown seam. Make gathered lace frills and stitch to the front edge of the bonnet and add ribbon ties to either side.

Knit the bootees on size 14 (2mm) needles. To make each bootee:

Cast on 43 stitches. Work 10 rows of st st. With right sides facing, k19, sl 1, k1, psso, k1, k2 tog, knit to end. *Next row* p. *Next row* k18, sl 1, K1, psso, K1, K2 tog, knit to end. Repeat the last two rows once more so that you have decreased six stitches altogether. Continue in st st for 1cm. Work 1cm in garter stitch, cast off. Press, fold in half and sew back and underfoot seams. If required, thread through narrow ribbons and tie in bows around the ankles.

The shawl is crocheted in 2-ply yarn using a size 12 (2.50mm) crochet hook. Make 85 chain.

1st row Into the 5th ch from hook work 1tr, 1ch and 1tr (called tr gp), * miss 2ch, 1tr gp into next ch, repeat from * until 2ch remain, miss 1ch. 1tr into last ch to form edge st, turn.
2nd row 3ch to form edge st, * 4tr into 1ch sp of tr gp of previous row, repeat from * 26 times more, 1tr into ch sp at edge to form edge st, turn.
3rd row 3ch to form edge st, * in between

2nd and 3rd tr of 4tr block of previous row, work 1tr gp, repeat from ★ 26 times more. 1tr into 3ch sp at beginning of previous row, turn. Repeat 2nd and 3rd rows until work is square.

Complete by making a border of 3 rows of dc. Pin out and press the shawl according to the instructions on the wool band.

If you wish to give the doll hair, stitch a fringe of mohair firmly into a length of bias-binding. Tack the fringe inside the brim of the bonnet, and comb gently to style.

For the pillow, cut two pieces 12×8in in cotton fabric and the same in lace (or fabric) for the cover. Seam the cotton pieces together to make a bag, turn through, stuff and over-sew closed. Stitch a gathered lace (or self-fabric) frill to the outside edge of one cover piece, then with right sides together, sand-wiching the frill, stitch the cover pieces together around one short and both long edges. Turn through, slip the cover over the pillow and, tucking in the raw edges, slip-stitch the other short side closed.

Mini Bye-lo Baby
(6in tall)
Difficulty 2/Colour picture page 102
Body and clothes pattern: Fig 85

small packet Fimo
core-ball (1in diameter) for head
pair of acrylic eyes (7mm)
narrow tape
¼yd calico (36in wide) for body
¼yd cotton (36in wide) for dress
¼yd lace (2in wide) for bonnet
tubular gauze finger bandage for bootees
scraps of lace, ribbon etc for trimming
shirring elastic

The miniature Bye-lo baby is modelled, painted and made up in exactly the same way as the larger version (*see* Fig 85 for body pattern). If you find setting acrylic eyes in a doll of this scale difficult, you may prefer to substitute painted eyes. Tie in the flange neck with narrow tape or strong button thread. The finished proportions of this doll should be: head circumference, 5in; length of face from hairline to chin, 1½in; length of hands from wrist to fingertips, ¾in. If the propor-tions of your doll are very different from these, you may need to alter the body pattern.

To make the baby's nappy, cut and hem a small triangle of cotton fabric and secure with a small gilt safety pin.

For the dress, cut one piece on the fold of the fabric (Fig 85) and cut open the centre back. Roll a narrow casing around the neck. Stitch the side seams from the sleeve ends, through the underarms and down the sides. Stitch the centre-back seam to 2in below the neckline, then hem the remainder of the back edges to form facings. Hem the sleeve ends and the lower edge of the skirt and trim with lace. Gather the sleeve ends with shirring elastic to form frills. Thread narrow ribbon through the neckline casing and tie in a bow at the back.

For the bonnet, cut a piece of 2in wide lace long enough to fit over the top of the doll's head plus ½in. Fold the piece in half, whip the back edges together, then stitch straight across, ½in below the point, to make a cap. Turn up the raw lower edge and hem to form a casing. Trim the front edge with a gathered lace frill. Thread narrow ribbon through the casing and tie in a bow under the doll's chin.

Make the doll a shawl from a scrap of lace or knitting and bootees from tubular gauze finger bandage.

The Moses basket is made of plaited raffia, using either natural raffia from garden-supply shops or artificial raffia from art and craft shops. Plait sufficient 6ft lengths of raffia to complete the basket – you will need six to eight of these lengths, depending on the thickness of the raffia. Cut an oval base 5×3in in stiff cardboard. Begin oversewing the raffia together with two or three rows straight up and down, 3in long, then work around these rows, oversewing each row of raffia to the previous one to shape an oval base a little larger than the cardboard oval. Glue the card-board base to the inside of the raffia base, then work the raffia upwards from the base to form the sides of the basket. Make the sides wider at the top than the base and continue until the basket is deep enough to hold the baby. Stitch the end of the raffia securely to the inside to fasten off. Make a handle at each side of the basket from lengths of plaited raffia, knotted at each end and stitched securely to the inside. Make a tiny stuffed cotton mattress and pillow to fit inside the basket, and add a knitted or fabric cover. To adapt these patterns and instructions to make a waxed Victorian baby, make the following

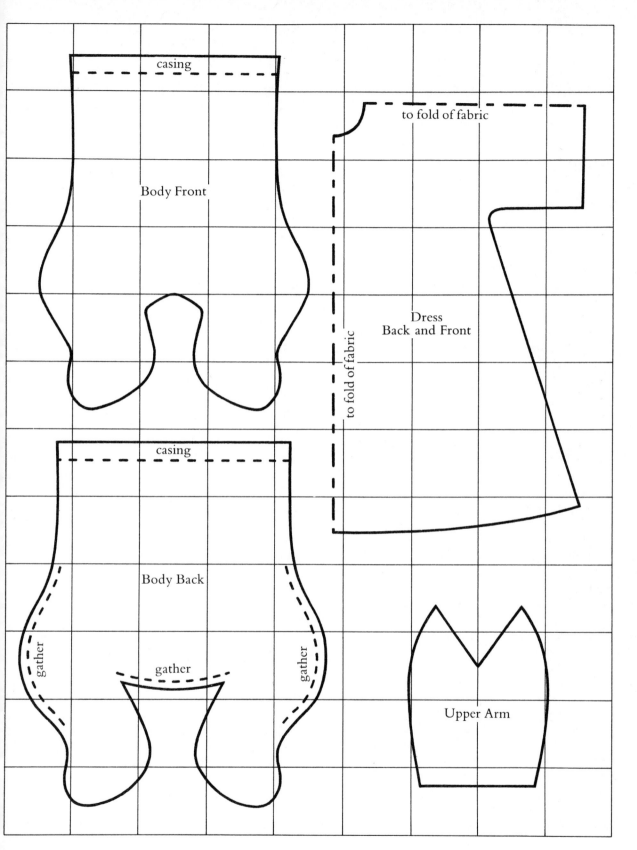

Fig 85 Body and clothes patterns for mini Bye-lo baby

changes (full wax instructions in Chapter 1).

When modelling the doll's head, aim for a pretty 'idealised' baby rather than a character baby. Remember that some definition in the modelling will be lost under the wax. Paint the head and hands flesh colour as previously described, but do not paint the features. Use larger eyes than for the Bye-lo baby.

The Bye-lo body pattern is not appropriate for a Victorian doll; a simple bag-shaped body should be used instead. See the patterns for the small rag doll in Chapter 4, and adapt these by cutting the body straight across at the neck and making a casing at the top edge to tie in the flange neck. Shorten the leg pattern from the top to the required length and cut the arms as simple tubes to tie in the modelled hands. Make the body in strong white cotton. This will not make an authentic Victorian doll, as they had wax shoulder-plates – usually including the shoulder and often part of the upper arm – and wax lower legs, but when the doll is dressed, these discrepancies will not show, and this method is a great deal simpler than the original!

Make a support for the head for dipping (see Chapter 1, page 18) and tie on the hands so that you can hold the arms to dip the hands. In a double boiler or pyrex jug inside a saucepan of water melt sufficient wax to cover the head. A mixture of one-third pure beeswax to two-thirds candlewax with a little pink colouring will produce the correct colour for this type of doll. Melt the wax slowly and carefully, taking note of the safety precautions on page 18. Turn off the heat before dipping. Dip the head and hands, once, twice or three times as you prefer and leave aside to cool. When the wax has hardened, cut it away from the eyes with a sharp craft knife and smooth away any imperfections with turpentine on a cotton cloth.

Paint the features with oil paints or acrylics (oil paint will require a week or two to dry properly) using a fine, good-quality brush. Paint in the eyebrows, lashes and mouth and colour the cheeks with oil paint or powder blusher rubbed in with the finger (the cheap brands of blusher are better for this purpose as they stain the wax more easily). I would recommend oil paints for wax – though one needs patience waiting for them to dry – as by

their nature they blend into the wax, rather than 'sit' on top as water-based colours do. Mixing the paint with a little turpentine will speed up the drying.

Wax babies should have hair wigs, either mohair or real hair. A cap wig may be glued to the head (UHU will stick to wax) or the back of the head may be re-dipped and the cap wig quickly applied while the wax is warm and soft. This latter method requires some dexterity but is very effective.

Alternatively you may prefer to insert small groups of hairs into small slits cut in the wax which are then sealed with a heated knife in the traditional manner. Work from the hairline to the crown of the head, smoothing the hair to lie naturally against the head as you work. This is a time-consuming (though not particularly difficult) process, which is one of the reasons why the original wax dolls of this type were so expensive.

The Victorian baby requires far more elaborate clothes, and more layers, than the twentieth century baby. A nappy, a wide binder pinned around the stomach, a cotton undershirt or chemise, bootees or soft leather shoes and several petticoats were worn under long, lavishly trimmed dresses with caps and shawls or cloaks. The clothes would be all white: cotton for the undershirt and top petticoat, flannel for the binder, nappy and under-petticoat. Lawn, trimmed with pintucks and lace insertion and frills should be used for the dress and cap. For a doll of this size, a dress 18–20in long from neck to hem would be appropriate. The most popular style had a small square bodice with a high waistline, a gathered skirt with an elaborately trimmed front panel and long sleeves with frills at the wrists. A matching bonnet, equally lavishly trimmed with lace, pintucks and frills, would be tied under the chin with a ribbon bow. A long cloak with a collar, trimmed with lace, marabou or swansdown would be worn for outdoor wear. (Fig 86 shows the type of clothes worn by Victorian baby dolls.)

Patterns may be adapted from this book, or you may prefer to design your own. Look out also for antique baby dolls' clothes in antique shops and markets and at doll fairs. Real Victorian babies' dresses might also be cut down to fit the doll.

Fig 86 Victorian baby clothes

12
THE 'CHAD VALLEY BAMBINA' (c1940)

Felt was first used in dollmaking in the 1890s. Knock-about dolls, distributed in America, had bisque heads and hands with felt bodies made to imitate gusseted kid bodies, and in Germany Margarete Steiff made dolls with felt heads and bodies. The Steiff dolls were character dolls, and are easily recognised by the seam down the centre of the face which gives the head its shaping. Steiff's factory claimed to be the first to make stuffed felt

Fig 87 Chad Valley Bambina

dolls. The range of characters was extensive; soldiers, workmen, Indians and dolls in folk costumes were popular, and examples of these dolls in good condition are much sought after by modern collectors.

During the early part of the twentieth century, felt continued to be a popular material, either for the whole doll or for the bodies of dolls with bisque heads as it was cheaper than kid. After World War I, several firms, particularly in Europe and England, produced dolls with pressed-felt faces. One of the best known was the Italian firm of Enrico Scavini who produced the 'Lenci' dolls ('Lenci' being the pet name of Scavini's wife Elena). The dolls were first produced in the 1920s and though they were expensive they were so popular that other firms began to imitate them. Lenci dolls were made all in felt, the faces moulded by pressure. The features were painted with the eyes glancing to one side. The bodies were beautifully proportioned to represent small boys and girls and the costumes were accurate copies of real children's clothes, often made entirely in felt. The wigs were mohair. These are probably the most popular of all felt dolls with collectors, and a modern version, though lacking the charm of the originals, is still available.

The English Chad Valley Company produced a large range of felt-faced dolls from the 1920s until after World War II. The Chad Valley dolls had pressed-felt faces, with inset glass or painted eyes and mohair wigs. The bodies were made of velveteen. The 'Bambina' range was first produced in 1927, though similar dolls, by then looking very old fashioned, were still being sold at the end of the 1940s. The Bambinas ranged in size from 14½ to 18½in and some were sold in boxes which could be used as a bed for the doll. They were dressed either in knitted suits, or in all-felt outfits in bright colours, trimmed with a contrasting colour. The large heads and limbs and small bodies are amusing to the modern eye but in their original clothes they are popular with collectors because they belong so utterly to the period between the wars. The Chad Valley dolls were considerably cheaper than the Lenci dolls, and though they lacked the artistic quality of their Italian rivals, the Bambinas were extremely popular. The 'Corina' range, sold during the 1930s, was dressed entirely in felt, or in flowered cotton, taffeta or organdie with large hats and frilled skirts, following the fashions of the day. The most expensive Chad Valley dolls wore silk party dresses, velvet cloaks and leather shoes and had long curly mohair wigs and sleeping glass eyes.

Other companies produced dolls similar to the Chad Valley range and it is often difficult for the modern collector to attribute dolls to a specific company. One of Chad Valley's designers, Norah Wellings, later started her own company, and produced a range of felt and velveteen dolls. During the 1920s, Deans Rag Book Company, which had been producing cut-out-and-sew rag dolls for some time, produced a range of felt dolls very similar to the Lenci dolls. These 'Posy' dolls had side glancing eyes and well-made felt clothes, designed to represent flowers. By the 1950s, however, firms could no longer compete with the cheap and popular plastic dolls which were now being produced and felt dolls ceased to be made commercially, though the material has remained popular with home dollmakers.

The doll in this chapter is a version of the Chad Valley Bambina, made entirely in felt. The head is shaped over a vinyl mask – a method I have devised after much experimenting and many failures attempting to press felt in a mould. I find that without the heavy industrial steam press, the felt mask will not hold its shape through stuffing, and the method produces an ugly seam around the doll's face particularly visible under the chin. By using the firm vinyl mask under the felt skin, the head can be made without distortion during stuffing and with only one seam at the centre back which is completely concealed by the wig. It is not an 'authentic' method, but it does produce very satisfactory results! The inset acrylic eyes are cut out of the mask before the head is made up, and then reset. The features are painted onto the face, and the wig is made of mohair. The body has the pro-

portions typical of this type of doll. The head and limbs are large, the torso small. The arms are pivot-jointed at the shoulders and the hands have fingers separated by stabstitching. The legs have stitched joints at the hips and the feet are large.

The doll is dressed in cotton knickers and socks, and felt dress, hat and shoes. I have used shocking pink trimmed with dark green for the clothes, but any combination of contrasting colours would be suitable. The hat and dress are trimmed with felt roses.

Use only the best-quality felt for both the doll and her clothes. Cheap felt is thin and patchy and tears when firmly stuffed. The wig should be mohair, bought as a length with a stitched parting (see Stockists), though you may prefer a different colour. Stuffing should be good-quality acrylic or polyester – not kapok or foam chips!

If you prefer to dress the doll in fabric rather than felt clothes, the patterns may still be used but you will need to add a ½in seam allowance and 1in to the length of the skirt for a hem. The shoes may also be made in leather without altering the pattern. For the best effect, choose suitable childish fabrics in plain colours, gingham or small prints.

The type of vinyl face mask used for this doll is widely available from art and craft shops. Do not be tempted to use the cheap stiffened fabric masks as an alternative, as they distort badly when soaked with glue. I recommend UHU for gluing the felt to the mask, as it does not soak into the felt.

Chad Valley Bambina (c1940)
(18in tall)
Difficulty 3/Colour picture page 102
Body pattern: Fig 88
Clothes pattern: Fig 89

vinyl face mask (4in long × 3½in wide)
½yd flesh-colour felt (36in wide)
14in mohair (6in wide)
2 × 1in 4-hole buttons
strong button thread
stuffing
paints

Note: Felt stretches slightly more from selvedge to selvedge than down the length, so ensure that body pattern pieces are all cut in the same direction, with the greater stretch from side to side for plump limbs.

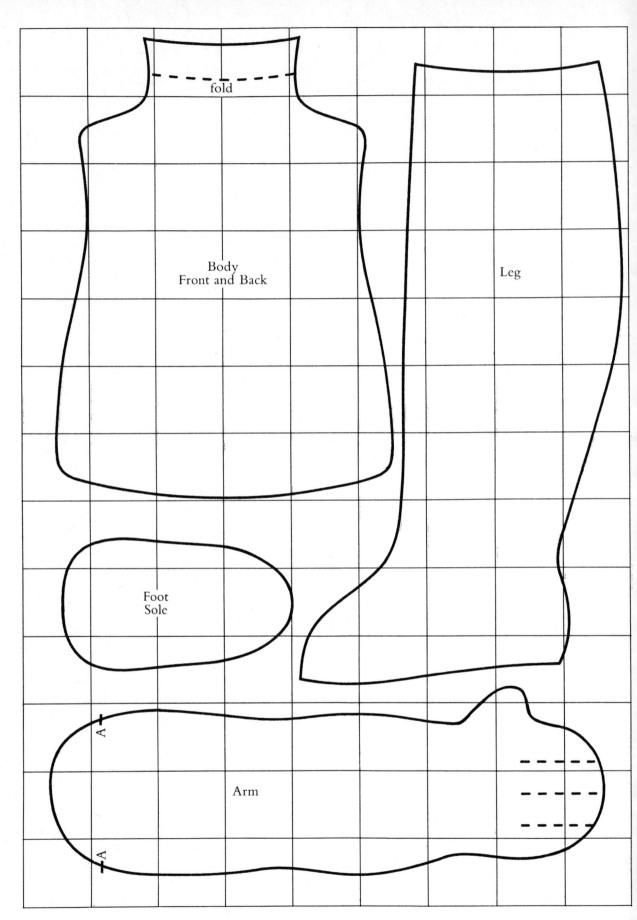

fold

Body
Front and Back

Leg

Foot
Sole

Arm

A

A

Cut two bodies, four arms, four legs and two soles from the pattern (Fig 88). Cut a rectangle of felt 10×6in for the head. To make the head, cut the acrylic eyes out of the back of the face mask, using a sharp craft knife, and pare the eye sockets level with the face. Set the eyes aside for re-use.

Coat the outside of the face mask liberally with glue (UHU) and press the centre part of the felt head piece over the mask. Smooth out all creases, and press the felt firmly into the contours of the mask. Allow the glue to dry thoroughly, then with a craft knife or small sharp scissors cut out the eye holes in the felt. (Check that the felt is firmly glued to the mask around the eye holes.) Paint the features onto the face with a fine brush. I have found acrylic or poster paint (used rather dry so that the colour does not soak into the felt) satisfactory. Outline the eye holes with brown, and paint short straight lashes above the eyes. Eyebrows should be small and curved, painted in single strokes in brown. Indicate the nostrils in brown or red. The mouth should be rosebud-shaped in a rather bright red. By painting the face at this stage mistakes are easily rectified. If you dislike the results, simply peel off the felt and make another face.

Allow the face painting to dry thoroughly, then reset the eyes. I have found the best way to do this is to use fabric adhesive plaster (ie Elastoplast). Cut two pieces about 2in long, stick the back of the eye firmly to the centre of the plaster, position the eyes in the sockets and press the plaster firmly to the inside of the mask. As these fabric plasters stretch, they follow the contours of the mask and hold the eyes securely in place and completely covered, so that they cannot be dislodged during stuffing.

Turn under the short back edges of the head at either side by ½in, and oversew the back seam closed. Using strong button thread, make a line of gathering stitches around the bottom edge of the head, immediately below the vinyl mask. Pull up the gathering as tightly as possible. Stuff the head firmly, easing out the puckers at the lower edge, and moulding the head to shape as you stuff. Gather around the top of the head above the mask with strong thread, and pull up tightly. The gathering on the top of the head will be concealed by the wig. Mould the head

Fig 88 Body pattern for Bambina

between your hands to shape it.

Stitch the front and back body pieces together to make a bag, leaving the neck edge open. Turn through and stuff firmly. Stitch the legs together in pairs, leaving the soles and top edges open. Stitch the soles into the feet, turn through, stuff firmly and oversew the tops closed, tucking in the raw edges. Stitch the arms together in pairs leaving the top curved edge AA open and turn through. Stuff the hands fairly loosely to allow for stabstitching and stuff the arm firmly to above the elbow. Sew a large flat 4-hole button to the top inside of each arm. With a mattress needle or a long darning needle and a long doubled length of strong button thread, sew through the button in one arm, right through the body at shoulder level, and through the button in the other arm. Work back and forth through the buttons in an X shape, pulling the thread tight enough to secure the arms to the shoulders without distorting the shape of the body. Fasten off the thread securely. Top up the stuffing in the arms and oversew the curved openings closed. The arms should swing freely from the shoulders, both thumbs facing forward.

Ladderstitch the head to the neck with strong thread, ensuring that the head seam is to centre back and pushing more stuffing into the neck as you go so that it is very firm and the head will not flop. Oversew the legs to the back lower edge of the body. Stabstitch through the hands to define the fingers.

To make the wig, stitch the mohair to the doll's head through the centre parting (or with a side parting if you prefer). Mohair cannot be brushed or combed, so ease it gently with your fingers to cover the head evenly, then, lifting one side at a time, cover the head with glue (UHU) and press the hair down over the glued head. Ease to style waves etc with your fingers and leave the glue to dry. Brush a little powder blusher into the doll's face to colour the cheeks.

BAMBINA'S CLOTHES
small piece white cotton for knickers
½yd narrow broderie anglaise for trimming
3×12in squares main colour felt
1×12in square contrasting colour felt
scraps of toning felt (for roses)
elastic
2 small buttons for shoes
small press studs

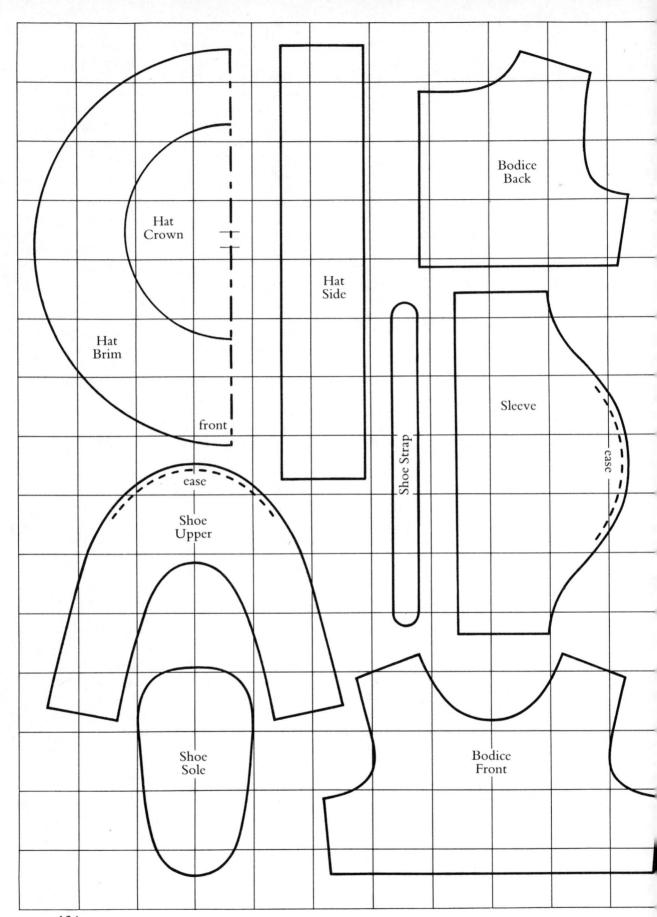

Hat Crown

Hat Side

Bodice Back

Hat Brim

front

Sleeve

ease

Shoe Strap

ease

Shoe Upper

Shoe Sole

Bodice Front

134

To make the knickers, use the pattern and directions given for the large felt girl doll on page 144. Widen the pattern by ½in at the folds to accommodate this doll's fatter body and legs. Trim the leg ends with broderie anglaise, and thread elastic through the waist and leg casings to fit the doll.

To make the dress, cut one bodice front, two backs and two sleeves from the pattern (Fig 89), and a skirt 22×6in in main colour felt. If you use 12in felt squares you will need to join two lengths for the skirt, and the seams should be at either side and at centre back. Stitch the bodice front to backs at the shoulder seams. Gather the sleeve heads slightly to ease and stitch the sleeves into the armholes. Stitch the side seams, from the sleeve ends, through the underarm and down the bodice sides. Gather the top edge of the skirt evenly and stitch to the bodice. Stitch the centre-back seam in the skirt to 2in below the waist, then turn back the remainder of the skirt and bodice back edges and hem to form facings. Bind the neckline and the sleeve ends with ½in wide strips of contrasting colour felt. Turn up the skirt hem and topstitch in contrasting colour. Fasten the back bodice with small press studs.

To make the hat, cut two brims, one side and one crown in main colour felt. If the felt you are using is floppy, the brim pieces may be stiffened with lightweight iron-on Vilene. Stitch the two brims together around the outside edge, turn through and press. (Check that the cut-out hole in the brim will fit the doll's head and enlarge if necessary.) Stitch the seam in the hat side piece, then stitch the side to the brim and the crown to the side, easing the felt gently to stretch as necessary. Topstitch around the brim in contrasting colour.

To make the felt roses, cut strips of felt approximately 1in wide × 3in long. Fold in half along the length and press. Round off the corners at both ends. With strong thread, gather along the cut edge and pull up tightly, coiling the felt to make roses. Stitch through the base to secure. Make two roses in main colour and four in toning colour. Cut four leaf shapes from contrasting colour. Arrange groups of three roses and two leaves on the hat brim and at the waistline of the dress and sew (or safety-pin) in place.

To make the shoes, cut one upper, one sole and one strap in contrasting colour felt. Stitch the centre-back seams in the uppers and gather around the toes to ease. Stitch the uppers to the soles and turn through. Try the shoes on the doll's feet, gently stretching the top edge to fit if necessary. Bind the top edges with main colour felt. Stitch the centre of the strap to the back of the shoe, cut small buttonhole and sew on small button to fasten the straps around the doll's ankles. If you wish, cardboard insoles cut from the shoe sole pattern may be fitted inside the shoes. This doll wears bought white socks (see Stockists) but similar socks may be made from tubular gauze bandage.

The method for making shaped dolls' heads over a vinyl mask described here can be used for a wide variety of felt dolls. If you prefer, the acrylic eyes may be left in place, and the eye holes not cut out of the felt face. If the shape of the eye is defined with a sharp pointed tool, ie a wooden toothpick, the eyes can be painted into this outline in the manner of the Lenci dolls. The body patterns may be lengthened to make a lady 'boudoir' doll of the type popular in the 1930s, perhaps dressed in a frilled full-skirted taffeta dress and 'picture' hat or marabou-trimmed lounging pyjamas. The method is not recommended for fabric heads, because the gathers under the chin will not ease out neatly in fabric.

Fig 89 Clothes patterns for Bambina

13

FELT CHILDREN (c1950)

Modern dolls fall fairly neatly into three main groups – commercial, homemade and professionally made. Of the three, the commercial dolls are by far the largest group. The vast majority of modern dolls are produced in factories and almost invariably made of some type of plastic. One only has to look around the local toyshop to see the enormous variety of dolls available and the innovations which have been made in the last decade or two. Baby dolls are still very popular, most of them now made in vinyl, but simply 'going to sleep' is not enough for the modern 'mother' who now requires a baby which will cry, kick, crawl and suck. I recently read of a baby doll which develops nappy rash! And of course, these fashion-conscious infants require large wardrobes of clothes suitable for every occasion, and as much nursery equipment as a real baby. 'Sindy' and her imitators seem to be so well established that one cannot imagine life without them – it seems that every little girl I meet has a Sindy doll with a vast wardrobe of clothes and accessories.

Figs 90, 91 and 92 Felt children

These are truly the 'fashion dolls' of our time, and though their clothes are very shoddy when compared to the beautiful garments of the dolls of the 1870s, at least they are no longer luxury toys, reserved for the very rich.

It is interesting to note the number of 'old-fashioned' dolls which are now being produced, ranging from the little Pedigree 'Sarah Kay' with her rather Edwardian clothes, to the expensive Italian dolls with their lavish 'Victorian' style outfits, all bonnets and frills. Several firms such as Arlesford Crafts are producing porcelain dolls dressed in retrospective styles including a range of babies, very like those made in the 1920s. Even the china manufacturers have decided to explore the doll market and several of them have produced a range of costume dolls.

The Italian dolls seem to be generally particularly good at the moment; they are not cheap, but most of them are very well made, both the plastic and porcelain types, with charming faces and well-designed clothes. Many of them are very 'old fashioned' – I have seen character children, similar to those made earlier this century, and elegant lady dolls dressed in the styles of the Twenties and Thirties in gorgeous fabrics, beautifully made. The English manufacturers tend to play safe, producing idealised babies and popular television characters. Small costume dolls are popular, both with the home market and the tourists, and several companies specialise in these.

An enormous number of commercial dolls are imported, ranging from the popular Sasha dolls, to reproductions of the Kathë Kruse cloth dolls from Germany. Vast quantities of cheap porcelain dolls are imported from Taiwan, varying in quality from good to quite appalling, and recently the outrageously overpriced but very lovable American 'Cabbage Patch' dolls, with all the American genius for sales technique, took Britain by storm!

The professional dollmakers produce a much smaller number of dolls – their output can be as low as only a dozen or so in a year, but the variety and standard of professionally made dolls is usually extremely high. Often called 'doll artists', these professionals work in a variety of mediums – cloth, felt, wood, wax, resin, clay or porcelain – making their own original or reproduction antique dolls. Many of them are well known inside their own profession, but largely unheard of by the general public. This is because their work is not usually available through shops, but made to commission or sold directly to the customer via a catalogue or a personal recommendation. Most professional dollmakers began as talented amateurs and their work often rivals that of the finest dollmakers of the last century. These are collectors' dolls, not intended as children's playthings, and as more people become interested in making and collecting dolls so the work of the doll artists is appreciated more.

The British Doll Artists' Association produces an annual directory, illustrating the work of its members (see Bibliography). The members of the BDA are all professional dollmakers, producing original work of an extremely high standard. Much of it is sold abroad, particularly to America where similar associations exist and dollmaking and collecting are enormously popular. These dollmakers set a standard for the amateur to aim for, and I thoroughly recommend that you obtain a copy of the directory as it is very inspirational!

There are, of course, many amateur dollmakers whose talents rival those of the professionals and who produce beautiful work for their own pleasure rather than for sale. It is my habit to 'test' all my patterns and methods on dollmaking friends (and my mother!) before they go into a book, and though some prefer to follow my patterns exactly, others enjoy experimenting and adapting to create their own versions of the doll. I have included the felt children in this chapter as they are the sort of basic dolls that lend themselves to all kinds of variations.

If you are making a modern doll, you are not restricted in any way by the styles, methods or fashions of any other period. The limitations imposed by each type of doll in the preceding chapters do not exist, and you have a completely free hand. I have chosen to make these 'old-fashioned' dolls to represent children of the 1950s, dressed in their Sunday best.

You might like to dress the dolls in the style of the 1980s – jeans and sweatshirts, Babygros and pinafore dresses. Ten years from now, they will probably look very old fashioned! Or you could adapt them to represent children of any period. Suitably wigged and dressed, they could be Regency, Victorian or Edwardian or belong to any decade of the twentieth century. The really adventurous might like to try Tudor or Stuart costumes. Recreate a particular outfit from your own childhood, perhaps school-uniform complete with blazer and cap for the boy and gymslips for the girls. It might be fun to try a Brownie or Cub uniform, a ballet tutu or football outfit. The possibilities are endless, and the choice is yours!

The dolls should be made in felt as this method for the head is not suitable for fabric, and as felt stretches slightly as it is stuffed, the head, body and limbs are nicely rounded. Use only the best-quality felt which is thicker than cheap felt and will not tear when stretched. Stuffing should be good-quality acrylic, terylene or polyester. I have used covered button-forms for the eyes; you can of course substitute any other method you prefer. Small shiny black buttons with shanks make effective eyes on simple dolls; they should be stitched right through the head with a long darning needle and strong button thread for security. The wigs are made from long pile fur fabric, seamed to make a cap shape and stitched to the doll's head. Curly pile fur fabric also looks effective, but choose a natural blonde, brown or auburn colour, and avoid black which looks very harsh and also attracts fluff. For babies, the lighter blonde shades are most suitable; darker colours tend to make their faces look older. Consider wool (particularly mohair) or bought or homemade hair wigs as an alternative. I have painted the doll's features with make-up pencils, a method suitable for dolls which will not get too much wear and tear, but for a small child's doll, embroidery would be a better alternative.

The noses are shaped by pushing a light-coloured bead, plastic or wooden, down under the 'skin' of the face. If you prefer, a 'bobble' nose made from a small circle of felt gathered around a little stuffing may be ladderstitched to the face instead.

Fabrics for the clothes are entirely a matter of individual preference, and should be chosen to suit whatever type of doll you are making. Period clothes should of course be made in natural fabrics, but modern clothes can be made of anything you please though as a general rule natural fabrics gather and hang better than man-made ones. The girls' dresses would look pretty in gingham, small prints, needlecord or velveteen (especially with lace collars). The boy's shorts may be lengthened to make trousers and made in drill, needlecord, denim or velvet. The baby's clothes could be knitted in any colour, or combination of colours. I have used white broderie anglaise for the girls' dresses, with white lawn for the boy's shirt and blue needlecord for his shorts. The baby's clothes are knitted in white, pure wool yarn. The girls wear bought straw hats (see Stockists) trimmed with ribbon bands and artificial flowers.

The pattern and instructions for the baby's teddy bear are also given in this chapter. Use velveteen or felt to make the bear – fur fabric is too thick.

Felt Children (c1950)

(16in, 13in and 11in tall)
Difficulty 3/Colour picture page 119
Body pattern: Figs 93 and 94
Clothes patterns: Figs 97 (boy), 98 (large girl), 99 (small girl)

FOR THE LARGE DOLL (BOY OR GIRL)
½yd felt (36in wide) for body
piece of fur fabric approx 12×6in for wig
2 covered-button forms (15mm) for eyes
strong button thread
stuffing (soft)
embroidery thread/make-up pencils
plastic or wooden bead (¼in diameter) for nose

Both dolls are made in the same way. Note: Felt stretches slightly more from selvedge to selvedge than down the length – lay out the pattern pieces following the direction arrows on the pattern so that the greater stretch is from side to side on each piece.

For each doll, cut two bodies, four arms, four legs and two soles (Fig 93), and a rectangle 9×5in for the head. Seam the body pieces together to form a bag, leaving the neck edge open. Turn through. Seam the arms together in pairs, clip between the thumb and fingers and turn through. Seam the legs together in pairs, stitch the soles into the feet and turn through. Stuff the legs and arms firmly (less firmly in the hands to allow for stabstitching) and, turning in the open edges, oversew closed. Stuff the body firmly, working the stuffing well into the hips and shoulders and up into the neck.

Stitch the centre-back seam on the head. With strong button thread, gather around the lower edge of the head and pull up tightly. Stuff the head very firmly, stretching out the gathers and moulding to shape as you work. Gather around the top edge of the head and pull up tightly. (If this thread pulls up easily there is not sufficient stuffing in the head; release it and add more stuffing until it requires some effort to pull up the gathers.) Select the least puckered end of the head for the chin, and ladderstitch the head to the neck, ensuring that the head seam is to the centre back. Push more stuffing into the neck as you go, so that it is absolutely firm and the head will not flop. The gathers on the top of the head will be concealed by the wig. Using strong button thread oversew the arms and legs to the back of the body. Stabstitch through the hands to define the fingers.

To make the wig, use long pile or curly fur fabric. Cut fur fabric from the back, using small sharp scissors and, taking care to snip only through the backing and not the pile, pull the pile apart gently. Cut a piece of fur fabric 9×3½in with the pile of the fabric overhanging one long edge (Fig 95a). This will be the front edge of the wig. Fold the fabric in half and stitch the centre-back seam (Fig 95b). Flatten the wig out as shown (Fig 95c) so that the back seam is uppermost and in the centre. Stitch a curved seam to round off the point and trim close to the seam. Still inside-out, pull the wig onto the doll's head and trim the front corners to a rounded shape to suit the doll's face. Turn right side out and pin to the doll's head to judge the best position for the eyes, but do not stitch the wig to the head until the eyes are sewn in.

To make the eyes (Fig 96), cover the button forms with closely woven white cotton and mark the eye lightly in pencil as a guide for the embroidery. Use satinstitch or buttonholestitch to work a coloured iris and black pupil, ensuring that you do not leave too large an area of white around them which would give a startled expression. Cut small felt semi-circles for the eyelids and buttonholestitch the straight edge across the front of the eye in black or brown thread to make the eyelashes. Gather around the curved edge of the felt and pull up tightly behind the eye.

Gauge the most attractive position for the eyes and mark lightly in pencil. Remove the wig and sew the eyes right through the head with a long needle and strong thread, pulling tightly to depress the eye into the face. (If

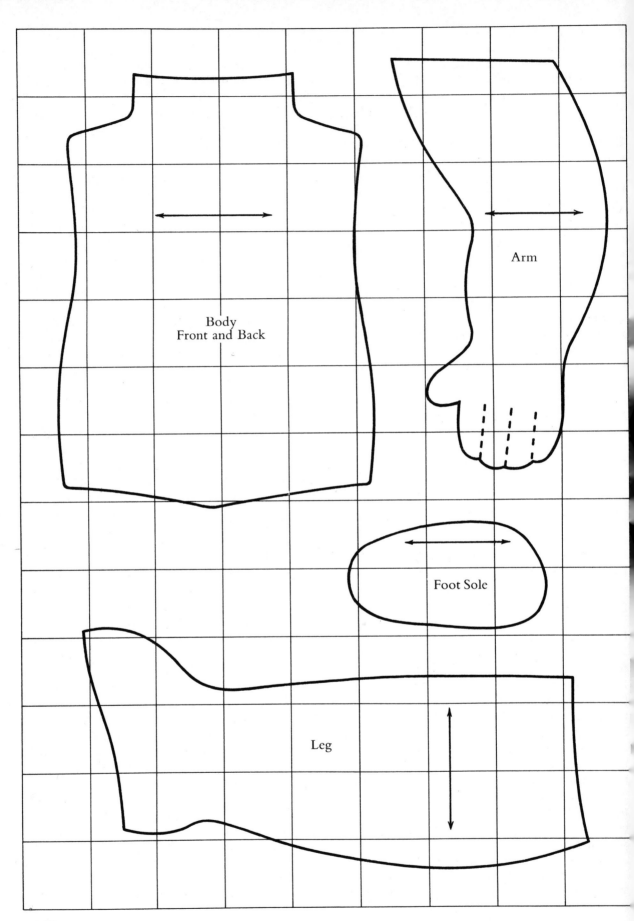

Body
Front and Back

Arm

Foot Sole

Leg

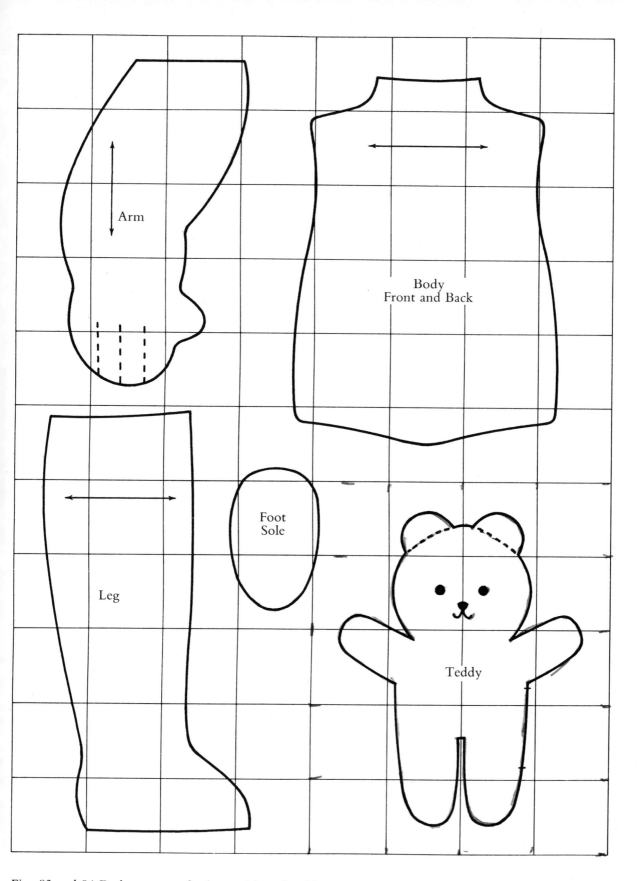

Figs 93 and 94 Body patterns for boy, girls and teddy

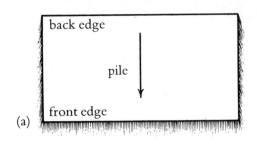

(a)

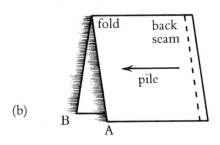

(b)

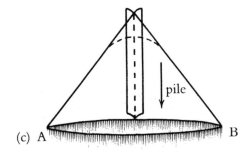

(c)

Fig 95 Making a fur fabric wig

Fig 96 Making covered-button eyes

necessary, smear a little glue on the back of the eyes to prevent them turning.)

Spear the nose bead on a knitting needle. Cut a small slit in the centre front of the doll's face above the hairline. Coat the bead with glue and push it down under the 'skin' to the correct position. Pinch the felt over the nose, draw out the knitting needle and oversew the slit closed.

Pin the wig in place, and stitch it to the head with small oversewing or blanket stitches all the way around. Embroider (or mark in make-up pencils) the eyebrows, nostrils and mouth, and dot lightly over the boy's nose and cheeks with brown pencil or felt pen for freckles. Colour the cheeks with powder blusher, brushed well in. Brush and comb the fabric wig to the required style (trim short for the boy) and, if necessary, hold with a little hairspray.

The materials and method are the same for the small girl with the following exceptions. The head piece is 4×7in, the eye buttons are ⅜in (11mm) and the wig is 6×2½in. (See Fig 94 for body pattern.)

BOY'S CLOTHES
¼yd cotton fabric (36in wide) for shirt
¼yd lace or broderie anglaise trimming (1in wide) for shirt front
4 small buttons
¼yd fabric (36in wide) for shorts
3×½in buttons
½yd ribbon (1in wide) for bow tie

To make the shirt, cut one back, two fronts, two sleeves and two collars (Fig 97). With right sides facing, sew the collars together, clip the curves, turn through and press. Stitch the fronts to the back at the shoulder seams. Gather the sleeve heads slightly to ease and stitch the sleeves into the armholes. Stitch the side seams from the sleeve ends, through the underarms and down the sides of the shirt. Turn back the front edges to form facings and hem. Stitch the collar to the neckline, enclosing the raw edges. Turn deep hems at the sleeve ends then turn back to form cuffs and press. Turn a small hem on the lower edge of the shirt. Work four small buttonholes on the left front to match small buttons on the right front. Trim the shirt front with lace or broderie anglaise trimming.

To make the shorts, cut two pattern pieces (Fig 97) and slash an opening on one side. Cut a waistband to fit the doll's waist with button and buttonhole fastening and two 1in wide straps to go over the doll's shoulders from front to back waist. Stitch the inside leg seams, then stitch the legs together at centre front and back. Roll a small hem around the slashed opening. Stitch the shorts to the waistband, pleating if necessary at the fronts to fit. Make buttonhole and sew button to

Fig 97 Clothes patterns for boy doll

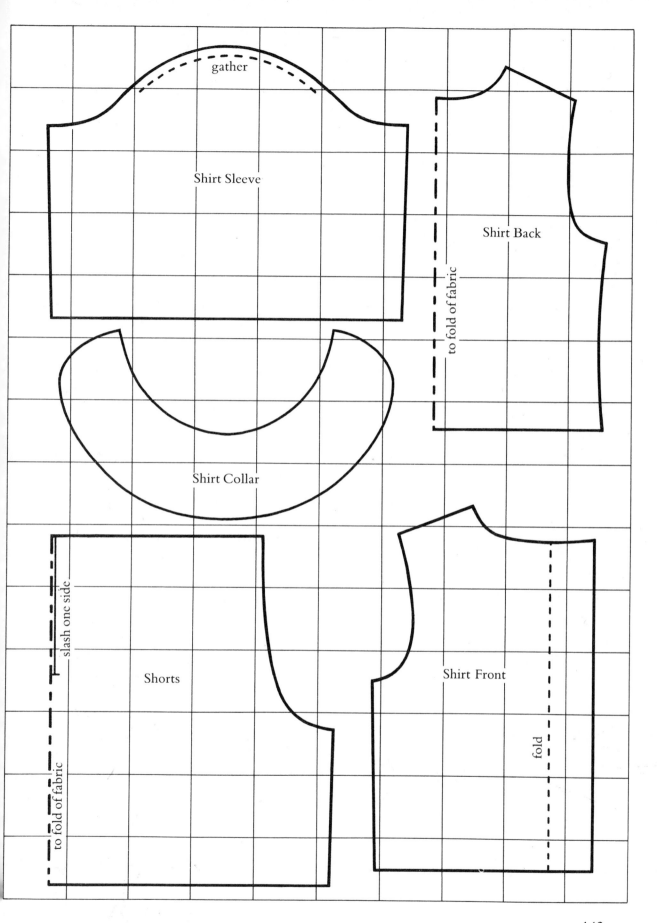

gather

Shirt Sleeve

Shirt Back

to fold of fabric

Shirt Collar

slash one side

Shorts

to fold of fabric

Shirt Front

fold

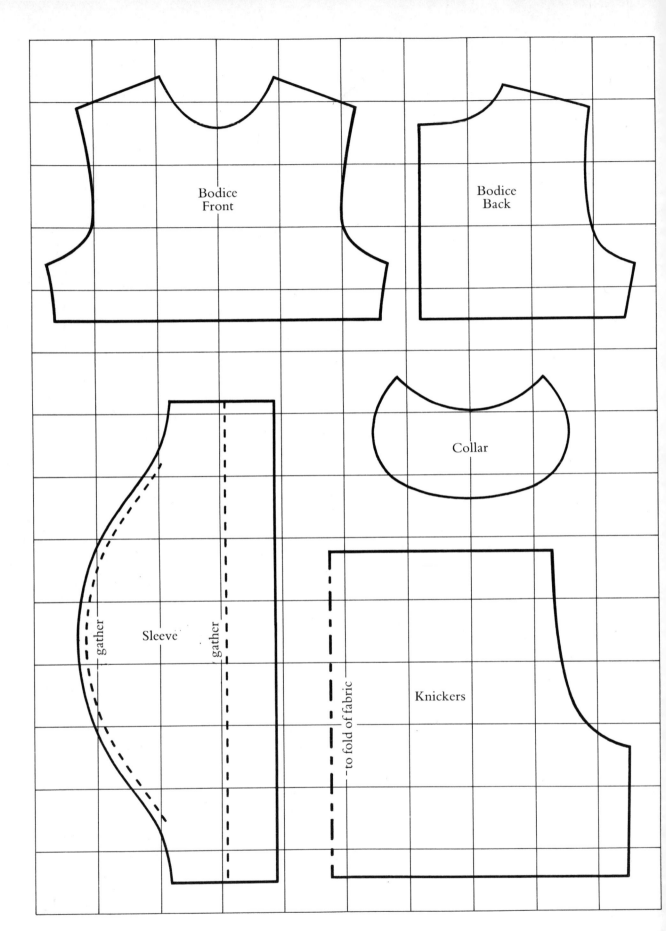

Bodice
Front

Bodice
Back

Collar

gather

gather

Sleeve

to fold of fabric

Knickers

144

waistband. Seam the straps, folding in half along the lengths, turn through, turn in the ends, oversew closed and press. Stitch straps to either side of the centre-back waistband. Make buttonholes at either side of the front waistband and sew buttons to the straps to fit. Turn up the leg ends and hem. Press creases into centre front and back of the shorts. Tie ribbon under the shirt collar into a neat bow at the centre front, trimming the ends.

LARGE GIRL'S CLOTHES
½yd white cotton (36in wide) for underwear
1yd broderie anglaise (1in wide) for trimming
1½yd broderie anglaise (8in wide) for dress
scraps of white cotton for lining
¾yd ribbon (1½in wide) for sash
3 small buttons
narrow and shirring elastic
bias-binding

To make the knickers, cut two pattern pieces in white cotton (Fig 98). Make casings at the leg ends and trim with broderie anglaise. Thread narrow elastic through the casings to fit the doll's legs and secure both ends. Seam each leg, then stitch the legs together at centre back and front. Turn a casing at the top edge and thread elastic to fit the doll's waist.

Cut a piece of white cotton 6×18in for the petticoat. Stitch the centre-back seam, hem the lower edge and trim with broderie anglaise. Turn a casing at the waist and thread elastic to fit the doll.

To make the dress, cut one bodice front and two backs in fabric and in lining (Fig 98). Cut the sleeves and a skirt 7×22in with the lower edges to the scalloped edge of the broderie anglaise. Cut four collar pieces. Stitch the bodice front to backs on both fabric and lining at the shoulder and side seams. With right sides facing, stitch the bodice and lining together at the centre-back edges and around the neckline. Clip the curves, turn through and press. Hem the centre-back edges of the skirt and gather the top edge. Stitch the skirt to the bodice, then oversew the lining over the seam to neaten. Stitch the centre-back skirt seam to 2in below the waist. Stitch the sleeve seams, gather the sleeve heads and stitch the sleeves into the armholes, sewing through both bodice and lining. Blanketstitch to neaten.

Fig 98 Clothes patterns for girl doll

Sew the collars together in pairs, clip the curves, turn through and press. Bind the raw edges of the collars with matching bias-binding, press to the inside of the collars and stitch the binding to the inside of the neckline. Gather the sleeves with shirring elastic to form frills. Make three small buttonholes and sew buttons to the back bodice to fasten. Tie a ribbon sash around the doll's waist in a bow at the back.

The materials and method are the same for the small girl's clothes, with the following exceptions. The petticoat piece is 4×12in. The dress skirt is 5×16in and the collar is omitted. The sash is ½in wide ribbon. (See Fig 99 for clothes pattern.)

The three dolls wear bought white socks and plastic 'Cinderella' shoes. If you prefer to make these, use tubular gauze bandage for the socks and see the patterns on page 31 for the shoes.

Baby
2×12in squares felt for body
piece of fur fabric approx 6×4in for wig
2 covered-button forms (⅜in [11mm]) for eyes
stuffing (soft)
embroidery thread/make-up pencils

Cut two bodies, two soles, four arms and four legs (Fig 100) and a piece 3½×7in for the head in felt.

Seam the body pieces together to form a bag and turn through. Stitch the arms together in pairs, clip between the fingers and thumb and turn through at AA. Stitch the legs together in pairs, stitch the soles into the feet and turn through at AA. Stuff the arms and legs firmly and, turning in the curved edges, slipstitch closed at AA. Stuff the body firmly, moulding a well-rounded tummy as you work and stuffing well up into the neck.

Make the head, eyes and wig exactly as for the other dolls. The wig piece is 6×2½in and the eyes and nose should be placed well down the face. Ladderstitch the head to the neck with strong thread, ensuring that the head seam is to centre back, and pushing stuffing into the neck as you work.

Ladderstitch the arms and legs to the body with strong thread. The tops of the arms are placed on the side seams, ½in below the neck, and the arms reach forward. The legs are placed on the side seams and sewn on at right angles to the body so that the doll sits. (If you

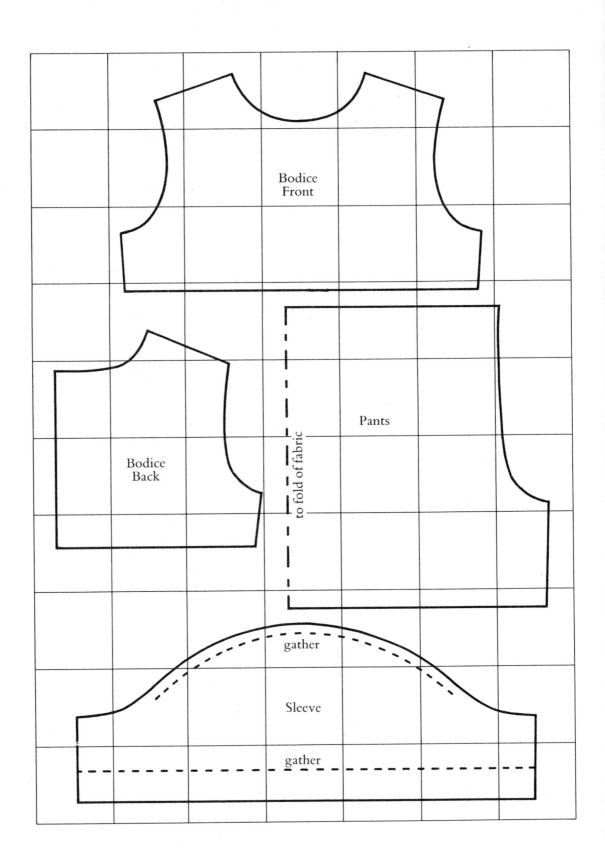

Bodice
Front

Bodice
Back

Pants

to fold of fabric

gather

Sleeve

gather

Fig 99 Clothes patterns for small girl

146

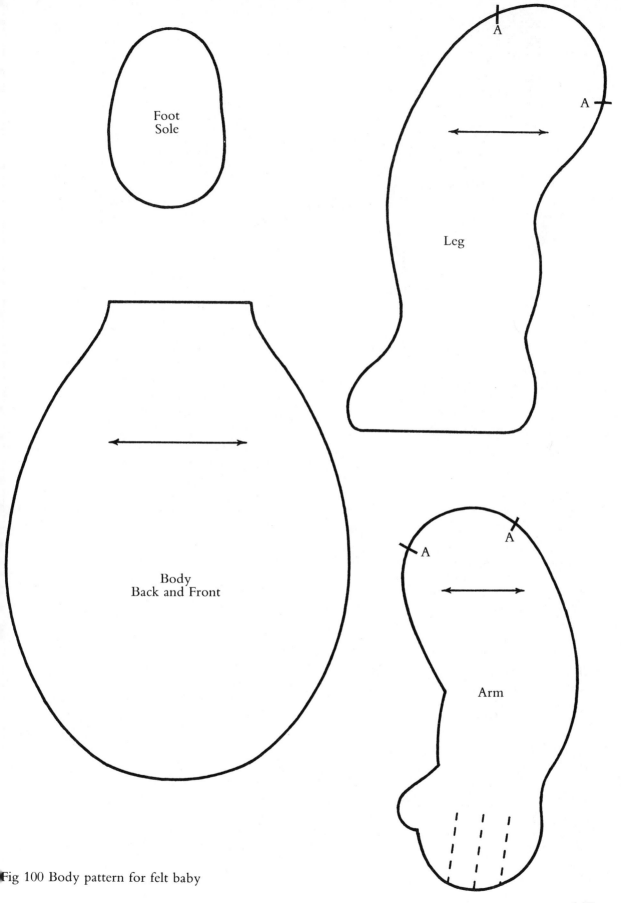

Foot
Sole

Leg

A

A

Body
Back and Front

A

A

Arm

Fig 100 Body pattern for felt baby

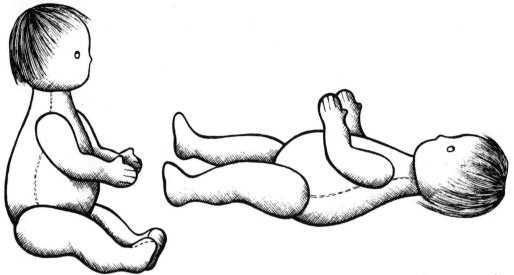

Fig 101 Assembly for sitting or lying felt baby

prefer the baby to lie down, sew on the legs in line with the body [Fig 101].) Stabstitch to define the fingers.

Colour or embroider the doll's features, and trim and style the wig as required.

BABY'S CLOTHES
2×25g 4-ply knitting yarn
1 pair size 10 (3¼mm) and size 12 (2¾mm)
  knitting needles
2 small buttons
1yd narrow ribbon
½yd ¼in ribbon

Leggings: Knit two pieces on size 10 (3¼mm) needles. Cast on 24 stitches. k1 p1 rib for two rows.

3rd row: k1 (wool forward k2 tog) across row, k1. This makes the holes for ribbon.

4th row: k2 tog, rib to end of row. Rib two more rows (24 stitches).

Change to stocking stitch and knit sixteen rows. Cast off two stitches at beginning of next two rows. k2 tog at beginning of next two rows (18 stitches). Knit twenty-four rows. Cast off.

To make up: Join leg seams from two cast-off stitches to foot. Fold so that seam is inside leg and stitch foot from toe to heel. Join centre seams from front to back.

Angel Top: This is knitted in five pieces and joined onto a yoke. (Also using size 10 (3¼mm) needles.)

Front: Cast on 50 stitches. St st four rows. 5th row: k1 (wool forward k2 tog) to end of row.

Knit twenty-one rows in st st ending on p row. Next row: k2 tog along whole row (25 stitches). Cut off wool leaving about 6in and slip stitches onto spare needle.

Back: This is knitted in two pieces but in the same way as the front. Cast on twenty-six stitches and follow pattern as for Front. (13 stitches left on each piece.) Cut wool 6in long and slip stitches onto spare needle.

Sleeves: Knit as for the two backs but cast on 20 stitches. Cut off wool leaving about 6in and slip stitches onto spare needle.

Yoke: Change to size 12 (2¾mm) needles and work in garter stitch as follows. With right side of work facing pick up stitches from first Back, first Sleeve, Front, second Sleeve, second Back. Knit three rows.

Shape the top as follows:

1st row: k4, k2 tog across row. 2nd and alternate rows: Knit. 3rd row: k3, k2 tog across row. 5th row: k2, k2 tog across row. 7th row: k1, k2 tog across row. Cast off.

To make up: Using the 6in lengths of wool join edges of Back and Sleeves and Front and Sleeves for ½in. Fasten off. Turn garment inside out and sew together sleeves and side seams. Sew back seam halfway up from the bottom. Turn up hem on cuffs and bottom to make picot edging and stitch loosely. Stitch buttons onto back of yoke.

Bonnet: Using size 10 (3¼mm) needles, cast on 40 stitches. Knit first six rows as for Front (above). St st eighteen rows ending on a p row.

To shape Back: 1st row: k4, k2 tog across row. 2nd and alternate rows: Purl. 3rd row: k3, k2 tog across row. 5th row: k2, k2 tog across row. 7th row: k1, k2 tog across row.

9th row: k2 tog across row. Do not cast off but cut off about 6in wool and thread on darning needle. Pick up the stitches left with the darning needle and pull up. Pull out knitting needle and sew together the edges of bonnet to where the shaping begins (about 1in). Turn up bonnet hem to make picot edging and stitch loosely.

This work looks better if it is pressed, but press only *very* lightly with a medium hot iron and damp cloth otherwise it will be flattened too much and the appearance will be spoilt.

Thread ¼in ribbon through the front edge of the bonnet brim to tie under the doll's chin. Thread narrow ribbon at wrists of angel top and ankles of leggings to trim. Thread elastic or ¼in ribbon through the waist casing of leggings.

Teddy Bear

small piece of velveteen or felt (approx 6×12in)
indelible black marker pen
scrap of narrow ribbon
stuffing

Fold the piece of fabric in half, right sides facing, and draw the outline of the bear (Fig 94) on the wrong side. Pin the piece, then stitch around the drawn outline with small tight stitches, leaving a gap below one arm to turn through. Cut around the bear, leaving as small an allowance as possible, and snip carefully up between the legs. Turn through – tricky, but not impossible – and stuff. Stitch through the lower ends of the ears and leave the ears unstuffed. Slipstitch the opening closed.

Mark the bear's face as shown with indelible black marker pen and tie a ribbon bow around his neck.

14

DOLL KITS AND ACCESSORIES

Dollmaking from kits has been described as 'cheating', 'not proper dollmaking' and 'painting by numbers' – all opinions I disagree with very strongly. For the amateur dollmaker, kits can be an excellent way of extending the repertoire, learning new skills and making the kind of dolls otherwise beyond one's capabilities. I hope to prove in this chapter to any sceptics that making dolls from kits can be very creative! To the doll collector who sees the prices of antique dolls rising yearly to even dizzier heights, the reproduction dolls and doll kits offer an ever more appealing alternative. Many firms who produce quality dolls produce kits of equal quality and many of our best doll artists are now producing their own original dolls in kit form at very reasonable prices. As these are likely to be among the antique dolls of the future they make a very worthwhile investment as well as giving the dollmaker much satisfaction. Although they are still a fairly recent innovation in England, kits have certainly earned their place in the dollmaking field.

I have chosen the kits for this chapter very carefully. They are only a small group from the wide range which is currently available, but they are a representative selection of what I consider the best of imported, reproduction and original doll kits in all price ranges. I have tried to show as wide a variety as possible ranging from the very simple to the elaborate, using several different body types and offering something to suit every level of dollmaking skill.

I had hoped to include a selection of rag doll kits as well as porcelain, but found to my surprise that the majority of commercial rag doll kits are very disappointing – most home dollmakers could do better! However, one company I can recommend is Crystal Calicos. This is a small firm based in Northampton that began in 1980 but has already established an excellent reputation which is not surpris-

ing as it makes a range of original rag doll kits in several sizes including 'Victorian' dolls, clowns and mini dolls. I made up the 20in Victorian girl (Fig 102) and found it extremely straightforward. It is a simple doll, but beautifully proportioned and the end result is charming. Everything you need (except the stuffing) is in the kit, including press studs, elastic and embroidery silks, and all the materials are of excellent quality. The making up instructions are clear and concise and the methods sensible. For anyone begin-

Fig 102 Crystal Calicos' 'Victorian girl' rag doll

ning dollmaking this would be a very good way to start. Crystal Calicos' kits are on sale in art and craft and needlework supply shops or can be bought directly from the firm (*see* Stockists).

So, other than this one representative of rag dolls, the rest of the kits in this chapter are porcelain. I make no apologies for that, as I think these are the type of dolls which most home dollmakers will be most interested in. As they tend not to advertise themselves very widely, the firms producing these doll kits seem to be largely unknown to many dollmakers so I intend to cover the various kits in some detail. I shall begin at the bottom end of the price range and work upwards. Obviously, in a book of this type it is not practical to give prices, but full details of every supplier mentioned here can be found under 'Stockists' at the end of the book. All the dolls described here are shown in colour on page 120. I have also given them each a difficulty rating on the same scale as the other dolls in the book.

The little pink Baby Bunting doll at the front of the picture is a 6in 'pocket-money' kit made by Frances Gray, a dollmaker from Warwickshire. Frances makes a range of original collectors' dolls in stoneware clay rather than porcelain and sells the Baby Bunting already made up as well as in kit form. The kit consists of the clay face mask with open or sleeping painted eyes and a good simple pattern for the body as a hooded suit (as shown) or with a long baby gown and bonnet. The faces are beautifully painted, and the kit is very easy and quick to make up. Frances recommends soft stuffing, but I have also tried it stuffed with lentils which made a delightfully poseable floppy baby. The doll has enormous charm, and I think would be good value at twice the price. (Difficulty: 1.)

The little boy baby at the bottom right of the picture is Ridings Craft's 12in 'William'. Ridings Craft is a Yorkshire firm which specialises in doll- and toymaking supplies of all kinds. It sells two ranges of doll kits – imported porcelain and English-made pottery – both ranges very reasonably priced. William is one of the lower-priced imported porcelain kits. He has moulded hair and inset acrylic eyes. His lower legs and arms are porcelain. The kit consists of the head with a flange neck and eyes ready set in, the legs and arms, and patterns for a seated body and baby clothes.

The clothes patterns are for a long baby gown, wrapper and bonnet. Both the body and clothes patterns are simple and well designed, the body nicely proportioned, and the making up instructions in booklet form are excellent. My one criticism would be the one which can be applied to most flange-neck dolls, that the arms tend to flop rather limply at the doll's sides, but that's not William's fault! It's a good kit, very reasonably priced and very satisfying to make, with an attractive end result.

I decided to dress William in rompers made in fine pale blue cotton lawn instead of the baby gown because I think they suit him rather well. He wears white socks, red leather shoes, and a nappy under the rompers! This is the sort of simple kit with which it is fun to experiment. Though his face suggests a small boy, a frilly bonnet or even a wig might make a totally different doll. As the face belongs to no particular period he can be dressed to suit your fancy. (Difficulty: 2.)

The young lady doll at the bottom left of the picture in cream and brown is the 12in 'Petite Princess' from Princess Porcelain Dolls in Derby. Run by Alison Wetton, Princess Porcelain sells a range of original and reproduction dolls. The Princess range has bone china heads made in Stoke-on-Trent and these vary from budget to medium price, according to size and whether they have painted or inset eyes. The Petite Princess is in the middle of the price range. The kit consists of a shoulder-plate head with the eyes ready set in, bisque lower arms and legs, an acrylic ringlet wig and a simple bag-shaped body pattern with making up instructions. Alison also sells clothes patterns if required.

The doll has a very sweet little face, delicately coloured and well painted. I felt that the acrylic eyes were a little large, and was tempted to change them for a smaller size, but this is a matter of taste. The wig is well chosen and suits the doll without limiting the choice of costume. The face is dateless – it belongs to no period or to any period, making this an excellent kit to dress. I thoroughly enjoyed making her a romantic long dress with a full-frilled skirt and lace yoke and undersleeves. The matching shirred bonnet is similar to the one worn by the bébé in Chapter 9. She has white lawn, lace-trimmed underwear and brown leather shoes. This is a good-size doll for costuming – small enough not to need too much fabric but large enough not to be fiddly. I would recommend this kit particularly to anyone who enjoys dressing dolls. (Difficulty: 2.)

The delightful miniature dolls are 5in lady and gentleman doll's-house doll kits from Sunday Dolls in London. Run by Sue Atkinson, Sunday Dolls specialises in doll's-house dolls, made up in exquisite clothes or in kit form. Sue also sells an excellent range of miniature clothes patterns in period styles and a very wide range of miniature haberdashery including silk ribbons, fine laces, buttons and buckles – in fact everything you need to dress these tiny dolls in perfect scale. The kits are very reasonably priced for fine-quality porcelain with superb detail. There is a large range including ladies, gentlemen and children; they are sold with moulded hair or to be wigged with homemade or Sunday Dolls' own tiny mohair wigs. The kit consists of a shoulder head, lower arms and legs with moulded shoes, and a body pattern and clothes patterns are available. The patterns are concise and the clever methods make dressmaking in this scale a lot easier than you would think. Using Sunday Dolls' patterns, the gentleman is dressed in a blue silk morning coat and 'salt and pepper' waistcoat and trousers with a silk cravat. His lady wears a pink and white silk dress in 1870s style with a tiny flower-trimmed straw hat. The wig is from Sunday Dolls. Of all the doll's-house doll kits I have seen I like these the best. The detail is perfect, and the range is so good it is easy to choose the right 'people' for any doll's house. They would also be fun to use in miniature 'scenes' like the conversation piece in Chapter 7, or as very special dolls' dolls. (Difficulty: 4.)

The elegant Edwardian lady on the right of the picture is an original kit from Gillie Dolls in Lancashire. Gillie Charlson is a well-known doll artist who produces a range of beautiful original and reproduction dolls in porcelain and wax. The 15in Edwardian lady is one of a small range of kits made to the same high standards as her dolls. The kit comprises a head with painted features and flange neck, very dainty lower arms and lower legs with modelled boots, a body pattern and clothes patterns. Also included is a swatch of mohair and instructions for making the wig. The painting on the face and the boots is beautifully done. The body pattern is excellent though I would recommend wiring the arms so the doll can be posed and I found the making up instructions rather brief especially as this is not a simple body. It is however very well designed and proportioned with the classic Edwardian shape – large bosom and hips and small waist. The clothes patterns are very simple and again the instructions are brief. I adapted the patterns to make a more authentic costume and made the hat in straw rather than fabric. There are no patterns for underwear but I have made drawers and petticoats in white lawn trimmed with lace and dressed the doll in lavender silk with a white embroidered 'front' and matching parasol. The boa is a length of lambswool trimming. Edwardian styles offer such wide scope for making pretty clothes. (Difficulty: 4.)

The large baby to the right of centre of the picture is a 14in reproduction of the Armand Marseilles 'Dream Baby' first produced in 1925. It is made by Recollect, based in Brighton. Run by Carol and Jeff Jackman, Recollect is a well-established firm which sells a large variety of dollmaking supplies of excellent quality and at reasonable prices. It makes a wide range of reproduction dolls and kits in fine-quality porcelain at prices to suit most budgets. The dolls are faithful copies of the originals, some with painted eyes, some with inset acrylic or glass eyes, or for a little extra, Recollect will set sleeping glass eyes in the head for you. The kits vary according to the type of doll – some have porcelain heads, arms and feet, others include the legs as part of the body. The Dream Baby kit comprises a head with flange neck and delightful hands and feet. The acrylic eyes come with full instructions and wax and plaster for setting them. The body pattern is a simple bag shape but well designed and beautifully proportioned. Recollect also sells clothes patterns and ready-made clothes. I have dressed the baby in a nappy, knitted bootees, a petticoat, and a dress and bonnet made in ivory silk trimmed with lace and embroidery similar to the ones on the baby in Chapter 11. Originals of this doll in good condition sell for several hundred pounds, so a fine reproduction like this is an excellent way of obtaining a lovely doll at an affordable price. As baby clothes are easier to make than lady-doll's clothes, this doll is also an excellent proposition for the home dollmaker who does not have a great deal of experience. (Difficulty: 3.)

The little girl in pink at the top right of the picture is a reproduction of the Bru 'Teteur' originally made in the 1870s. This lovely little bébé, 14in tall, is sold by Hello Dolly of Cornwall. Pat Holbrey of Hello Dolly sells a range of budget-priced imported and medium-priced English-made reproduction doll kits, including this Bru which is sold as 'Anne-Marie'. The kit consists of a socket head with a swivel neck ready mounted on a deep shoulder-plate. The head has an open crown with a cardboard pate and the acrylic eyes are ready set in. The lower arms and legs with bare feet and a simple 'bag' body pattern with making up instructions in booklet form are also included. The porcelain is good quality and the face painting is most effective. Anne-Marie comes with a blonde acrylic wig which is well chosen and suits her delicate colouring. Pat also sells a pattern for a full set of clothes including combinations, dress and bonnet specially designed for the doll. I have used these patterns (my own) to dress the doll shown in the picture. The low-waisted French dress with the shirred front panel is made in pale pink lawn and trimmed with cream lace. The dress and the matching shirred bonnet are versions of the types worn by the bébés in Chapter 9. She has cream leather shoes with pink ribbons, made from the pattern on page 31, though Hello Dolly can supply laced boots if you prefer. This is a charming doll, and one which I am sure most dollmakers would enjoy making and dressing as much as I did. (Difficulty: 3.)

The larger girl doll at the top left of the picture is an 18in reproduction of a Jumeau bébé of the 1880s. It is made by Reflect Reproduction Dolls in the West Midlands. Ron and Val Lacey of Reflect make a large range of reproduction dolls, all of them available either made up and dressed or in kit form. The range contains copies of the most popular French and German antique dolls including babies, girls and a lady fashion doll. The porcelain is a very good quality and the face painting is most effective. I chose this 'long-face' Jumeau for her appealing expression and because for a doll of this size I felt that the price was particularly reasonable.

The kit consists of an open crown socket head (the pate was not supplied, but part of a polystyrene ball proved most effective) with ready-set acrylic eyes. The shoulder-plate is not attached, but the nylon 'nut and bolt' are supplied and it is a simple matter to screw the swivel neck into the shoulder-plate. The arms and legs and a seated body pattern are included. The kit comes with an acrylic wig as standard in a choice of colours, or real hair wigs can be supplied if you prefer. There are no making up instructions included so perhaps this is not a good choice for the beginner, though this type of body has been used on several dolls in this book, so the instructions for them could be used as a guide. I felt that the kit was straightforward enough to make up in spite of the lack of instructions and I like the finished doll very much. Her solemn face and dark ringlets and the sturdy child-shaped body closely resemble the original. These kits are particularly good for the home dollmaker especially as each part can be bought separately. The hands, heads, shoulder-plates, legs, eyes, wigs etc are all listed and priced individually so the dollmaker can choose whatever parts she wishes and design her own bodies and clothes to suit them. Reflect also sells hand-made boots and shoes to fit each kit.

There are no clothes patterns, so one is left with a totally free hand to design and make costumes to suit the individual kit. I have dressed the Jumeau in a coffee-coloured low-waisted French dress with a short pleated skirt. It is trimmed with pale blue satin ribbon and cream lace. The large-brimmed bonnet is made on a stiffened bonnet form from 'Beth' (see Stockists), covered with ruched blue chiffon and trimmed with flowers and feathers. She wears white lawn underwear lavishly trimmed with lace and beige leather buttoned boots. (Difficulty: 4.)

The large doll in the centre of the picture is an exquisite, 22in reproduction of a Bru lady doll of the 1870s, from Creations Past in Worcester. Maureen Martin of Creations Past specialises in very high-quality reproduction and original portrait dolls. Her range includes Bru and Jumeau bébés and fashion dolls, character dolls and babies, also portraits of Diana, Princess of Wales and Henry VIII. Though she sells mostly made-up dolls, often with kid bodies and dressed in antique fabrics, many of her dolls are available in kit form. Eyes and wigs are sold separately, so the customer may choose the more expensive mohair or cheaper real hair ringlet wigs as she prefers and buy the beautiful (but expensive) paperweight glass eyes instead of the standard crystal glass ones. This is a sensible arrangement as the basic kit is very reasonably priced for such high-quality bisque and the doll-maker can spend as much as she wishes on the wig and eyes.

The basic Bru 'Shandele' kit comprises an open crown socket head with cardboard pate which is ready set onto the shoulder-plate with a swivel neck, the lower legs and arms, clothes patterns, and a good body pattern, designed for a firm sawdust stuffing. (On a doll of this size, a heavy body is needed to balance the weight of the head.) Creations Past's crystal glass or paperweight eyes arrive ready set into the head. I chose the hand-made mohair wig because it suits the doll perfectly and is totally in keeping with the period. The face painting is superb, the colouring soft and delicate. The fingernails on the lovely Bru hands with their drooping fingers are outlined, as are the toenails on the beautifully shaped feet. I found the making up instructions for the body very clear and concise and though it is not a simple body, and probably not suitable for a beginner, it posed no problems. Stuffed with sawdust it has a very satisfying 'feel' and the proportions are good. I made the standing version as I feel the doll needs to be displayed standing to do justice to her costume, but a seated adaptation is also offered in the instructions.

The clothes patterns are a little disappointing – they are for very simple rather girlish clothes and I feel a doll of this quality deserves something much more sophisticated and elaborate. Instead, I have dressed her in a walking costume of the early 1870s over layers of underwear, including a corset, combinations and several petticoats. The basque jacket has a collar and high waistline and centre-front fastening. The frilled skirts are looped up in the fashionable 'polonaise' bustle. The doll wears a flower-trimmed straw hat and carries a lace parasol. The costume is made in a delicately flower-patterned fine cotton lawn. A string of pearls around her throat covers the neck joint and there are matching pearl drop earrings in her pierced ears. I had enormous pleasure in dressing this doll; she is large enough to cut completely authentic patterns for and so beautiful that she amply rewards any amount of time spent making her clothes. The originals of this doll are very rare and, when they can be found, are sold for thousands of pounds. This superb reproduction, though not cheap, is only a fraction of the cost and it certainly gives me as much pleasure as owning the original would, without any of the worry attached to a doll so valuable that it cannot be handled! (Difficulty: 5.)

Adapting Kits

Up to now I have discussed a variety of doll kits which are so well designed and made that they need no more than making up and dressing to produce very attractive finished dolls. There are, however, a very large number of cheap imported doll kits (largely from Taiwan) which in their basic form are not very prepossessing but provide excellent raw material for experimenting and adapting. The cheap kits are usually made in a rather heavy white porcelain and have crudely painted faces or sometimes inset acrylic eyes, generally brown or orange! The same type are also imported as made up dolls and sold very cheaply. The bodies are badly proportioned and crude, and the clothes and wigs usually very cheap and tatty. Because they are so cheap, one can afford to dismember them, throw away the body and clothes, and use the porcelain parts to create something better. Here then are the 'raw materials' for the doll-maker who cannot or does not wish to model heads and hands but would like to make the types of doll described in Chapters 8, 9, 10 and 11 of this book. Providing the basic shaping of the heads, hands and feet is good, these cheap porcelain parts can be repainted, rewigged, made up on attractive bodies and dressed to make lovely 'original' dolls.

The face painting is usually done on the surface of the porcelain (not fired-in) and can easily be wiped off with nail varnish remover (acetone). If the wig is worth re-using, peel it off carefully and keep it. Decide what type of doll the modelled head best represents (this will not necessarily be the form in which the doll was originally sold). Often a head and limbs made up and dressed as a 'lady doll' are better proportioned for a child and vice-versa.

Follow the painting instructions in the relevant chapters. Humbrol enamel paints work very well on porcelain, using two or three coats to paint the head, shoulder-plate and limbs. If the doll has modelled shoes or boots, paint these as realistically as possible, following the shape of the modelling but ignoring the original painting which is

154

normally very crude. Try colouring the shoes to match the doll's dress (in this case, leave the painting until you have decided on the clothes), remembering that the sole of a shoe is a different colour from the upper, and define any moulded decoration.

If the doll has inset eyes and you don't like the colour, remove them (they are usually just stuck in with glue and are easily prised out) and replace them with a new pair in the colour of your choice (*see* Stockists). Check also whether a larger or smaller size showing more or less iris might not be more attractive. I would recommend removing inset eyes anyway before painting the head, to save them getting smeared with paint.

When you have a nice even flesh colour on the head, paint the features as you wish. Use good-quality fine brushes and whatever type of paint you prefer. With water-based colours, mistakes are easily removed with a damp cloth so you can try a lot of different effects. Use the drawings and photographs in the book as a guide for 'period' dolls, or cosmetic advertisements in magazines for a modern face. See the individual chapters for advice on features and colouring if you are planning a specific type of doll, eg a bébé. When the painting is satisfactory, including such details as the finger and toenails, spray the head, shoulder-plate and limbs with a coat of matt varnish (Humbrol is good) to seal the colours. If you wish, shoes or boots might be given a coat of gloss varnish (Das or colourless nail varnish work well).

For the body, I suggest checking the measurements of your doll's head against those of the modelled dolls in the book and selecting the size and type best suited, altering the proportions if necessary. Or you could, of course, design your own body. I recommend calico and a soft or sawdust stuffing made up in the same way as the modelled dolls in the book. The limbs will have grooves or sewing holes for tying or sewing on to the upper limbs, but check whether the proportions of the upper limbs need altering to make the arms and legs the right length. The shoulder head may be glued onto the body or sewn on with button thread or narrow tape.

If you have retained the original wig, check that it still suits the doll (and the proposed costume). New wigs may be bought in acrylic, mohair or real hair (*see* Stockists). Gauge the size by measuring around the hair-line. If you prefer to make your own wig see Chapter 1 for ideas.

If you have used a body pattern from the book, the relevant clothes patterns should fit, though minor alterations may be needed. If the styles are unsuitable, use the book patterns as a guide for size to cut your own. Fabrics are a matter of personal choice, but I strongly recommend natural fabrics and trimmings for all old-fashioned dolls. If your doll needs shoes, see page 31 or buy her shoes and boots from one of the specialist stockists.

Having discussed making a whole doll from bought parts, it is also worth mentioning that many of the doll-supply stockists sell individual heads and limbs. If for example you find that you can model attractive heads but you simply cannot make hands, it is worth considering buying a pair of hands in porcelain or composition. If these are painted to match the head, the difference in material will go undetected. Alternatively you might like to make all-cloth dolls with bought porcelain heads (the patterns for the rag dolls would adapt easily to this method). Baby dolls, like the Bye-lo baby in Chapter 11, are often made entirely of cloth except for the heads and hands and it might be fun to design your own body and clothes patterns to suit a particular commercial head.

Notes on Buying Kits
When buying a kit (if you buy by post, check it as soon as it arrives) make sure that the limbs are good matching pairs – of equal lengths and a right and left of each. Check that the tying-on grooves are cleanly cut and deep enough, or that the sewing holes are all cleanly cut. With inset eyes, check that the eye holes are the same size. You cannot expect perfection from a very cheap mass-produced kit, but these things should be correct or the finished doll will be disappointing. When you make up the kit, cover the open ends of the limbs (and particularly the open end of a flange neck) with thin cardboard discs, glued in place, to prevent the stuffing shifting into the limb (or up into the head). If the cloth body is ready cut out, check that the pieces are squarely on the grain of the fabric, if not, use them as a pattern to cut another body. (If you make up a body which is out-of-true it will take on a distorted shape when stuffed.) Always use strong button thread to tie on limbs and check by

pulling that they are completely secure. If the lower limbs have sewing holes rather than grooves either push the stuffed upper limb down into the lower limb and sew in place, or, better still, seal the open end of the lower limb with a card disc and pull the edge (preferably cut on the selvedge) of the upper limb down over it, then sew through to secure. (This second method is neater and allows more flexibility at the joint.) It is worth stitching all seams twice for extra strength and clipping curves carefully before turning through. Stitched elbow and knee joints are a matter of individual preference, but only make them when the joins between upper and lower limbs are low enough to allow the stitched joints to be in the natural place (elbows which bend just below the armpit look most odd!). Decide whether you wish to display the doll sitting or standing, preferably before you stuff it, and if it is required to sit, stabstitch through the body at the top of the legs. A seated body can easily be displayed standing (with the aid of a doll stand) but one with rigidly stuffed hips and legs cannot be forced to sit.

Consider, also, using bought doll parts (or commercial dolls) to make your own plaster moulds. For example, the face of a bought doll's head may be pressed into wet plaster to make a face-mask mould. Fimo, rolled out to an even thickness, is then pressed into the greased mould and baked. When the edges are trimmed with a craft knife, the result is a well-defined face mask which can be painted and glued to the front of a stuffed doll's head. Similarly, a whole head may be made by making separate moulds of the back and front and pressing Fimo into each. When the two halves are baked, they are trimmed and joined together with more Fimo and then baked again to seal the join. Limbs may be made in the same way. Commercial plaster moulds may also be used for this method, though they are designed for use with porcelain slip and are expensive.

One small word of warning. If you decide to join a doll club and enter doll competitions, dolls made from kits, however much you have altered the basic kit design, are not usually judged as original dolls. To be truly original in this context, the doll must have a head, limbs, body and clothes all designed and made by yourself.

Accessories

At the end of the book you will find a very comprehensive list of suppliers, not only of the doll kits and parts already discussed in this chapter but also of many items such as wigs, eyes and shoes of which the home dollmaker may be unaware. I therefore propose to outline some of the goods which are available, and hope that readers will find it useful. I have personally used items from all the listed stockists, many of which appear in the photographs in this book, so I recommend them with confidence.

There are three types of doll's wig currently available – mohair, acrylic and real hair. Acrylic wigs are the cheapest and the most widely available. They come in several colours and styles made on either a flat non-stretch base or a stretchy cap. The majority of these wigs are imported from places like Taiwan where they can be produced cheaply, so they are very good value. Many of the listed stockists supply acrylic wigs, usually in blonde or brown, in long hairstyles with a centre parting, fringe and ringlets or short curls. The quality varies quite considerably – some examples are very good, with the hair evenly distributed and firmly sewn in; others are quite poor, some having almost 'bald' patches. Obviously, if you order such a wig and it is not satisfactory it should be exchanged for a better one. The minor inconvenience of an occasional exchange is more than outweighed by the low price and these are the wigs which most home dollmakers will find useful.

Acrylic wigs are permanently styled, though they can be brushed and trimmed to shape. Washing will not affect the curls, but they cannot be 'set' with heated rollers or tongs as heat frizzles the 'hair'. Hairspray is as efficient on acrylic as real hair, which is useful as some acrylic wigs are rather fly away. I have found them effective on modelled dolls, where they are glued to the head (check that a stretchy cap base does not have to stretch too much to fit or it may well come unstuck), and also on soft dolls, where the base is oversewn to the head around the edge. My main objection to acrylic wigs in the context of old-fashioned dolls is that many of them look too modern. The blonde colours especially have a rather artificial look and they are all just a little too shiny. However, this is a matter of personal taste so I suggest that you try them first and see if you like them.

Real hair wigs, whether imported or made in England, are considerably more expensive than acrylics, often at least twice as much. Most real hair wigs are made on non-stretch cap bases (though some stretch) and should be chosen to fit the doll's head as closely as possible. The quality varies, from coarse Asian hair (usually bleached) to much finer European hair which is usually used in its natural colour. Generally, the finer the hair, the more expensive the wig. The range of colours is wider than with acrylic wigs and varies from one stockist to another. A real hair wig is usually ready styled, but it can be washed and set, even permed, like your own hair. Heated rollers or curling tongs and hairsprays can all be used for styling. In spite of the greater cost, hair wigs are recommended for most of the modelled dolls in the book because they are much more realistic than acrylic. I have used a cheaper type (bleached Asian hair) for the small bébé in Chapter 9 and an expensive, but very beautiful, fine-quality one for the fashion doll in Chapter 8. I think that on a well-modelled, elaborately dressed doll, the extra cost is justified.

Mohair wigs are especially suitable for old-fashioned dolls as they imitate the wigs found on many antiques. Prices vary a great deal – from the example used on the Edwardian child in Chapter 10 which is the same price as a real hair wig to the elaborate and beautiful but very expensive example shown on the large Bru doll in this chapter. It is ironic that in the nineteenth century mohair wigs were used as a cheaper alternative to real hair, but nowadays they are generally the most expensive. The simpler types are available in soft blonde and chestnut brown shades in several styles and are made on non-stretch cap bases (see Kinloch and Sellers). Select the size to fit the doll's head as closely as possible. More elaborate mohair wigs are styled with ringlets, frizzed curls, plaits and chignons and, though they are expensive, they are exquisitely made and give the doll an utterly 'period' look. A beautiful wig can so improve the looks of an ordinary doll that sometimes extravagance is justified! A word of warning about mohair wigs – they cannot be brushed or restyled, only smoothed gently with a comb, so choose a style which suits the doll.

As well as the oval flat-backed acrylic eyes which I have used for the modelled dolls in the book, several of the listed stockists also supply glass eyes. Because of their round shape, I have found them of little use for modelled dolls, but they are excellent for most doll kits. Only the most expensive kits supply glass eyes as standard, but you might prefer to substitute them for acrylic eyes as they have greater depth and give the doll a more life-like expression. Prices, range of colours and sizes vary from one stockist to another.

Another item many dollmakers prefer to buy rather than make are dolls' shoes. Several of the listed stockists supply a range of dolls' shoes and boots, varying from the budget-priced plastic shoes I have used for the felt dolls in Chapter 13, which are available in many sizes in black, white, pink and blue, to the lovely little leather buttoned boots on the Jumeau doll kit in this chapter. These little boots are very similar to those worn by antique dolls and are available in a range of colours and sizes (see Recollect). When buying dolls' shoes, draw around the foot for a pattern for size and compare this with the size chart in the catalogue or measure the length of the doll's foot and order the closest size. You cannot usually squeeze the doll's feet into shoes which are too small without stretching or tearing them, but you can stuff the toes of shoes which are too large with a little cotton wool to make them fit. Select shoes carefully – the cheaper plastic type are only suitable for simple dolls; a fashion doll or bébé needs good-quality leather in the appropriate style and colour. Consider also adding your own trimmings to bought shoes. Simple, plain leather shoes can be much improved by adding a buckle or ribbon bow to the fronts to match the dress.

Socks and stockings are also often better bought than made. Many of the stockists supply white nylon socks and stockings but Hello Dolly also has knitted cotton stockings in black and white which are more suitable than nylon for old-fashioned dolls. These are available in several sizes and though more expensive than nylon are reasonably priced.

Apart from the bonnets supplied by 'Beth', several other stockists sell straw hats in a wide range of sizes, similar to the ones I have used on the felt children in Chapter 13. These hats are sold untrimmed, are inexpensive, and suit a variety of dolls. There are also straw boaters, of a better quality and slightly more expensive, which look good on 'period' dolls. These little straw hats look very pretty trimmed with ribbon bands and flowers, and with the brim pulled down at either side by ribbons tied under the chin they also make very acceptable straw bonnets.

If you prefer to buy dolls' clothes rather than make them, Recollect and Granny's Goodies sell sets of clothes in a variety of styles, sizes and prices suitable for most types of doll, some of them reproductions of the clothes found on antique dolls. Doll fairs are also a good hunting-ground for both antique and reproduction clothes.

Finally, doll stands. Most dolls look their best displayed standing so that their clothes may be seen to advantage. Many of the listed stockists supply doll stands suitable for all sizes of doll. They are not expensive and can usually be discreetly hidden under the dolls' skirts, while at the same time keeping the standing doll perfectly stable. Select the size appropriate to the height of the doll and fit the 'arms' of the stand around the doll's waist. These metal stands are usually supplied painted white, but they can easily be re-painted any colour you wish (Humbrol enamel paints are ideal for this purpose) and if the stand shows, ie on a boy doll, it can be painted to blend in with the costume. I have also found it a good idea to glue felt to the underside of the base to prevent any possibility of scratching polished surfaces.

To any dollmaker who was previously unaware of the existence of these stockists and the goods they supply I strongly recommend obtaining their catalogues and price lists. As with any other kind of shopping, it is worth comparing prices and sizes before choosing those best suited to your own dolls. To anyone who until now has only used home-made wool wigs or felt shoes, the commercial ranges open up a host of new possibilities, and one can also learn a great deal by studying how commercial wigs, clothes or shoes are made and perhaps copying or adapting methods to one's own dollmaking.

It should be noted when ordering from specialist suppliers, that though many items are kept in stock, others are made to order. Imported doll kits or wigs etc can usually be delivered quickly, but hand-made wigs, high-quality doll kits or leather shoes may require a few weeks to make. Therefore, if you need something urgently it is as well to check with the supplier that there will be no delay, but be prepared to be patient if you have ordered something special.

15
DOLLMAKING COURSES
AND DOLL FAIRS

For the home dollmaker who wants to make her own porcelain dolls, there are now a number of dollmaking courses available in all parts of the country. Whether you just want to make one doll, for your own pleasure, or learn to make dolls to sell, these courses are an excellent way to learn. Classes are graded from absolute beginners to experienced dollmakers, with expert tuition and personal attention at all stages. The courses are run by professional dollmakers who are happy to pass on their skills, teaching from practical experience the methods they use themselves. Classes are usually small and friendly and the atmosphere is conducive to learning in a relaxed, informal manner.

Two of the best-known teaching programmes are run by Recollect at its studio in Brighton, and Living Dolls which holds classes in Bexhill-on-Sea but also works with other dollmakers all over the country. The costs vary, from very modestly priced beginners' classes, to the more expensive week-long course for teachers. Kilns, moulds and porcelain slip are fairly expensive to buy, and anyone considering making porcelain dolls would be well advised to take a course before making the investment. Not only will you have the opportunity to try the techniques for yourself and see if you have the ability, but also the chance to gain expert advice on the types of kilns and moulds etc which are available and those best suited to your needs.

Recollect also runs courses in the restoration and repair of antique dolls which is a craft many dollmakers enjoy and one in which the more knowledge you have, the better, as many antique dolls are ruined by clumsy 'restoration'. Many people believe that if you can make dolls you can repair old dolls, and this is of course not the case. Good repair work requires a knowledge of methods and techniques which the average dollmaker does not use, and restoration is usually a far more delicate and painstaking process than making a doll from scratch.

To give some idea of what the home dollmaker might expect, I will give a brief description of the types of course available. At Recollect, for example, the courses are held in its studio in an old village school, nine miles outside Brighton. It offers courses for all standards of ability in dollmaking and in Hobby Ceramics.

The hobby dollmaking courses are designed for beginners upwards who take one class a week for five weeks and make one doll on each course. They are designed for people who do not intend to buy their own kilns, but prefer to take advantage of the facilities offered at the studio. As a different doll is made at each five-week course, students may attend several courses and make a variety of dolls. The fees for these courses are very modest, and students provide their own tools and materials which can be bought at the studio. The dolls you can make on these courses include: a 12in fashion doll with bisque swivel head and lower limbs on a cloth body which is perfect for costuming; a small all-bisque chubby toddler; and the Armand Marseilles 'Dream Baby'. You will learn how to pour a mould, trim and clean the greenware (unfired clay), mix and use china paints and assemble the body. Simple wig-making, stringing and setting eyes are also taught for the appropriate dolls. This is the ideal course for the dollmaker who wants to try her hand at porcelain dollmaking without any further commitment.

For the more serious dollmaker who wants a very thorough grounding with a view to making her own porcelain dolls and buying her own kiln, there is a full-time one-week course. Each course is limited to ten students who receive a great deal of personal attention and learn the techniques involved in making the three basic types of doll: a bisque head on ball-jointed body, bisque head and limbs on a cloth body and an all-bisque doll. You will learn how to pour moulds and how to care for them, how to clean greenware, cut eyeholes and how to load and fire a kiln. All aspects of china painting are covered, and full tuition on assembling and stringing bodies and fixing eyes is given. This course also includes guidance on costing dolls for sale. All the materials and the tools you need are provided and are yours to keep, and you take home the three completed dolls you make on the course which include a character child, an all-bisque doll and a baby or fashion doll. This course teaches you everything you need to know, both the practical skills and the commercial aspects involved in dollmaking, and gives you the ability and the confidence to set up on your own. Guidance is offered on moulds, slip and kilns and you will also have the opportunity to see the wide range of doll-making equipment supplied by Recollect. For full details of the courses described here, and dates of the next season's courses, contact Recollect (see Stockists).

Living Dolls, based in Bexhill-on-Sea, offers two apprentice courses. The first, suitable for beginners, covers two days, during which you learn how to prepare and pour the slip, clean the greenware and cut eyeholes, load and fire the kiln and then paint the finished head and fix the eyes. On this course, you make the Armand Marseilles 'Dream Baby' and the Bye-lo baby, both with bisque heads and limbs on cloth bodies. The course is reasonably priced, all materials and tools are provided and you take home the two completed baby dolls. The second two-day apprentice course is for making two German character dolls with jointed papier mâché bodies, glass eyes and real hair wigs. The fees are considerably higher than for the first course, but everything you need to complete the two dolls is provided.

There is an intermediate course for more advanced students on which you will make a Jumeau bébé with a jointed body and a Kestner girl doll with a leather body. Both dolls have glass eyes and real hair wigs and again everything you need to complete the dolls is provided. There are also two advanced courses and a teacher's training course for professionals wishing to learn how to teach others to make dolls. These courses are an excellent way to acquire good reproductions of some lovely antique dolls at a very reasonable price and have the pleasure of making them yourself. Living Dolls is a distributor for the German Wanke dollmaking products, and also works in collaboration with other professional dollmakers all over the country who offer similar teaching courses to students of all abilities using the Living Dolls products and methods. For details of the courses in Bexhill, or of teachers in your own area, contact Living Dolls (see Stockists).

Doll Fairs

One of the best places to see both antique dolls and the work of professional dollmakers is at a doll fair. As the making and collecting of dolls becomes ever more popular, so more and more of these fairs are being held all over the country. They are advertised in the doll magazines (see Bibliography) and there are at least one or two each year within reasonable travelling distance of almost everywhere. Obviously, most of the major events are in London, like the annual fair organised by Living Dolls, and the fairs organised by Granny's Goodies. These usually take place in large hotels and are large affairs with exhibitors coming from all over the country and abroad, but smaller fairs are held in hotels and village halls in every county, organised by local dollmakers clubs or craft guilds.

Even at the largest fairs, the admission price is modest and one can have a delightful day just looking – there is no pressure at all to buy. You will find stalls of antique dolls ranging in price from the affordable to the astronomical, all of them offering inspiration to the dollmaker and miniature dressmaker. There will be stalls of modern reproduction and original dolls, ranging widely in price and providing a glorious opportunity to pick up new ideas. Unless you belong to a doll-making club, you do not see much of other people's work and can feel a bit isolated, but at a fair you have the chance to see what other people are doing and compare notes. Most of the exhibitors are happy to discuss their work and many of them are very generous with tips and advice. You invariably leave a fair knowing a little more than when you arrived!

As well as the stalls of dolls you will find many stalls selling dollmaking accessories, fabrics and trimmings, and clothes both old and new. Here you have the opportunity to see the latest wigs, eyes, shoes and hats and to browse through the dollmaking books on sale. Many of the fairs also include other items such as trains, soldiers, clockwork toys, dolls' houses and miniatures, so there is usually something to interest most people, even the dollmaker's most reluctant husband!

For the home dollmaker, the doll fair or craft market offers the best place to sell. Shops usually put high mark-ups on goods to cover their costs and this means that the dollmaker must either pare her prices to the bone or see her dolls selling in the shop at higher prices than she feels reasonable. The shop may buy on a sale-or-return basis which is unfair to the dollmaker as the goods are not paid for until the shop sells them, possibly months later, or they are returned, often grubby, spoilt and unsaleable. I would not advise anyone to sell on this basis; if the shop owner has sufficient faith in his own judgement of what is good and saleable then he should be prepared to back it by buying the goods outright. If the dolls sell well, then the dollmaker is often pressured into making more and more, usually to the extent that her time is so committed to producing the dolls which sell that she no longer has time to experiment and develop any further and what began as pleasure can rapidly turn into drudgery. Never commit yourself to supplying certain dolls to certain shops on demand – unless this is what you want to do. It may seem like a heaven-sent chance to make an income, but it can turn into a nightmare. If the shop likes your dolls well enough, then sell on your own terms. Set your own price and do not commit yourself to making more dolls than you reasonably can, and decide at the outset whether you find the shop's selling price acceptable, bearing in mind that you can sell the same dolls direct to the customer at half the price!

The doll fair or craft market offers the opportunity to sell direct to the customer, thus cutting out the middleman and enabling you to sell at a reasonable price. The major doll fairs can be expensive and generally one has to be invited to exhibit, but small local events are a different matter. Take a stall at an event organised close to home to begin with. This might be a market organised by the WI, a playgroup fundraiser or a street fair. There is usually a small charge for the stall, or the organisers will ask for a modest percentage of the takings. Obviously you will need suf-ficient goods to stock the stall and preferably a few extras to replenish the stock as the goods sell. At least twenty dolls would be needed, fewer if you share a stall with some-one else. Display them as attractively as possible. Cover the stall with a coloured sheet (a good strong colour is eyecatching and will draw people your way) and arrange the dolls so that they can be seen easily. A few doll stands are a good investment (they can be removed and used for others when a doll is sold) so that you can make pleasing groups of sitting and standing dolls and display their clothes to the best advantage. Label each doll clearly with the price – swing tickets tied round the wrist is a good method. Be sensible about pricing. You must cover your costs and make a profit otherwise selling is pointless, but at a small local event you must accept that people will not pay high prices.

It is virtually impossible to run a stall at a craft market on your own so you will need help. Customers come in waves, not one at a time, and you may lose them if you can only serve them individually. You must be prepared to talk to your customers – at some markets you will do more talking than selling. Have a stock of large paper bags or tissue paper to wrap the sold dolls and keep a good float of change in a tin. Look friendly and approachable but don't be over-eager or pushy. If you are lucky you will sell a good percentage of your stock and have a reasonable recompense for your efforts.

Selling at markets is tiring because you are 'on duty' all the time, but it is very rewarding. You can see exactly how the customer reacts to your dolls and often eavesdrop on some informative criticism! If your work does not sell, consider three points. (a) Are you making the sort of thing people want to buy? This can be difficult to judge; often something will simply not sell in one place and go like hot cakes somewhere else, but time and experience will provide the answer. (b) Are you making it well enough? (c) Is the price right? And that doesn't always mean you are charging too much – sometimes if something is underpriced it is undervalued and doesn't sell.

After a few markets, you will have got the hang of things; you will be able to judge your goods, your prices and your customers, and be ready to spread your wings and try bigger markets and fairs further afield. Selling this way gives you independence – you make as much as you want to and set your own prices. You book stalls at as many fairs as you wish and after your stall fee is paid, the profits are yours. You also meet other dollmakers and various other craft workers with whom you can exchange ideas. You may not have much opportunity to see other people's work, especially when the fair is busy and you are tied to your own stall all day, but the atmosphere is generally friendly and people are usually willing to help and encourage the beginner. Consider joining a local craft guild or doll club. Many guilds have their own shops and markets where they ask only a small commission and most doll clubs organise doll fairs.

Specialist doll magazines publish details of doll clubs, fairs and exhibitions and they also contain advertisements for the suppliers of dollmaking equipment and accessories, excellent articles about dolls and doll events, reports of auctions and a wealth of small advertisements. Magazines like this are not just useful and informative, they also combat the sense of isolation that many home dollmakers experience. It's nice to know that there are thousands of other dollmakers out there! Most of the magazines are international, so there are new ideas from abroad as well as Britain and it is interesting to read about the current trends in dollmaking in other countries. Usually the magazines are sold by subscription, and as the circulations are comparatively small, the subscription rates are fairly high. I feel that the expense is justified by the information and pleasure one gets from reading the magazine, but if in doubt, write and ask for one issue before committing yourself to a full year's subscription (see Bibliography). The Kinloch and Sellers Catalogue is a delightful and informative quarterly magazine, beautifully illustrated, which deals with both antique and modern dolls. The International Doll's House News is published quarterly and though its primary interest is dolls' houses, it often has articles, advertisements and reviews relating to dolls. Popular Crafts is a splendid monthly magazine (available from newsagents) which has some doll oriented articles in most issues. Dolls – the Collector's Magazine is a lavish, glossy American quarterly which has a section devoted to British dollmaking in each issue. The Granny's Goodies Catalogue, published quarterly, has good photographs of all the antique dolls currently for sale in the shop and is very useful for copying antique dolls and their clothes, and the annual British Doll Artists' Association Directory shows photographs of the work of the BDA members which are not just interesting but also inspiring.

Collecting Antique Dolls

You may find that you would like to start collecting antique dolls, so I offer a word of advice. Read, look, feel and learn all you can before you start to buy. Visit your local museum and see if they have some antique dolls you can study. Usually if you make an appointment, the museum will allow you to handle the dolls and examine them properly. When in London, visit the Bethnal Green Museum, which has a superb collection of dolls and a very knowledgeable, kind and friendly staff. Ask in the local antique shops if they have dolls you may look at. Ask around among your friends and relations – it is quite extraordinary how many people have old dolls tucked away and never guess how interested you would be to see them.

Make sure that you only buy from a reputable dealer (they advertise in the specialist magazines). The man in the junk market probably knows very little about old dolls and because the prices of some of the rarer examples have risen so high some people think that all old dolls are very valuable – they are not! It is very easy to cheat an unwary customer who can end up paying a lot of money for a doll in very poor condition just because it is 'old'. There are also a lot of fakes on the market – heads and bodies which do not belong together, new clothes sold as old, and reproductions passed off as originals. Any respectable dollmaker signs her reproductions so they may be identified, but there are disrespectable dollmakers! Also, avoid auctions unless you know exactly what you are doing. It is still possible to pick up bargains in country auctions or small junk shops, but more often than not the unwary pay high prices for attractive but not particularly valuable dolls, carried away by the bidding or the hope of a bargain. To some degree intuition and your senses of sight, touch and smell will guide you, but there is no substitute for experience. Only buy what you are sure of and at a price you know is reasonable. Good hunting!

BIBLIOGRAPHY

Arnold, Janet *Patterns of Fashion – 1660–1860 and 1860–1940* Wace (1966)
(Now out of print) Superb books containing scale patterns of real clothes of each period and a wealth of costume and dressmaking information.

Byford, Peggy *Wooden Dolls* (private publication available from: Key Books, Box 88, 43 Franklin Road, Haywards Heath, Sussex RH16 4DQ)
A delightful and fascinating book about wooden dolls from Roman times to the twentieth century, illustrated with sketches and photographs.

Coleman, Dorothy etc *The Collectors' Book of Dolls' Clothes* Robert Hale (1978)
The Collectors' Encyclopedia of Dolls Robert Hale (1968)
Two enormous, expensive, but absolutely invaluable books, full of information, photographs, measurements and patterns.

Dodge, Venus A. *Making Collector's Dolls* David & Charles (1983)

Ewing, Elizabeth *History of Children's Costumes* Batsford (1977)
The best book I have read on the subject, illustrated with photographs throughout.

Johnson, Audrey *Dressing Dolls* Bell and Hyman (1978)
Particularly useful for the beginner.

Victoria and Albert Museum *Four hundred years of Fashion* V. & A. and Collins (1984)
Glorious book full of colour and black and white photographs and descriptions of clothes.

King, Constance Eileen *Dolls and Dolls' Houses* Hamlyn (1978)
Lots of information about antique dolls and both colour and black and white photographs. Helpful as reference for modelling dolls.

Tozer, Jane and Levitt, Sarah *Fabric of Society* Laura Ashley (1983)
A super book, full of colour photographs of fabrics and clothes from the collection at Platt Hall (Manchester).

Westfall, Marty *Doll Repair and Restoration* Robert Hale (1981)
Primarily intended for doll repairers, but is also enormously useful to the maker of old-fashioned dolls. Also contains wigmaking and bodymaking instructions etc.

Willet, C. and Cunnington, Phillis *The History of Underclothes* Faber (1981)
An excellent book, both amusing and informative. Illustrated with sketches and photographs throughout.

Yarwood, Doreen *English Costume from the 2nd Century BC to the Present Day* Batsford (1979)
An extremely good costume reference book, illustrated with sketches throughout and a section of photographs.

Magazines

Dolls – the Collector's Magazine (available on subscription from: Mrs Susan Haines, PO Box 125, London SW13 0BE)
A lavish glossy American magazine, published quarterly and now available in Britain, full of articles about and photographs of antique and modern artist dolls. Illustrated in colour.

Granny's Goodies Catalogue (available on subscription from: 8 Harold Road, Upper Norwood, London SE19)
A quarterly magazine showing the antique dolls currently on sale at Granny's Goodies. The dolls are all shown in black and white photographs, some wearing original clothes.

International Doll's House News (available on subscription from: 56, Lincoln Wood, Haywards Heath, Sussex RH16 1LH)
A quarterly magazine for doll's-house collectors, but also contains doll articles and use-

ful advertisements. Illustrated in black and white.

Kinloch and Sellers Catalogue (available on subscription from: 80 Grove Hill Road, Tunbridge Wells, Kent TN1 1SP)
A quarterly magazine for doll collectors, but also contains much to interest the dollmaker and has excellent small ads. Illustrated in black and white and colour.

The British Doll Artists' Directory, c/o Ann Parker, 67 Victoria Drive, Bognor Regis, Sussex PO21 2TD (tel: 0243 823 538)

(Write to the above addresses, enclosing sae for details of subscription rates.)
See also Popular Crafts published monthly, available from newsagents. Contains doll articles most months and also has regular special offers of doll kits.

STOCKISTS

Because of the large number of specialty stores and catalogs that carry dolls and doll parts, we suggest you consult your local telephone directory or look through the ads in many specialty magazines.

INDEX